Family Support in Cases of
Emotional Maltreatment an

Studies in Evaluating the Children Act 1989

Series editors:
Dr Carolyn Davies, Prof. Jane Aldgate

Other titles in the series include

From Care to Accommodation

Parental Perspectives on Care Proceedings

The Last Resort

Leaving Care in Partnership

Safeguarding Children with the Children Act 1989

The Best-Laid Plans

Supporting Families through Short-term Fostering

Expert Evidence in Child Protection Litigation

STUDIES IN EVALUATING THE CHILDREN ACT 1989

Family Support in Cases of Emotional Maltreatment and Neglect

June Thoburn
Jennifer Wilding
Jackie Watson

London: The Stationery Office

First published 2000

ISBN 0 11 322292 0

Published by The Stationery Office and available from:

The Stationery Office
(mail, telephone and fax orders only)
PO Box 29, Norwich NR3 1GN
Telephone orders/enquiries 0870 600 5522
Fax orders 0870 600 5533

www.itsofficial.net

The Stationery Office Bookshops
123 Kingsway, London WC2B 6PQ
020 7242 6393 Fax 020 7242 6412
68–69 Bull Street, Birmingham B4 6AD
0121 236 9696 Fax 0121 236 9699
33 Wine Street, Bristol BS1 2BQ
0117 926 4306 Fax 0117 929 4515
9–21 Princess Street, Manchester M60 8AS
0161 834 7201 Fax 0161 833 0634
16 Arthur Street, Belfast BT1 4GD
028 9023 8451 Fax 028 9023 5401
The Stationery Office Oriel Bookshop
18–19 High Street, Cardiff CF1 2BZ
029 2039 5548 Fax 029 2038 4347
71 Lothian Road, Edinburgh EH3 9AZ
0870 606 5566 Fax 0870 606 5588

The Stationery Office's Accredited Agents
(see Yellow Pages)

and through good booksellers

Printed in the United Kingdom by The Stationery Office
TJ563 02/00 C10 485058 19585

Contents

List of figures and tables

Figures

Tables

Foreword

The Children Act 1989 was implemented on 14 October 1991. At its launch the then Lord Chancellor, Lord Mackay, described the Act as 'the most radical legislative reform to children's services this century'. Shortly after the launch the Department of Health put together a strategy to monitor and evaluate the initial impact of the Act. Taking a tripartite approach, this drew on evidence from statistical returns, inspections and research to develop a rounded appreciation of early implementation. The subsequent strategy plan was published and circulated to relevant bodies, including social services and the major voluntary agencies, in 1993. This plan formed the backcloth for a programme of research studies commissioned by the Department of Health to explore early evaluation in more depth. It is these studies, some 20 in all, which form this new series.

The programme studies investigate the implementation of key changes introduced by the Act and evaluate the facilitators and inhibitors to the meeting of key objectives. A longer-term goal of the programme is to review the aims of the Act in the light of implementation with a view to reconsideration or amendment should this be felt necessary. Finally, a more general and important scientific aim is to consider how far change could be achieved successfully by changing the law.

There are several principles underlying the Children Act 1989 that permeate the research studies. An important strand of the Act is to bring together private and public law so that the needs of all children whose welfare is at risk might be approached in the same way. This philosophy is underpinned by the principle of promoting children's welfare. There should be recognition of children's time-scales and, in court cases, children's welfare should be paramount. To aid this paramountcy principle there should be a welfare checklist, and delays in court hearings should be avoided.

The promotion of children's welfare takes a child development focus, urging local authorities to take a holistic and corporate approach to providing services. Departments such as health, education, housing, police, social services and recreation should work together to respond to children's needs. Children, the Act argues, are best looked after within their families wherever possible

and, where not, the continuing support of parents and wider kin should be facilitated by avoiding compulsory proceedings whenever possible. Parents should be partners in any intervention process, and children's views should be sought and listened to in any decision-making affecting their lives. To promote continuity for children looked after, contact with families should be encouraged and children's religion, culture, ethnicity and language should be preserved.

Local authorities have a duty to move from services to prevent care to a broader remit of providing family support, which could include planned periods away from home. However, family support services should not be universal but target those most in need. The introduction of Children's Services Plans in 1996 has made the idea of corporate responsibility a more tangible reality and seeks to help local authorities look at how they may use scarce resources cost-effectively.

The themes of the Children Act have relevance for the millennium. The concern with combating social exclusion is echoed through several of the studies, especially those on family support and young people looked after by local authorities. The value of early intervention is also a theme in the studies on family centres, day care and services for children defined as 'in need' under the Act. Further, the research on the implementation of the Looking After Children Schedules emphasises the importance to children in foster and residential care of attaining good outcomes in education. Lastly, attending to the health of parents and their children is another strand in both the family support and 'children looked after' studies.

To accompany the 20 individual studies in the research programme the Department of Health has commissioned an overview of the findings, to be published by The Stationery Office in the style of similar previous publications from HMSO: *Social Work Decisions in Child Care 1985*; *Patterns and Outcomes in Child Care 1991*; *Child Protection: Messages from Research 1996*; and *Focus on Teenagers 1997*.

The editors would like to express their appreciation to the members of the research community; professionals from different disciplines, and service users, among others, who have contributed so willingly and generously to the successful completion of the research studies and to the construction of the overview. Without their help, none of the research would have been written or disseminated.

Carolyn Davies
Jane Aldgate

Preface and acknowledgements

Most research-based publications are the result of teamwork and that is especially the case with this one. Jane Gibbons designed the original research and it was under her direction that the first round of interviews, the survey of family support services in the three areas, and the interim report were completed (Gibbons and Wilding 1995; Wilding and Thoburn 1997). We pay tribute to Jane's flair, energy and creativity as a researcher, not only in this project but over many years. We are also grateful to Melvyn Evans for the work he put in at that stage, preparing a report on family support resources in the city areas, and for his later work in compiling lists of neighbourhood resources which were used in the Stage 2 interviews.

Before Jane's retirement it had already been decided that the research design should be altered. Originally a second cohort of families was to be recruited into the study and a major focus was to be the impact on families of *changes* made in response to what has become known as the 'refocusing initiative'. It was anticipated that these changes would lead to a larger proportion of families referred because of concerns about neglect and emotional maltreatment being helped subsequently under the provisions of Part III of the Children Act 1989. In all three authorities the proposed changes happened less quickly than had been planned originally. After consultation with the Advisory Group it was agreed that the research design would focus more on any changes to the well-being of the families already recruited into the study during a 12-month period (during 1994–95). Alongside this there would be group and individual interviews with social workers and managers to ascertain their views about the impact on practice of the changes that were gathering pace.

Since our research started, most local authorities have undertaken surveys of the cases crossing their threshold and there have been several studies and two major Social Services Inspectorate reports. We owe a particular debt of gratitude to Clare Mann for permission to make liberal use of her literature review on the role of the voluntary sector with children in need (Mann 1997).

The particular contribution of this research report to the growing volume of literature is fourfold. First, it focuses specifically on referrals where concerns are expressed about emotional maltreatment and neglect, and is the largest

British cohort study providing detailed information on this group of families. Data were collected not only from records but also from interviews with over half of all those referred for these reasons. We would like to acknowledge the professionalism, determination and sensitivity of the research interviewers: Mary Baginsky, Kalwant Bhopal, Christine Bignell, Suzanne Cohen, Samantha Creighton-Gutteridge, Valerie Golding, Suzanne Hood, Sasha Josephides, Hasina Khan, Naresh Sharma, Maria Skinner and Sara Woodward. Without them the insights into the lives of these families and their views about the services they received – or failed to receive – would be far less powerful. The data is even stronger because the families were interviewed on two occasions, and there is comparative material from families referred for reasons other than neglect and emotional maltreatment. Second, the sample includes the largest group ever studied in detail of families of minority ethnic origin who came in contact with UK social services departments because of concerns about maltreatment. These data are presented in summary here but will be examined in more detail in subsequent publications. Third, the study follows earlier work by Jane Gibbons linking data on child maltreatment and child protection services with information about the family and community support systems available to parents. Fourth, detailed information is provided on the families who were *not* offered a service as well as those who were.

Many other people have made this study possible. The research was commissioned and funded by the Department of Health: we are especially grateful to Dr Carolyn Davies of the Research and Development Division for chairing the Advisory Group and steering us through the changes in research design and direction. Members of the Advisory Group included Rosemary Arkley, Elizabeth Fradd, Jenny Gray, Anne Gross, Felicity Leenders, David Matthews, Wendy Rose, Peter Smith and Kathleen Taylor of the Department of Health; and Michael Little and Harriet Ward of the Dartington Social Research Unit. Some attended meetings throughout whilst others moved on and were replaced. We thank them all for their lively and informed contributions. Also members of the Advisory Group were staff of the social services departments and health services of the three local authorities chosen for the survey. Their names are not included here in order to protect confidentiality, but we recognise our huge debt to them for their time and the advice given throughout the project. Through them we also acknowledge the individual social workers and managers who gave so generously of their time.

Without the parents who talked through their sadnesses, and in some cases their victories over adversity, this study could not have been completed. We tell their stories with some details changed in order to protect confidentiality.

In Norwich, colleagues and students on qualifying and post-qualifying courses at the University of East Anglia (UEA) have provided encouragement and helpful suggestions. We particularly thank Jo Connolly and Jacquie White for help with data processing; and Ann Lewis, Beth Neil and Ann Way for help with the records search, interviewing the social workers and for their thoughtful analyses of the cases they discussed. Heather Cutting, research secretary, remained cheerful under pressure as she carefully typed up the data and coped with numerous redrafts. Anne Borrett was a tower of strength during the final stages and Mark Barton was largely responsible for data inputting and checking. To all of these we extend warmest thanks for playing their part with good humour.

In their different ways all have made a contribution to this report, but the faults, omissions and opinions expressed are ours alone and not necessarily those of the Department of Health, nor of the agencies taking part.

Finally, our thanks go to our partners and families for their patience and encouragement.

June Thoburn
Jennifer Wilding
Jackie Watson

University of East Anglia

1 The study in context

This study was commissioned by the Department of Health in the context of its research programme on child protection, published as *Child Protection: Messages From Research* (Dartington Social Research Unit 1995a). The studies in that programme raised a number of questions about the purposes of the child protection system while confirming that child protection procedures were, for the most part, being followed by local agencies. One such question concerned the appropriate threshold for investigations. Had the balance in social services departments tilted too far from needs assessment and provision of support, and too much towards investigation of particular incidents which might signal that a child was at risk of significant harm? The Children Act 1989 placed a duty on local authorities in England and Wales to safeguard and promote the welfare of children in need by means of family support services (Section 17). Under the Act local authorities also have a duty to make (or cause to be made) such enquiries as are necessary to enable them to decide whether they should take any action to safeguard or promote a child's welfare (Section 47). The *Child Protection: Messages From Research* studies indicated that this duty was usually seen as a requirement to investigate under the formal child protection procedures set out in *Working Together under the Children Act 1989* (Home Office et al. 1991). Although there is no contradiction between these two duties, there is evidence of some tension between them. *The Children Act Report 1993* (Department of Health and Welsh Office 1994) stated that:

> local authorities perceive often serious difficulties in achieving the intentions of S17 of the Children Act in the face of a high level of demand for action regarding child protection cases. (p.16)

The *Child Protection Messages from Research* studies were all undertaken before, or in the very early stages of, implementation of the Children Act 1989. This book presents findings from one of several research projects commissioned by the Department of Health to study post-Children Act policy and practice (Aldgate and Statham, forthcoming).

This research focuses on families with children under 8 years of age who were referred to 15 child and family teams of three social services departments because of concerns about neglect or emotional maltreatment. For comparative purposes, identical information was collected on children referred to the same teams for a service which was not, at least initially, identified with a 'child protection' label.

In their Child Protection Registers study Gibbons et al. (1995) found that a large majority of children referred because of child protection concerns were quickly filtered out of the system and received no protective or support services. This was particularly marked when the reason for referral was concern about emotional maltreatment or neglect. The research reported here takes a closer look at this type of referral and in so doing focuses on those complex cases where the key issues are not only those of 'need' and 'support' but also 'risk' and 'protection'. In all except a tiny minority of the most serious cases of neglect and emotional maltreatment both family support and child protection services are needed, either sequentially or in tandem. In setting our study in its context, we first explore the situation regarding family support services. The literature and debates about the place of the formal child protection system in meeting the support and protection needs of children who have been or are at risk of being neglected or emotionally maltreated are considered next. In the light of this knowledge and these debates, our research then describes cases which raised concerns about neglect or emotional maltreatment in the context of all referrals of children under 8 years of age. This is done in order to give an account of the needs, risks and delivery of family support resources, and to present the outcomes for the families 12 months after referral. Finally, our conclusions and the implications for policy and practice are put forward.

The context of family support

The term 'family support' is now widely used in the child welfare literature to describe interventions that enable a family to function as a unit, or for the members to remain as healthy as possible in times of difficulty. Such support can involve financial assistance, alternative accommodation for children, or various services to relieve stress upon the family. The means and goals of this practice have varied since the creation of Children's Departments in 1948, but were not consolidated as a clear duty until the Children Act 1989.

In 1948, child care officers had a responsibility towards children needing 'care', but they had no power to intervene before breakdown occurred. The power to assist a family before such a crisis was laid down in the Children and Young Persons Act 1963, but only if it diminished the need for reception into care. 'Prevention' was thus born, albeit with a narrow focus. Frost (1997) argues that this encouraged reactive practice, responding only to what was already happening – families were pathologised as failures and social work done *to* them. However, from 1948 onwards, having to look at family circumstances and seeking to return children home as soon as possible raised questions. For example, if certain family issues were tackled earlier, the need for care would not arise. Prevention thus broadened first into 'preventing neglect', then to preventing child physical abuse (and later on to other forms of abuse). And finally, in the period after 1969, to 'preventing delinquency' when 'ring-fenced' grants for 'intermediate treatment' were more widely used to bolster preventive family support services (Thoburn 1993).

During the 1980s the debate about prevention broadened out further. The Short Committee Report (House of Commons Social Services Committee 1984) and the ensuing *Review of Child Care Law* (DHSS 1985) reiterated the Curtis Committee Report conclusion (Home Office 1946): that the family is the best place for a child, and that social work services should be provided to strengthen the family unit. The Children Act 1989 required family support services to be provided to *groups* of children at risk in the community, and not simply identified 'high-risk' families. The use of medical rhetoric by Parker (1980) and Hardiker et al. (1991) clearly defines this downward shift along the continuum of preventive practice: from reactive (quaternary intervention), as in 1948, to the more pro-active support of today.

The requirement in the Children Act 1989 to provide family support was therefore to prevent long-term family breakdown or the need for more formal child protection interventions (Gibbons 1990; Parton 1991; Tunstill 1996). In their assessment of the 1989 Act, Aldgate and Tunstill (1995) argue that family support is positive social work, responding to all levels of need, not just crises, so having the potential to ease the stigma felt by families seeking help. Tunstill (1995) explains the basic principles of the Act as being the protection of the welfare of children, in light of the importance of the views of the child and of his/her family. The goals, as defined by Gardner (1992), are to identify need, emphasise parental responsibility, promote the upbringing of children by their families, provide services to prevent ill-treatment occurring, and reduce the need for care proceedings. In short, to consider the alternatives and select those that are in the best interest of each child 'in need', or of children and their families comprising a 'need' group because of the potentially harmful circumstances or environment in which they live. These alternatives were to be looked for within the informal, self-help, voluntary, private and state sectors. The 'mixed economy' of child welfare is vividly described in an account of Birmingham social services department's response to the Act's implementation (Coffin 1993).

As our research has progressed the language of 'targeting' statutory services has become more pronounced, as in a recent Department of Health report:

> Statutory social services have been and should remain a service whose resources are targeted at those whose needs cannot be met through these [family and friends] networks. (DoH 1997a, p. 9)

It is also likely that the 'too little too late' conclusions of enquiries into child deaths (summarised in Reder et al. 1993) prompted the move towards more support being offered at earlier primary and secondary stages. Utting (1998), in a contribution to a Treasury-led debate about cost-effective policies to reduce social exclusion, further refines the concept of targeting and locates it in the context of high-quality, non-stigmatising health and education services for all children.

The mechanism for delivering these supportive services is the definition of 'children in need' found in Part III of the Children Act 1989. It places on local authorities the duty:

> to safeguard and promote the welfare of children within their area who are in need; and so far as is consistent with that duty, to promote the upbringing of such children by their families. (Section 17(1))

It further clarifies that a child is in need if:

- he [or she] is unlikely to achieve or maintain, or have the opportunity of achieving or maintaining a reasonable standard of health or development without the provision for him [or her] of services by a local authority under this Part;
- his [or her] health or development is likely to be significantly impaired, or further impaired, without the provision for him [or her] of such services; or he [or she] is disabled. (Section 17(10))

'Such services' comprise financial assistance, accommodation, day care and child-minding, and services set out under Schedule 2, which include family centres; home help; occupational, social, cultural or recreational facilities; advice, guidance and counselling; and travel to enable the use of facilities.

The Audit Commission (1994) concluded that the concepts of 'family support' and 'children in need' are inextricably linked, as the former cannot exist without the definition of the latter. The point of the 'child in need' definition is to act as a filter: 'prevention' in previous legislation related to targeted recipients and something specific to be prevented, but 'support' is more diffuse and general in its aims. The acceptance that families should receive appropriate help in order to maintain themselves establishes the principle that at some time or other many families may cross the 'in need' threshold and benefit from family support services. Indeed, to make it absolutely clear that it is *family* and not just *child* support which is required, the Act states that any Section 17 service:

> may be provided for the family of a particular child in need or for any members of his [or her] family, if it is provided with a view to safeguarding or promoting the child's welfare. (Section 17(3))

However, filtering through a threshold of needs can be argued as realistically necessary, or 'the potential scale of family support might be infinite' (Tunstill 1996, p. 156). Sutton (1995) agrees:

> A broad interpretation of need would affirm the clear intentions of the Act to provide a non-stigmatising, user friendly range of family support services, rather than the preventive services demanded by previous legislation, but would run the risk of raising hopes which the available resources would never fulfil. (p. 24)

In the run-up to implementation of the Act, the Department of Health recognised the tightrope to be walked between a too-broad interpretation leading to disappointment in the light of finite resources and an over-restrictive interpretation (child protection cases only). A 'Dear Director' letter from the Chief Inspector of Social Services, the advice of which was repeated in Volume 2 of the *Guidance* on the Act (DoH 1991a, paras 2–4) stated:

> The definition of 'need' in the Act is deliberately wide to reinforce the emphasis on preventive support and services to families. It has three categories: a reasonable standard of health or development; significant impairment of health or development; and disablement. *It would not be acceptable for an authority to exclude any of these three – for example, by confining services to children at risk of significant harm which attracts the duty to investigate under Section 47. . .* [our emphasis].

Problems of definition

Noble and Smith (1994) pick up this debate and note that 'child in need' is an ambiguous concept. Support services are specified to children who are in need, but the criteria for determining need is wide and prospective, and being 'unlikely to achieve or maintain . . . a reasonable standard of health or development' (Section 17(10) of the Children Act 1989) could stretch to every child. The whole notion of 'support' is surrounded by paradox: the services that can be offered to families to support them are increased by the Act, but the eligibility for them is then narrowed to those judged to be 'in need' (Tunstill 1992). Despite being a duty, the deliberately wide nature of 'child in need' allows for wide discretion in deciding who shall receive family support services, for as Jones and Bilton (1994) point out:

> The key limitations of the definition [of need] hinge on what standards of health and development are to be regarded as reasonable, and on what degree of impairment of health and development is to be regarded as significant. (p. 12)

This is backed up by the official guidance:

> This guidance does not lay down firm criteria or set general priorities because the Act requires each authority to decide their own level and scale of services appropriate to the children in need in their own area. (DoH 1991a, para. 2.4)

Despite being clearly told that they may not rewrite the Act's definition of 'in need', local authorities, influenced by individual environments, politics and resources, drew up their own threshold procedures for prioritising the provision of services to those who crossed the 'in need' threshold. Very quickly it was these procedures that were referred to by social workers making decisions about who crossed the 'in need' threshold, rather than the language of the Act itself, as found by Brandon et al. (1999). Almost always at the top of these priority statements was 'children in need of protection' (Aldgate and Tunstill 1995). As Gardner (1992) notes, social services departments are subject to opposing pressures. Resources are either at a standstill or being reduced; but legislation such as the Children Act 1989 moves ahead and demands remain high, the consequences of which are highlighted by Aldgate and Tunstill (1995):

> It was also clear that, in a world of finite resources, choices had to be made to cover the work that was most pressing. To put it bluntly . . . no-one wants a dead child on their caseload. (p. 38)

Thus the discourse of 'need' became inextricably linked with the discourse of 'protection'. Rose (1994) showed how resource pressures led to a division of Part III and Parts IV and V of the Act, with family support being seen as secondary to protection concerns. It was not uncommon to find social workers and managers saying that they had to concentrate on their 'statutory duties', thus ignoring the wide-reaching intentions of the Act, and that Part III duties are just as 'statutory' as any others:

> The Children Act and Guidance . . . leave no doubt that children in need of protection and their families should be offered support services under Part III of the Children Act. Only when voluntary methods of helping are unable to provide adequate protection should the compulsory powers of Parts IV and V of the Act be invoked. (Thoburn and Lewis 1992, p. 49)

> There is a fundamental misunderstanding of the meaning of statutory responsibility under S17 which warrants more guidance from central government. . . . Family support services are often seen as optional and a luxury rather than as an integral part of S17 services, thereby helping to exclude children in need in the community. (Aldgate and Tunstill 1995, p. 41)

If anything, child protection concerns have become the gatekeeper to support services, rather than the other way around. The Social Services Inspectorate found that social services departments were prioritising children as being 'at risk' in order to receive services:

> In seven of the eight local authorities it was very difficult to gain access to services unless child protection concerns were expressed. (DoH 1997b, p. 1)

Many commentators have argued that the focus on risk and significant harm cases, for whatever reason, is deleterious to child welfare, by allowing needs to go unnoticed and problems to recur, or by dealing with cases via a Section 47 investigation that is not needed. Rose (1994) argues that this again means support needs are unmet, while leaving a legacy of trauma and stigma of abuse upon the family where initially there was only a cry for help. Bilson and Thorpe (1997) found that 85% of child protection referrals were unsubstantiated and a further half of the remainder did not require protection under Parts IV and V of the Act.

Thoburn et al. (1995), in a study of family participation in child protection work at the time the Act was implemented, showed that while 42% of children who were abused suffered poor developmental outcomes, so did 19% of children who were not thought to have been maltreated by parents. Drawing from several research studies, the *Child Protection: Messages from Research* overview (Dartington Social Research Unit 1995a) concluded that the environment in which a child grows up, particularly one of high criticism and low emotional warmth, can produce long-term negative effects in children.

Brandon et al. (1999), in a study of cases of significant harm undertaken three years after the implementation of the Children Act 1989, found that a large proportion of the children newly identified as 'suffering or likely to suffer significant harm' were already known by social workers to be living in such an environment but were not provided with services.

Since the publication of *Child Protection: Messages from Research* the Dartington Social Research Unit has worked with several local authorities to help them refine the way in which needs are categorised (Dartington Social Research Unit 1995b). The Social Services Inspectorate has undertaken inspections of family support work (SSI 1997b; 1998) and researchers have done further work on the categorisation of 'need'. Sinclair and Carr-Hill (1997) examined a stratified random sample of all children in contact with 25 local authorities on a specified day. They found that around 6% were registered as children in need of protection, 13% were 'looked after' by the authorities, 12% were children 'in need' because of a disability and 70% were 'other children in need receiving services'. This study indicates that the frequently repeated statement that 'we only do child protection work' may have given a false impression of the extent of work with children 'in need'. Of particular relevance to our study is their grouping of the causes of children 'in need':

- as a result of their own physical condition, disability or developmental difficulties;
- as a result of deprivation, poverty or social disadvantage;
- as a result of parents'/carers' disability, illness or addictions;
- (of protection) as a result of abuse or (wilful) neglect;
- as a result of living within unstable, stressed, conflictual, emotionally or developmentally damaging families;
- as a result of breaking the law;
- as a result of rejection from, estrangement from, or collapse of their own family; and
- none of these categories. (Sinclair and Carr-Hill 1997, p. 4)

They further reduce these down to:

- the intrinsic health and development of the child (e.g., the child's disability, mental health problems, substance abuse);
- the child's family circumstances (e.g., child suffering as a result of family conflict, abuse by parents); and
- the child not meeting the expectations of the wider community (e.g., child's anti-social behaviour, delinquency, truancy, linguistic or cultural difficulties (refugee status). (pp. 4–5)

The 'cause' most frequently mentioned (in 59% of cases) was 'living in an unstable or otherwise detrimental family' followed by 'deprivation, poverty or social disadvantage' (mentioned in 40% of cases).

A wider perspective on 'need' and 'support'

A bench-mark study, carried out by Bebbington and Miles (1989) of children in care found that half of them were from lone-parent families, compared with just 7% of children who did not need to be looked after by the local authority. Those living in overcrowded conditions were three and a half times more likely to be in care than those in houses with more rooms than people. Living in rented accommodation tripled the odds, whilst council housing, as opposed to owner-occupation, doubled the likelihood. Receiving benefits tripled a child's chances of being in care, an association also found by Burrell et al. (1994). Having a mother under 21 doubled them. Half of the children in care also came from 'poor' neighbourhoods.

This study reflects a USA study by Garbarino and Sherman (1980), who conclude that lack of an adequate income – which influences housing and living and working environments – in turn determines access to quality health, education, leisure and social facilities. Families with lower means suffer relatively poor environments, comparatively higher isolation and an increased likelihood of child maltreatment. Disadvantage may impede parents from meeting their children's physical and developmental needs (Martin and Waters 1982) leading to neglect or stress and anxiety, impairing parents' emotional care (Hegar and Yungman 1989). Wilson and Herbert (1978) found similar outcomes in a study of parenting in an inner city in the UK. Hashima and Amato (1994) report how the poor are more likely to experience greater economic uncertainty and inadequate living conditions, leading to crises, stress and social isolation which affect their relationships with their children. Coulton et al. (1995) found that children living in poverty and experiencing the lack of resources, in areas with a high concentration of other children and lone-female-headed families, were at the highest risk of maltreatment. Long (1995) and Parton (1995) note that a third of UK children were living in households of below half the national average income in 1991–2, a figure that has trebled since 1979.

The subject of emotional abuse is linked to attachment theory. Goodyer (1990), Shaw and Vondra (1993) and Feeney and Noller (1996) all cite Bowlby's (1971) conclusion that there is a connection between early life events and the ability to cope with stress. These studies are but a few to point out that parents' ability to provide the basic needs of love, protection, food and security can be impaired by low finances and poor environment, loneliness and the depression and anxiety they can create. The resulting lack of care, or anxious and inconsistent parenting may result in children being afraid of intimacy and rejection; having low self-esteem, self-control and confidence; being unlikely to trust others or ask for help; becoming frustrated and aggressive, or dependent, attention-seeking individuals, generally unable to cope with everyday demands (Egeland, Sroufe and Erickson 1983). Claussen and Crittenden (1991) found that wherever there was physical abuse there was often psychological maltreatment associated with the behaviours described. Crittenden (1999) and other authors in Dubowitz (1999) link emotional maltreatment and neglect. They also note that psychological maltreatment occurs independently of other forms of maltreatment. Weismann-Wind and Silvern (1994) found abused children were more likely to have had parents who were cold, unsupportive and exposed to life stresses. These research findings imply a cycle: that life stress affects child-rearing thus adversely affecting the child emotionally and psychologically, the behavioural results of which may then contribute to the stressed parent moving on to more extreme, physical reactions. Not only are socio-environmental factors and stress levels instrumental in the occurrence of child abuse, but by the time physical harm manifests itself the low warmth/high criticism environment, the harmful effects of which are flagged up in *Child Protection: Messages from Research,* is likely to have already damaged the child. This literature on emotional harm adds weight to the earlier point, that concentrating on child abuse and using narrow criteria such as tangible harm as a ticket to services is failing many children in need.

Evidence on the nature and importance of support

All the authors cited in this chapter thus far, as well as Seagull (1987), Gibbons (ed.) (1992), and Moncher (1995), offer the same solution – social support to help to break the cycle. It may not be possible to alter a parent's physical environment or financial situation, but reinforcing their cognitive, emotional and practical competencies may leave them more able to cope with stress, thus avoiding letting it spill over on to their children.

Smith (1998), in a paper prepared for a series of UK government seminars on social exclusion, has summarised the research on parenting education programmes, early child enrichment programmes (such as High/Scope in the USA), and more general family support services. Most research is American and includes evaluations of large-scale programmes and smaller initiatives. As an example of the latter Olds et al. (1986) found that a home-visiting service in the early months of a child's life may not reduce existing habits of maltreatment but could *prevent* it from occurring among disadvantaged families.

There is much British literature on the importance of support services in countering parental depression (for example, Brown and Harris 1978; Brown et al. 1986). More recently Harris (1993) and Sheppard (1997) have related this literature to parents who maltreat their children. Harris describes a cohort study of mothers in a socially disadvantaged area of London who had children not yet at school and husbands in manual occupations. Complex interactions are explored among childhood adversity, including maltreatment and neglect; the mothers' depression; support or being 'let down' by a current partner; and support from a less-intimately related person such as a close friend. A particular focus of the study was women who had lost a parent by death during their childhood. She concludes that:

> It was not the loss of mother as such, but the indifference and poor support that so often followed such a loss which were implicated in adult depression. (p. 101)

Women who had experienced maltreatment or neglect as children were more likely to have low self-esteem as parents, and an association was found between low self-esteem and the lack of emotional support from a partner, relatives or friends. In such circumstances episodes of depression lasted longer than if support was available and/or there were no reported incidents of maltreatment or neglect in childhood.

Eight years on, a sub-group of the daughters of these mothers was interviewed (Andrews et al. 1990). Disorders amongst the daughters and reports by them of incidents of maltreatment (usually by a father or stepfather) were associated with depression in their mothers. In a summary of the findings from this series of studies, Harris (1993) concludes:

> What stands out then from this set of studies is the notion of a conveyor belt of unsupportiveness, beginning in childhood and leading to depression in adulthood. (p. 102)

When discussing the nature of support Harris identifies two key protective factors:

> First is the crucial link between true support and self-esteem, highlighting the importance of the support figure not just listening but doing so with respect, if what is offered is truly to make some difference. Second is the way in which,

> even when true support is available, it can be overruled by what is happening in other more core relationships, for example, being let down. Both themes (respectfulness and preventing 'let down') can be seen as consistent with the [Children Act 1989], with its emphasis on the importance of parental involvement in child protection work. In practice the two themes often overlap, in that respect for the victims [of marital conflict or child maltreatment] should involve acknowledging they may have deep-seated loyalties to their abusers. (p. 140)

Harris highlights the marital or partner relationship as a protective or negative factor that interacts with other sources of support. As we shall see, marital conflict (with or without accompanying violence) is found in a high proportion of cases of emotional maltreatment or neglect, but it is rated fifteenth out of 17 in the list of circumstances in which family support is likely to be provided by social services departments (Aldgate and Tunstill 1995). In an article on child care and maternal depression, Sheppard (1997) concludes that:

> Lack of instrumental (practical) support and emotional support, as well as the absence of support with child care, has been generally related to maternal depression . . . Where women remain the primary caregivers, as is the case with social work service users, a focus on maternal depression is particularly important. (p. 817)

Sheppard's study of 116 child care clients of two district teams found, using as a screening instrument the Beck Depression Inventory (Beck et al. 1988), that '36% of mothers suffered a depression of clinical severity'. There was a significant association between maternal depression and cases being categorised by a social worker as involving potential danger of physical or emotional harm to a child. Linking together with the work of Harris:

> nearly all the depressed women suffered isolation and limited social networks, and for half this was a severe problem. Nearly a quarter had persistent and severe disruption of, and arguments with, their extended family. Over half of these women had marital problems and for nearly a third these were severe. (Sheppard 1997, p. 830)

Evaluative studies on support and help with parenting when child maltreatment is an issue are beginning to appear in Britain. Earlier work in this area is reviewed by Gibbons (1990; 1991), and Macdonald and Roberts (1995). Most concern small projects based in family centres, often with a volunteer home-visiting element. Roberts (1996) concludes that:

> family support provided by home visitors reduces the incidence of childhood injury, improves maternal psychological well-being, and has positive effects on the parent–child relationship (p. 222)

This suggests that combating parents' isolation and providing some educational feedback on child care can have an impact on the chain of abuse by helping to alleviate situational stress. By improving parents' relationships with their children incidents that may precipitate verbal or physical maltreatment are reduced. The argument is thus for continuing, low-level support for parents, such as good day care provisions:

> This type of family support perhaps leads to greater resilience and ability to resolve problems, and links isolated parents to other sources of support in local communities. (Gibbons 1991, p. 225)

Jones (1985) assessed a foster care prevention project in New York and found that support in coping with life stresses reduced the likelihood of children entering care, while those children also out-performed the control group in terms of child well-being and functioning. A crucial point is that unmet needs at case closure proved to be one of the most significant factors in a child's later entry to care. Baldwin and Spencer (1993) conclude from an evaluation of the voluntary agency NEWPIN (a home-visiting and befriending scheme for depressed mothers of young children) that there was a reduction in abuse and neglect amongst the clients of that agency. Mortley (1999) summarised the, as yet inconclusive, UK research on parenting education, another model of family support that aims to decrease the incidence of child neglect.

Children in need of protection

The place of the formal child protection system

We noted in the introduction to this chapter that one of the questions raised by several of the studies summarised in *Child Protection: Messages from Research* (Dartington Social Research Unit 1995a) was whether the thresholds for entry into the formal child protection system, as governed by *Working Together under the Children Act 1989* (Home Office et al. 1991), were appropriate. In this book a distinction is made between child protection aspects of family support packages for children assessed as 'unlikely to achieve a reasonable standard of health or development' unless the services are provided under Part III of the Children Act; and the *more formal* enquiries, assessments and conferences required by the *Working Together* guidance. It has been suggested by ministers, civil servants, practitioners and researchers (see especially the reports of the influential Sieff conferences: Sieff Foundation 1994) that some social services departments have tilted the balance too far from the assessment of need and the provision of support, placing too much emphasis on the investigation of particular incidents. In so doing they may have included too many children in the costly and, in the eyes of many parents and children, stigmatising formal system. From a study of almost 2,000 referrals investigated for child protection concerns Gibbons et al. (1995) showed that three-quarters were filtered out before an initial conference and only 15% were placed on a Child Protection Register. They suggested that the threshold for invoking child protection procedures might be too low. Referrals for neglect were particularly unlikely to be recorded as needing an interagency protection plan: only 7% of nearly 400 such referrals were recorded as needing one. These authors found that, although parents and children often seemed to need family support and services, 70% of the neglect cases filtered out before an initial conference were not allocated to a social worker nor referred for other statutory or voluntary sector services. Most investigations started under the provisions of Section 47 of the Children Act apparently revealed no need for the formal child protection system; other needs were apparently not assessed.

In 1978 the Central Council for Education and Training in Social Work (CCETSW) emphasised that:

> scanning wider than the immediate referral problem should be part of any social work visit so that preventive or supportive help can be offered before crises arise. (CCETSW 1978, p. 15)

A too-exclusive focus on 'protection' may deny family support to the much larger numbers of children in families where 'good enough parenting' is a struggle. Brandon et al. (1996; 1999) and Thoburn et al. (1997), reporting on one of the post-Children Act studies that focused on cases of significant harm, identified a further problem related to this preoccupation with specific incidents of maltreatment. They describe cases where protection plans were formulated that were too narrow and did not lead to the provision of services to counteract the *emotional* harm which children were suffering or likely to suffer. It has already been noted that, as early as 1994, the Audit Commission called for a rebalancing of services for children who may need protective services, away from individually focused investigations and towards more broadly based supportive provision. Many, however, expressed concerns that shifting the balance in this way would incur an unacceptably high level of risk, so the Department of Health called for a period of debate before any changes were made to the formal guidance (Sieff Foundation 1994).

When the study reported in this book was commissioned the treatment of 'neglect' represented a good starting-point for such a debate. At present, 'neglect' and 'emotional abuse' are specifically listed in child protection guidance as reasons for a formal enquiry and registration of children as being in need of protection, yet there are arguments to be made (Glaser and Prior 1997) that only a small minority of such children need or will benefit from formal protective intervention. They might be more appropriately helped in the first instance as children 'in need', through family support provision but with careful attention given to alleviating problems that carry risks to their health or development. However, more information is necessary about the risks and needs of children referred for neglect before firmly arguing that many of them could be offered more appropriate and cost-effective help outside the formal child protection procedures.

Defining 'neglect' and 'emotional abuse'

'Neglect', as one of the categories of abuse for registration, is defined as follows:

> The persistent or severe neglect of a child, or the failure to protect a child from exposure to any kind of danger, including cold or starvation, or extreme failure to carry out important aspects of care, resulting in the significant impairment of the child's health or development, including non-organic failure to thrive. (Home Office et al. 1991, para. 6.40)

'Emotional abuse' is defined as:

> Actual or likely severe adverse effect on the emotional and behavioural development of a child caused by persistent or severe emotional ill-treatment or rejection. (Home Office et al. 1991, para. 6.40)

At the start of the data collection phase of our study, approximately 7,000 (30%) of children on protection registers in England were categorised as 'neglected' and 3,500 (13%) as 'emotionally abused' (DoH 1995a).

The identification in 1980 of neglect as a specific category of abuse warranting registration may have been influenced by the general process of 'net-widening', whereby child protection procedures were extended to more groups of children in need; by the occurrence of neglect as a factor in child deaths, which raised public and professional concern through inquiries; and by concern within the Department of Health that neglect was not being taken seriously enough by some local authority social workers precisely because it was not identified specifically in procedural guidance. A DHSS synthesis of findings from 18 inquiry reports emphasised the need to investigate allegations of neglect as a matter of urgency, and specifically identified children being left alone as a 'warning sign' of abuse (DHSS 1982). Parton (1995) argues that the change in policy and practice from viewing neglect as a child welfare issue to considering it as a child protection issue must be understood in the changing political and economic context of the period.

At the start of our study there were few recently published articles specifically addressing this issue, although it was referred to in most general studies of child maltreatment and the child protection services. In the USA there had been an attempt to develop a more systematic range of operational definitions of types of child maltreatment (US Department of Health and Human Services 1988; Brière et al. 1996). *The National Incidence and Prevalence of Child Abuse and Neglect (NIPCAN)* categories listed under emotional abuse and neglect were:

Emotional abuse

- *Close confinement:* restriction of movement or confining a child to an enclosed area as a means of punishment
- *Verbal or emotional assault:* habitual patterns of belittling, denigrating or other forms of non-physical overtly rejecting behaviour, as well as threats of physical maltreatment
- *Other:* overtly punitive, exploitative treatment other than those specified elsewhere

Physical neglect

- *Refusal of health care:* failure to provide or allow care recommended by a health care professional
- *Delay in health care*
- *Abandonment:* desertion of a child without arranging reasonable care
- *Expulsion:* turning a child out of the home without making arrangements for care
- *Other custody issues:* for example, repeatedly leaving a child with others
- *Inadequate supervision:* child left unsupervised for extended periods
- *Other physical neglect:* conspicuous inattention to avoidable hazards in the home, inadequate nutrition, clothing or hygiene; reckless disregard of safety and welfare

Educational neglect

- *Permitted chronic truancy:* at least five days a month
- *Failure to enrol/other truancy*
- *Inattention to special educational needs*

Emotional neglect

- *Inadequate nurturance/affection:* marked inattention to a child's need for affection, attention
- *Chronic/extreme spouse abuse:* domestic violence in a child's presence
- *Permitted substance abuse:* encouraging or permitting a child to use drugs or alcohol
- *Permitted other maladative behaviour:* for example, chronic delinquency where the parent does not attempt to intervene
- *Refusal of psychological care:* failure to allow available treatment for a child's behavioural or emotional difficulties
- *Delay in psychological care*
- *Other emotional neglect:* for example, markedly over-protective restrictions.

These definitions have not been tested in British settings although, as research has proceeded, O'Hagan (1993), Glaser and Prior (1997), Iwaniec (1995; 1997) and Stevenson (1996; 1998) have refined our understanding of these concepts and definitions in the UK context. Two special editions of *Child Abuse Review* brought together UK writing on emotional maltreatment and neglect in 1997 and 1998.

Although until recently there was little British research into child neglect, the concept was bound up with the large amount of much earlier research into the 'problem family'. Such families were usually characterised by child neglect, large family size, poverty and low social status, poor physical and mental health, relationship problems and social isolation (Philp and Timms 1957). Worries about such families in Britain can be traced back to the Poor Law and the publications of the Eugenics Society (Lidbetter 1993). Stevenson (1996; 1998) explores the relationship between poverty and other aspects of parental deprivation and child maltreatment. Cleaver and Freeman (1995) scrutinise the history of parents whose children were the subject of allegations of maltreatment and conclude that 43% of the 83 sample cases could be categorised as families with 'multiple problems'. Using a similar definition, Brandon et al. (1999) conclude that 40% of a cohort of 105 children newly identified as 'suffering or likely to suffer significant harm' had parents who had 'multiple and long-standing problems'.

Research from the USA has generally found that neglected children (as compared to children in the general population or physically abused children) are more likely to show developmental delays and poor academic performance (Egeland et al. 1983; Wodarski 1990; Claussen and Crittenden 1991; Kurtz et al. 1993; Eckenrode et al. 1993). Margolin (1990) stated that neglected children were more likely to be killed in accidents. This research is often difficult to interpret as no details are given of the nature or degree of the child neglect involved, but it does suggest that neglect may have longer-term adverse consequences for child development.

Having reviewed the literature on family support, neglect and emotional maltreatment, in the following chapters we contribute to this growing volume of research by focusing on seven types of questions:

1. How big a problem is neglect and emotional abuse, when set in the context of the whole range of the needs of children and families referred to social services departments? How do neglected children come to the attention of social workers? Who frames their needs in these terms? What types of behaviour are subsumed under the labels of 'neglect' and 'emotional abuse'?

2. Are neglected and emotionally maltreated children separate groups? Are there differences, for example, between their circumstances and those of referred children who require assessment for service provision? Or is there more of a continuum? Do parents of neglected or emotionally maltreated children have different problems from other parents living in similar environments?

3. What sorts of assessment do children receive when there is concern about neglect or emotional maltreatment? Do social workers describe risks that require protective interventions as well as, or instead of, needs which require the provision of family support services? What plans for family support are made and how do parents feel about the help offered?

4. What types of services are provided in what sorts of cases? How are decisions taken to close some cases, refer others elsewhere, and allocate others for specific services or longer-term support?

5. Considering the data, does it appear that children referred because of concerns about emotional maltreatment or neglect are receiving an appropriate and a cost-effective service? Do the data suggest changes

in policy, procedures or assessment, supportive or protective services that might diminish the extent of impairment to the health and development of neglected and emotionally maltreated children?

6 Do families find the services helpful and does the provision of services appear to lead to lower levels of maltreatment?

7 In the light of events during the first 12 months, interim outcomes for the parents and children, and the opinions of the parents, do the initial decisions of social workers and managers appear to have been consistent with the Children Act duty 'to safeguard and promote the welfare of children in their area'?

Summary

The research was commissioned in the context of the Department of Health's research programme on child protection, published as *Child Protection: Messages from Research* (Dartington Social Research Unit 1995a). A question raised by that earlier research concerned the appropriate threshold for investigations of allegations of child maltreatment, particularly those involving concerns about emotional maltreatment and neglect.

This report presents findings from one of several research projects commissioned by the Department of Health study *Research on the Implementation of the Children Act 1989* (Aldgate and Statham, forthcoming). It focuses on families with children under 8 years of age who were referred to 15 child and family teams of three social services departments because of concerns about neglect or emotional maltreatment.

The growing body of research and practice literature on family support services is reviewed alongside the more extensive literature on child maltreatment.

In the first year or so after the implementation of the Children Act 1989 the emphasis in practice was on child protection, and referrals that came with the child protection label were prioritised. More recently, encouraged by the Department of Health, social work managers have found more creative ways to sift the large volume of referrals of children who may be in need – including those who may be in need of protection – and to seek more rational ways of allocating scarce resources.

Most of the research on family support services has focused on family centres and on family-visiting services. These studies are not always clear about the threshold for those using their services, which makes comparisons on the effectiveness of different models of support problematic.

There is little information about the way in which families referred because of concerns about emotional maltreatment or neglect use general family support services. When they are referred to specialist resources (provided for those referred because of child protection concerns), they are rarely differentiated as a group from those referred because of concerns about sexual or physical maltreatment.

A second body of research, which is relevant to this study, is that on the importance of social and emotional *support* as a protective factor for adults, particularly mothers, at risk of developing serious mental health difficulties. This work initially tended to concentrate on depression amongst mothers but has been developed as a framework for studying child maltreatment across the generations. This literature considers the impact of practical support (including the provision of day care) and emotional support, especially in so far as it is available from or withheld by husbands or partners.

The literature review ends with a discussion of the research and practice literature on emotional abuse and neglect. These subjects have been more fully researched in the USA and we used an American categorisation in this study, as British writing was just beginning to appear. More recent British studies have concentrated on how a particular group of families are referred because of concerns about emotional maltreatment and neglect – those families characterised as 'low on warmth and high on criticism', whose problems are long-standing. There has been less emphasis on referrals where the main concern expressed is physical neglect and inadequate supervision.

2 The methods used in the study

The study areas

Our research took place in three areas: two inner-city, urban areas with ethnically diverse populations and a mainly rural county area with a predominantly white population. This mix of communities enabled defined research issues to be considered in different geographical and social contexts. The areas were selected because all three were seeking to improve their family support services and encourage the provision of community support by voluntary agencies and self-help groups.

Large parts of both city areas had undergone comprehensive post-World War II redevelopment, which meant that much of the housing was in the form of system-built tower blocks, with clear implications for family life patterns and child-rearing. Whilst parts of City 1 were affluent, pockets of severe deprivation existed on particular housing estates.

The area called County included in our study is not traditionally viewed as a deprived location. It is well known for its pretty villages and areas of natural beauty. These tend to hide the fact that many sections of County suffer from economic disadvantage and relative poverty. The research covered one of the three social services divisions in the county, including some declining rural areas as well as a coastal town.

The structure of the research

The research employed a mixture of qualitative and quantitative methods, and information was gathered from a range of sources in four phases. Figure 2.1 gives a diagrammatic representation of these research phases.

For Phase 1 (the referral study), information was obtained from 15 social services teams in the three areas on all referrals of children under 8 years of age. Social services staff completed a monitoring form for each child referred over a period of 20–30 weeks in 1994–95. The monitoring form included the

Figure 2.1 ***The research process and samples***

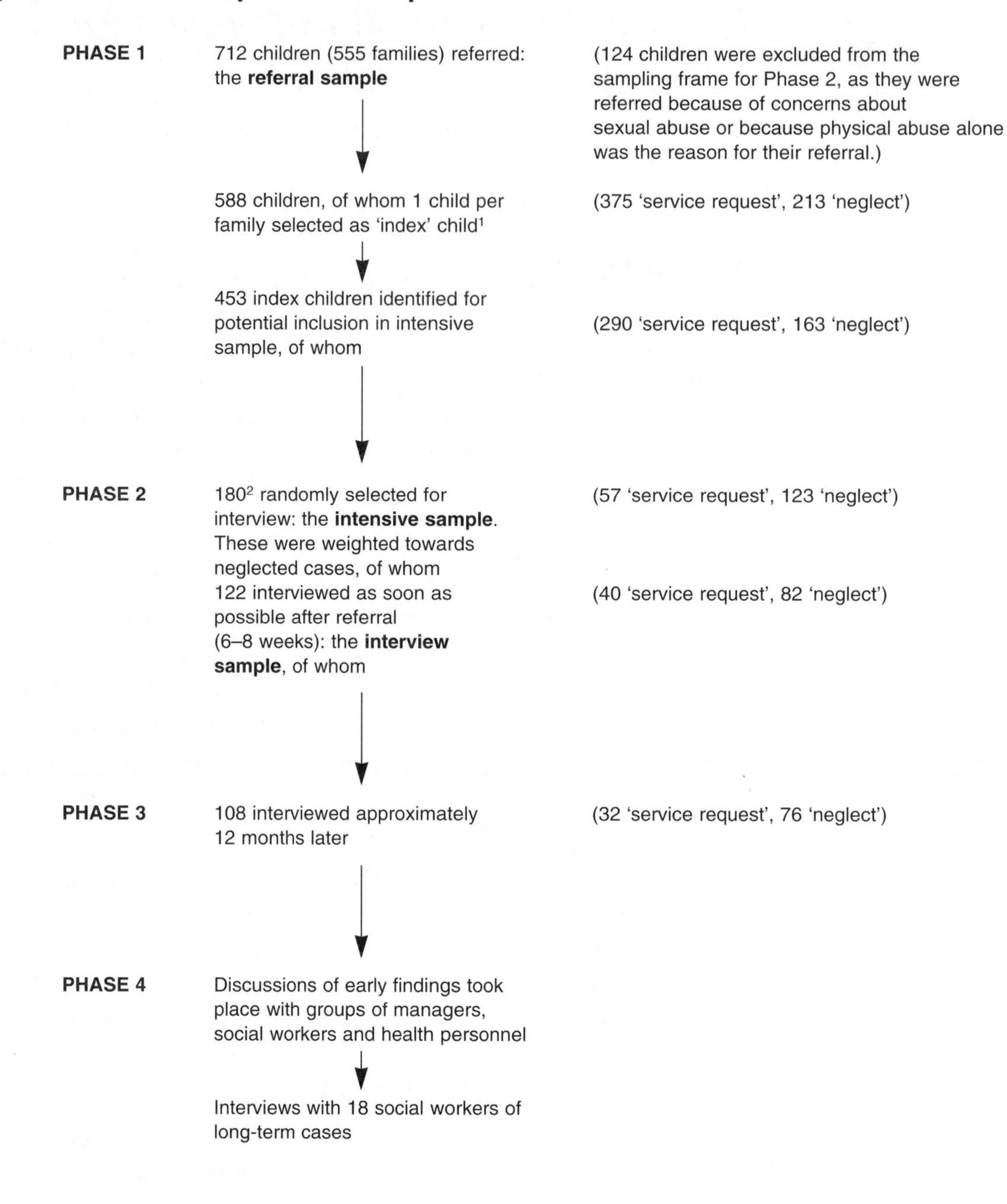

[1] The index child was the one about whom most concern was expressed (confirmed during a file search) or the youngest of those referred. The numbers from which the sample was selected were further reduced by the unavailability of some addresses (for example, an anonymous referrer did not know the child's address).

[2] The social services' records for these 180 families were scrutinised during Phases 2 and 3 and these data contribute to the Stage 1 and Stage 2 analyses.

reasons for the referral, selected from a list of nine possibilities, and the team manager's initial decision on the action required. It also included the child's name and address, age, sex, ethnic group and the main language spoken in the family. The monitoring form produced data on 712 children in 555 families. (The results of the referral study are summarised in Wilding and Thoburn 1997.) Within each family the 'index' child was the one about whom most concern was expressed or the youngest of those referred.

Before identifying a sample of families who would be asked to take part in the research, all referrals for which the monitoring form mentioned sexual or physical abuse, but not neglect or emotional abuse, were excluded. Families were then randomly selected. However, a higher proportion were selected from those referred because of concerns about emotional maltreatment and neglect (75% of such families for whom addresses were available) than those referred for a service (20%).

Phase 2 (the intensive study) had the following components:

- One hundred and eighty families were randomly selected from the referral sample and comprised the 'intensive sample', on which more detailed data were collected. Of those 180 families, 123 were referred because of concerns about neglect or emotional maltreatment (the 'neglect' group), and a smaller sample (57), for comparison purposes, were families requesting a service (the 'service request' group).

- The 'main parent' or carer in each family was invited to take part in the research. Interviewers, whose ethnic background was similar to that of the families, were recruited locally and briefed about the study. The interviewers successfully contacted and interviewed 122 of the 180 families (the interview sample) (a 68% success rate for Stage 1 interviews). A small number of the Stage 1 and Stage 2 interviews were completed by one of the main researchers in order to give more familiarity with the nature of the data.

- The social services' records on the families in this randomly identified 'intensive sample' were examined. Useful information was extracted for 176 of the 180 families, but for the remaining four, only basic information was available from the referral form.

- With the permission of the 122 families interviewed, health visitors and school nurses were contacted to complete a health record on each child. One hundred and seven families gave permission, and information was obtained on 97 children, a 91% success rate.

Phase 3 involved the following aspects:

- Those interviewed in Phase 2 were re-contacted 8–12 months later for a follow-up interview (Stage 2 interviews). One hundred and eight of the 122 families were successfully re-interviewed: an 89% success rate, and 60% of the 180 randomly identified intensive sample families.
- Updated information was extracted from the social services' records for 163 of the 180 families originally selected for interview.
- With the permission of the 108 families re-interviewed, health visitors and school nurses were re-contacted to update the health record on each child. One hundred and six families gave permission, and information was obtained on 77 children, a 73% success rate.

Phase four provided a social services' perspective and comprised:

- Group interviews with intake social workers to discuss their initial decision-making systems
- Interviews with individual social workers dealing with 18 families who received a longer-term service
- Interviews with managers about agency policy, including changes in policy and practice since the sample was identified.
- In addition, information was collected on the social and economic characteristics of the three areas, and the family support resources available in each area.

Table 2.1 summarises the different sample sizes and success rates for Phases 2 and 3 of the research.

Referral information on the monitoring forms was used to make comparisons between those identified for interview and those who could potentially have been included in the 'service request' or 'neglect' groups. There were no statistically significant differences in age, gender or ethnicity. The differences in the proportions of those contacted who were then interviewed in City 1, City 2 and County are statistically significant (56%, 62% and 82% respectively, $p<.01$). To some extent this is explained by the number of families in the city areas living in 'controlled access' flats, which made it more difficult for the interviewers to contact them. We were able to compare interviewed with allocated, but not interviewed, cases on 13 variables extracted from social services department records and found no statistically significant differences.

Table 2.1 ***Sample sizes and interview success rates for intensive sample***

	Stage 1	Stage 2
Interviews		
Number of families in the sample	180	122
Number of families interviewed	122	108
Success rate for interviews	*68%*	*89%*
Health records		
Number of families giving permission for health records to be obtained	107	106
Number of health records obtained	97	77
Success rate for health records	*91%*	*73%*
Social services' records		
Number of families in the sample	180	180
Number of social services' records providing information	176	163
Success rate for social services' records	*98%*	*91%*

The intensive study in more detail

The 180 families in the 'intensive' sample were *either* referred due to allegations of neglect or emotional maltreatment *or* the referral requested assessment, support or a specific service, with no child protection concerns specifically mentioned. Generally, the youngest child referred to Social Services from each family was selected as the 'index child'.

Families in the intensive sample were contacted first by letter and then in person to see if they would be willing to participate in the research. The success rate in the city areas was considerably lower than in the county area (59%, compared with 82% in County). This was in large part because the interviewers found it much harder to track people down in the city areas and there was more suspicion about the purpose of the research. Access to flats in tower blocks and intercom systems that sometimes appeared not to be functioning posed particular difficulties, as did multiple occupancy at addresses.

Interviewers asked specifically to talk to the main carer of the index child, and tried – not always successfully – to interview the same carer on the second occasion. Of the 122 families in which a parent was interviewed, 84 were from the 'neglect' group and 38 were from the 'service request' group, a similar proportion to the 180 families approached for interviews during Phase 2.

Each interview took about an hour, and questions were asked about:

- contact with the social services department (how it came about, what, if anything, the family had wanted);
- the families' social and economic situations;
- knowledge and use of local resources;
- the families' more personal social support systems;
- family problems;
- the physical and emotional well-being of parents and children; and
- their use of, reactions to and satisfaction with the social services department and other statutory and voluntary services.

Detailed questions about the child's health and development were also asked. For these, parts of the behaviour section of the *Looking After Children* 'Assessment and Action Records' (Ward 1995) were used.

Those interviewed were of different ethnic backgrounds and some interviews were conducted in Punjabi, Hindi/Urdu, Bengali, Spanish and Portuguese, by the trained interviewers themselves or through interpreters. The interview material was translated into eight different languages: Punjabi, Gujarati, Bengali, Hindi, Urdu, Turkish, Somali and French.

The characteristics of the families in the intensive and interview samples are described in detail in Chapter 3. In brief, 67 of the families interviewed lived in the two city areas and 55 in County. Mothers were interviewed in 109 cases; eight fathers were interviewed; and one stepmother, three grandmothers and a sister spoke with interviewers. The numbers of female and male children were roughly equal. Thirty-eight per cent of the families were of minority ethnic origin but this disguises big differences between the city areas, with 50% and 80% respectively of families of minority ethnic origin, and County, with only 2%.

Examination of the social services' records

The social services' records on the 180 families in the intensive sample were examined and information extracted using a structured schedule. This focused on previous contact with Social Services, the details of the referral, whether assessments were made and whether services were identified. Updated information from the social services' records on the 180 cases originally selected for interview was sought after 12 months. This particularly looked at whether families had been re-referred to Social Services, whether assessments were made, whether families were allocated a social worker and whether services were provided in response to either the index or later referrals. Dispersal of records to different social services teams, or case closure, sometimes made it difficult to track down the records. We had to give up on some of them as time ran out.

Summary

The study took place in two inner-city areas with ethnically diverse populations and a county comprising rural and urban populations of mainly white British descent.

In Phase 1, basic information on 555 families with 712 children under 8 years of age, referred over a 20–30 week period in 1994–95, was collected on a monitoring form. These data included the reasons for referral and the team managers' initial decision on the action to be taken.

In Phase 2, a random sample of 180 families was identified, including 123 referred because of concerns about neglect or emotional maltreatment (the 'neglect' group), and 57, for comparison purposes, requesting or referred for family support services (the 'service request' group). Stage 1 interviews were successfully completed with 122 of these families (of whom 108 were interviewed again a year later).

If parents consented, health visitors and school nurses provided data on the health and development of the children on two occasions.

Social services' records were examined during Phases 2 and 3 and data collected on the types of service provided and significant events in the lives of the family members.

Between 12 and 18 months after referral, Stage 2 interviews took place with groups of social workers and managers in each area, and with 18 social workers who undertook longer-term work with some of the families.

Quantitative data were analysed using the 'Statistical Package for the Social Sciences' (SPSS) program. The qualitative data covered the opinions of family members on their circumstances and on the services provided. Their views were also sought on the nature of their parenting and any particular parenting difficulties in the areas in which they lived. They were asked their opinions about 'need', 'risk', 'neglect' and 'abuse'. These data and qualitative data from other sources were analysed with the help of the Non-numerical Unstructured Data Indexing, Searching and Theorising (NUDIST) package.

3 The families before and after interview

Introduction to the families

In this chapter basic information about the 555 referred families and their 712 children under the age of 8, taken from the monitoring form, is presented. More detailed information then follows about the 180 intensive sample cases. (For some variables and for the qualitative data, the number of families about whom information is available is 122, that is, those interviewed at least once.) The 180 families in the intensive sample are similar to the full cohort except in two respects. This was a purposive sample that omitted families referred because of concerns about sexual or physical abuse if not accompanied by concerns about emotional maltreatment or neglect. Also, since concerns about emotional maltreatment or neglect tend less often to lead to referrals for children under 1 year, the youngest children are under-represented when compared to the full referral cohort (see Table 3.1).

Table 3.1 ***Age profile of children (referral and interview samples)***

Age of children	Referral sample		Interview sample	
	No.	%	No.	%
<1	117	17	12	10
1–2	157	23	35	29
3–4	213	31	39	32
5–7	201	29	36	30
Total	**688**[1]	**100**	**122**	**100**

[1] Missing=24 in referral sample

Table 3.2 shows that nearly three-quarters of the children lived in the city areas. Although the monitoring form included a question about the child's ethnic group, this information was not provided for over 40% of cases. Information on the child's ethnic group *was* provided for 73% of the children in the two city areas. There was a strong emphasis on the provision of ethnically sensitive services in the city areas and thus on the recording of data on

Table 3.2 ***Children under 8 years referred to social services teams during the research intake period***

Research area	No. of teams	Families		No. of children	
		No.	%	No.	%
City 1	7	192	35	266	37
City 2	3	200	36	266	37
County	5	163	29	180	25
Total	**15**	**555**	**100**	**712**	**100**

ethnicity. Interviews in the area teams as the research progressed, and scrutiny of the initial referral forms for the intensive sample, suggested that a lack of information on ethnicity from the referrer was the major reason, in the city areas, why area team staff failed, at the very early stages of the case, to complete this part of the monitoring form. Therefore, it is likely that cases where information was missing in the two city areas will have included a cross-section of ethnic groups, and that the 73% of city cases for which information on ethnicity is available is reasonably representative. In consequence, where appropriate in this report, the data on ethnicity for the two city areas were analysed separately as a sub-group of 386 referrals (see Table 3.3 and Figure 3.1).

Table 3.3 ***Ethnic backgrounds of the children in the city areas (referral sample)***

	% City 1	% City 2
African–Caribbean	13	10
Black African	14	21
Black other	8	–
Asian	22	39
White	39	23
Mixed-race parentage	4	4
Other	1	2
Base n=100%	**214**	**172**
Missing data	**52**	**94**

Since, at the start of the study, around 40% of the under-fives population in City 1 and 50% of the under-nines population in City 2 were of minority ethnic origin, it appears that these groups were over-represented among those considered by their parents or others to be in need of help from a social services

Figure 3.1 ***Ethnic origins of children, city areas only (referral sample)***[1]

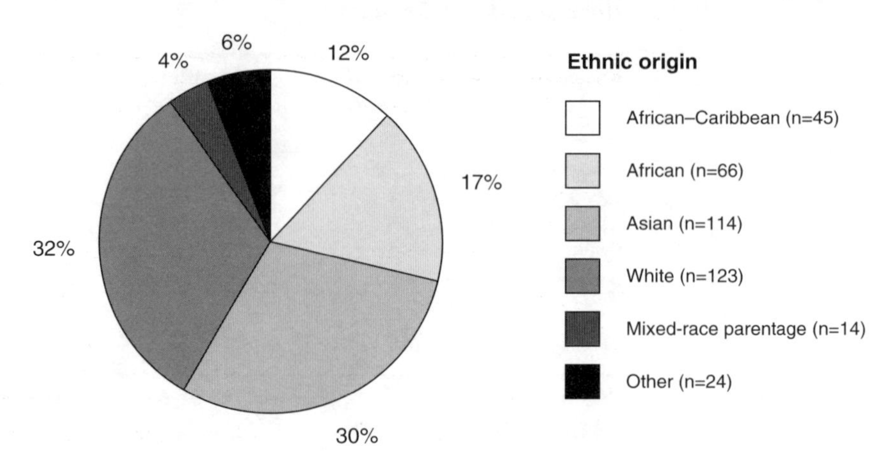

[1] n=386; missing data=146

department. Because data on age were not available for the different ethnic groups served by each social services team, it was not possible to know whether all minority ethnic groups were over-represented or just some of them.

In the County area, information on the child's ethnic group was provided for only 9% of the children. Since 98% of County's population is white, it is likely that nearly all the children in County were white other than two specifically recorded as of mixed-race parentage and one as 'white other'.

The ethnic composition of the families referred and those in the interview sample was broadly similar. The proportion of minority ethnic families in the two city areas in the intensive sample closely mirrored that in the referral sample (69% and 68%, respectively).

It was much harder to enlist families into the study in City 1 and City 2 than in County. The response rate in County was 82%, compared with 62% in City 2 and 56% in City 1, giving an overall rate of 68%.

Before giving a more detailed picture of the family circumstances of the intensive and interview samples and the reactions to their problems and to the social services intervention, we consider the reasons for referral for the 555 families and 712 children in the full cohort.

Table 3.4 shows that more than one cause for concern or reason for referral was noted in many of the cases. Just over half (53%) of the referrals of the 712 children (375) involved a request for general support or a specific service, or other matters not seen as coming within the framework of child protection.

Table 3.4 ***Concerns leading to referral of children under 8 years (referral sample)***

Reason for referral	No.	%
Concerns *re* child safety/child left alone	90	13
Concerns *re* unborn child	4	1
Other child protection concerns	67	9
Possible neglect	82	12
Possible emotional abuse	37	5
Possible physical abuse	82	12
Possible sexual abuse	47	7
Request for a service	285	40
Other	134	19
Total responses	**828**[1]	–

[1] The percentage is based on the total number of children referred – 712. The total is more than 712 and the percentage adds up to more than 100 as some children were referred for more than one reason.

Concerns about child safety or a child left alone were mentioned in 13% of the referrals and concerns about possible neglect and about possible physical abuse were each recorded in 12% of cases. Possible sexual abuse and possible emotional abuse were less frequently recorded (7% and 5%, respectively).

There were 337 monitoring forms that mentioned one or more child protection concerns (Figure 3.2). Those where the main concern was about sexual or physical abuse comprised just over a third of these child protection referrals (37%), whilst neglect, child safety, emotional maltreatment or other child protection concerns were the main reason for referral in 63%. Figure 3.2 also shows that concerns about less clear-cut child protection issues (including four referrals of unborn children) were also common at this very early stage (18% of the child protection referrals).

It is interesting to compare these proportions with the child protection referrals to eight authorities in 1991 reported by Gibbons et al. (1995). Perhaps surprisingly, in view of greater attention now being paid to neglect and emotional maltreatment as factors impacting on long-term child development, differences were not marked. The proportion of referrals for emotional abuse alone is the same as that reported in the earlier study (3%). The proportion of child protection referrals in which neglect was the main reason for referral is also similar (19% in this study and 21% in the earlier study by Gibbons et al. (1995)). However, referrals mainly because of concerns about child safety were up from 4% in the earlier study to 23% in this study.

Figure 3.2 ***Main type of maltreatment (child protection referrals only)***[1]

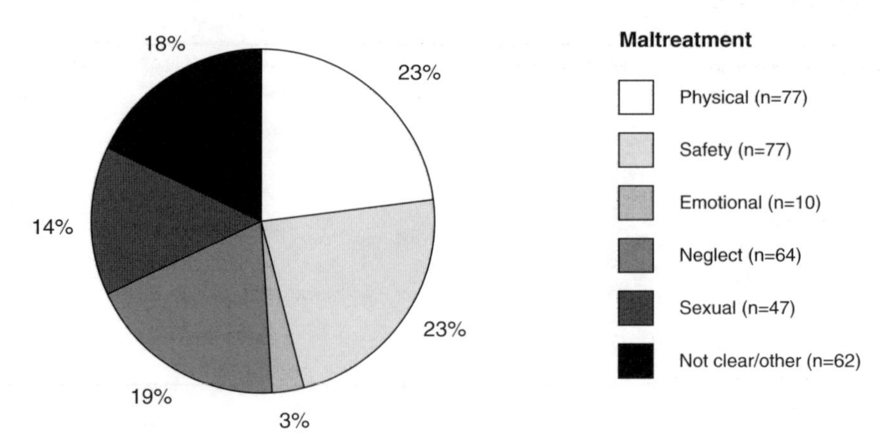

[1] n=337 children

The changes in policy and practice noted in Chapter 1 will have affected referrals in two ways. The increasing concern about the harmful impact on children of living in neglectful or 'high criticism, low warmth' families, as characterised by the authors of *Child Protection: Messages from Research* (Dartington Social Research Unit 1995a), might have been expected to lead to more 'neglect' referrals. However, the impetus given by the 'refocusing debate' and the questioning of the need for or value of the formal child protection system in cases of neglect and emotional maltreatment may have led to more of these cases being treated as 'service request' cases. These data suggest that those referring cases are continuing to identify neglect as a reason for referral.

The overlap in reasons for referral is demonstrated in Table 3.5. For example, the 37 referrals about possible emotional abuse also mentioned:

- possible neglect in seven cases;
- concerns about child safety in ten cases;
- the possibility of physical abuse in ten cases;
- other less specific child protection concerns in five cases;
- requests for a service in two cases; and
- referrals for 'other' reasons in two cases.

This demonstrates that concerns about the care and safety of children cannot be neatly pigeon-holed into mutually exclusive categories. The main exception to this pattern was the 47 referrals for possible sexual abuse. It is worth noting here that, on the monitoring forms, information usually referred to the *abusive behaviours* leading to referral. It is now recognised that sexual and

Table 3.5 ***Combinations of reasons for referral of children under 8 years (number of children, referral sample)***

Reasons for referral	Neglect	Emotional abuse	Safety/ child alone	Unborn child	Physical abuse	Sexual abuse	Other child protection concerns	Service request	Other
Possible neglect	**82**	7	–	–	–	–	3	7	1
Possible emotional abuse	7	**37**	10	–	10	–	5	2	2
Concerns *re* safety/child left alone	–	10	**90**	–	–	–	2	2	2
Concerns *re* unborn child	–	–	–	**4**	–	–	–	2	–
Possible physical abuse	–	10	–	–	**82**	–	1	3	2
Possible sexual abuse	–	–	–	–	–	**47**	–	–	–
Other child protection concerns	3	5	2	–	1	–	**67**	10	3
Request for a service	7	2	2	2	3	–	10	**285**	–
Other	1	2	2	–	2	–	3	–	**18**

physical *abuse* are often associated with or lead to emotional *harm* to the children. Crittenden's work (summarised in Crittenden 1996; 1999) is important in understanding the links between parental behaviour and emotional harm. Brandon et al. (1999) explore this complex issue in the UK context.

Our interview and file data on the 180 cases followed up after 12 months indicate that other child protection concerns emerged for an important minority of the cases, including a substantial proportion of the 'service request' cases.

Figure 3.3 shows the pattern of referrals in the three areas. Although City and County research areas were very different in socio-demographic terms, the balance between 'child protection issues' and more general child and family welfare concerns was remarkably similar, with social workers in all three areas categorising less than a fifth of all referrals as involving physical or sexual abuse. Concerns about neglect, emotional abuse and other less clear-cut protection issues were most common in each of the three areas. However, there were statistically significant differences between the areas in respect of the types of child protection concerns referred. In City 2 fewer referrals were categorised as involving neglect, more were categorised as 'other child protection' and none involved emotional abuse. The proportions referred with definite allegations concerning physical and sexual abuse were similar in each of the areas, and the proportion seeking support or a service was around 50% of all referrals.

Figure 3.3 ***Type of referral by area (referral sample)***[1]

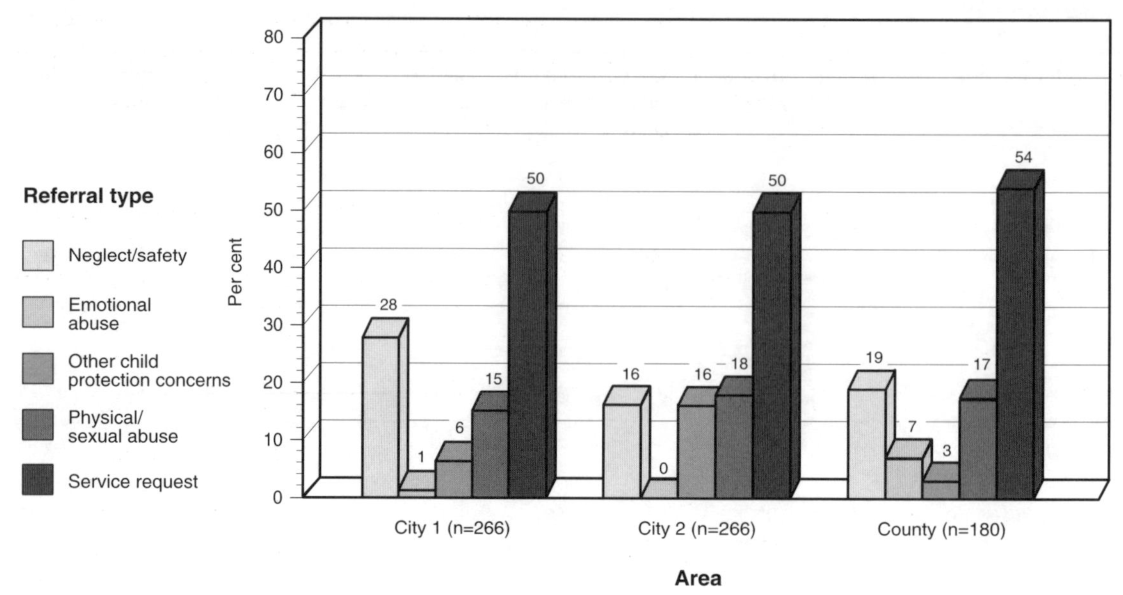

[1] n=712

Figure 3.4 ***Pattern of referral by ethnicity, city areas only (referral sample)***[1]

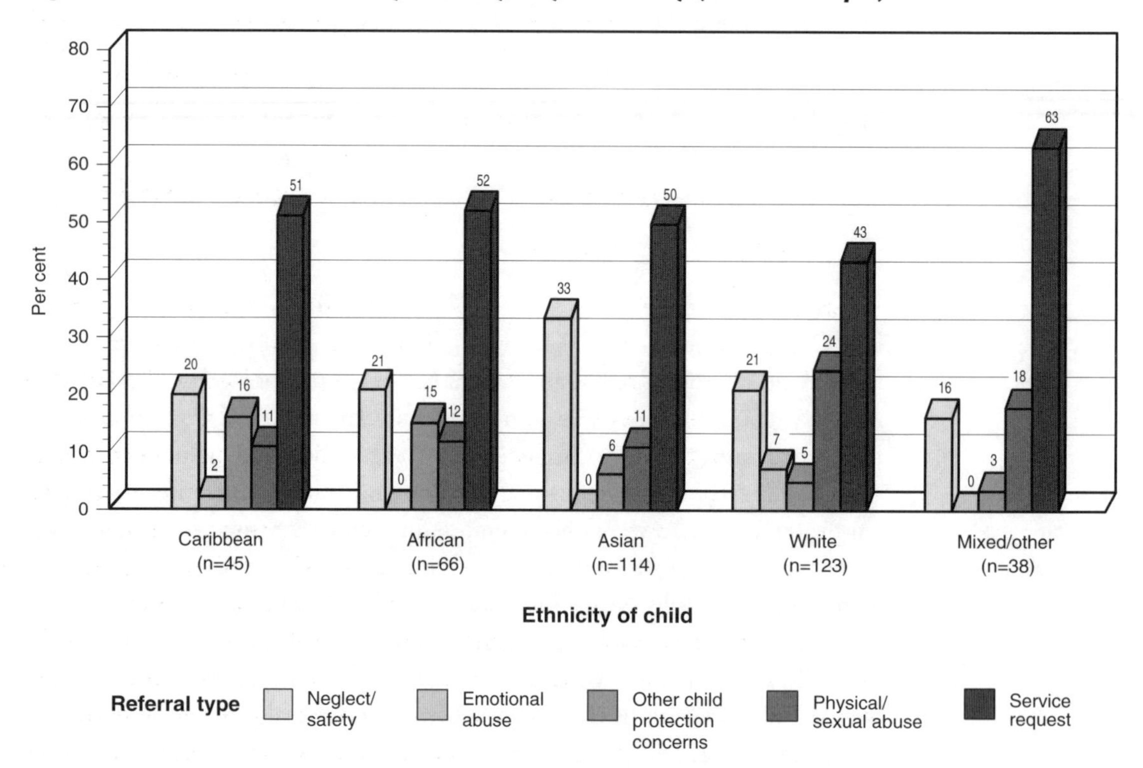

[1] Main reason for referral; n=386 cases for which ethnicity known; x^2:16.987 df:4 $p<.01$

When those of minority ethnic origin are considered together and compared with white children, there is a statistically significant difference between the two groups in that the former were less likely to be referred or to seek assistance because of concerns about sexual abuse, emotional maltreatment or neglect (Table 3.6 and Figure 3.4).

Table 3.6 ***Reason for referral by ethnicity, city areas only (referral sample)***[1]

Concern about	Ethnic origin of child				Significance (x^2 test)
	Minority ethnic origin		White		
	No.	%	No.	%	
Physical abuse	29	11	22	18	ns
Sexual abuse	7	3	14	11	p<.001
Other child protection	73	28	21	17	p<.05
Neglect	30	11	25	20	p<.05
Emotional maltreatment	5	2	11	9	p<.01
Child safety/'home alone'	41	16	14	11	ns
Service request	95	36	45	37	ns
Base n=100%	**263**		**123**		

[1] Number of children in city areas whose ethnicity is known=386. Total and percentages do not add up to 386 or 100% because more than one reason for referral was given in some cases.

The intensive sample families in more detail

Reasons for referral

Because the focus of this study was mainly on referrals that included concerns about neglect or emotional abuse, it is from cases where these concerns were noted on the monitoring forms that the largest group of families in the intensive sample was drawn. From the 235 cases in which neglect, child safety, emotional maltreatment or other less specific child protection concerns were mentioned (sometimes as a secondary reason for concern alongside physical abuse or other concerns), 123 were selected for interview. Interviews were successfully completed with 82 of these (over two-thirds of those approached and half of all referrals mentioning concerns about neglect, child safety or emotional maltreatment for which addresses were available). Fifty-seven of the 290 families where 'service request' was the main reason for referral mentioned on the monitoring form and whose addresses were available (20% of these families) were selected for interview and 40 were successfully interviewed (70% of those approached and 14% of all the 'service request' families).

Table 3.7 shows the distribution of families by main reason for referral and area for the 122 interviewed families. Just over half (55%) of the families interviewed lived in the two city areas and the remainder in County. (It has already been noted that there was a higher contact and positive response rate from County than city families.) There was a fairly even distribution of types of cases across the three areas, although there were slightly fewer 'service request' cases in City 1.

Table 3.7 ***Type of case by area (interview sample, Stage 1)***

Type of case	City 1		City 2		County		All	
	No.	%	No.	%	No.	%	No.	%
Neglect/ emotional abuse	21	75	25	64	36	66	82	67
Service request	7	25	14	36	19	34	40	33
Total	**28**	**100**	**39**	**100**	**55**	**100**	**122**	**100**

Not untypical straightforward 'service request' cases were recorded on the interview schedules as follows:

> The mother referred her 2-year-old child. The child is disabled with spina bifida. He is on the special needs housing register and she would like him to be on the register for children with a disability. The mother receives good support from the grandmother and voluntary agencies.
>
> Request came from the Education Welfare Officer for funding for a playgroup place for a child aged 3 years. Four weeks after the referral there had been letters and phone calls with a social worker but no face-to-face contact. There was no record of any resources being provided.

A more complex 'service request' case, which might in other circumstances have come in as a 'neglect' case, was noted as follows:

> The Deputy Head reported that the mother had told the teacher that she was very concerned about her son's behaviour at home. He is disruptive, wets the bed, won't dress or undress, so attends school in the clothes he slept in without shoes on, empties food on the floor and is disruptive. In desperation the mother took him to a hospital. The driver had to put other passengers off the bus and call an ambulance because the child was out of control. He was sedated at hospital and sent home with mother. School fears that mother could flip and harm her son. His behaviour at school was said by the referrer to be 'normal'.

Cases in which neglect or emotional maltreatment were the main reasons for referral were even more varied. This not untypical referral was described in the researcher's notes in the words of the mother of a 4-year-old:

> Someone reported me for swearing at my son. They called it verbal abuse. He had been screaming and I shouted back at him to make him realise. I never swear at him – he would pick it up. I felt very angry; it upset me a lot.

She received a letter warning her about her behaviour and she wrote back a detailed refutation:

> Then I got another letter which made me feel better. The only thing that worries me is that I am on their list. I'd like them to take me off.

In another case:

> The police came. Someone complained I wasn't looking after the children and they were unattended, but they weren't. I don't want anything to do with Social Services . . . I was very distressed. I was scared they would take my children away from me. Their attitude is bad. They don't understand my situation.

Some of these cases could clearly have been reframed or, indeed, referred originally as family support cases:

> A mother accused of leaving the children said, through an interpreter: 'I am very worried because I must work and I feel Social Services may take the children away.' She was facing eviction, the child was ill, the house was damp and there were many financial problems.

> A mother referred by the general practitioner because of difficulty coping with the child said: 'We wanted advice, maybe a new way of dealing not only with his behaviour but also we are getting so tired because he won't sleep.' A social worker visited but she then had a letter from the child care manager: 'A rather shitty letter criticising rather than helping. I felt I'd opened up a can of worms for myself after a half-hour visit from a bloke who didn't even meet the whole family. I feel I have got to clear my name. I feel hurt because of the things they said in the letter about how I bring up my children.'

The short case summaries show that most families in both groups *wanted* help. Some in the 'neglect' group did not consider that they had problems and would not have responded positively to offers of help. From the accounts of the interviewers, some of these children were clearly 'in need', and the parents might have accepted help had it been offered in a more positive way.

However, in other cases the referral had been an inappropriate one and it subsequently became clear that neither the family nor the child were 'in need' as defined by the Children Act 1989.

Figure 3.5 gives the main reason for referral of the 180 initially selected for interview. More than one concern was noted on the monitoring form in respect of several of the index children in the 'neglect' group. For example, of

Figure 3.5 ***Main reason for referral (intensive sample)***[1]

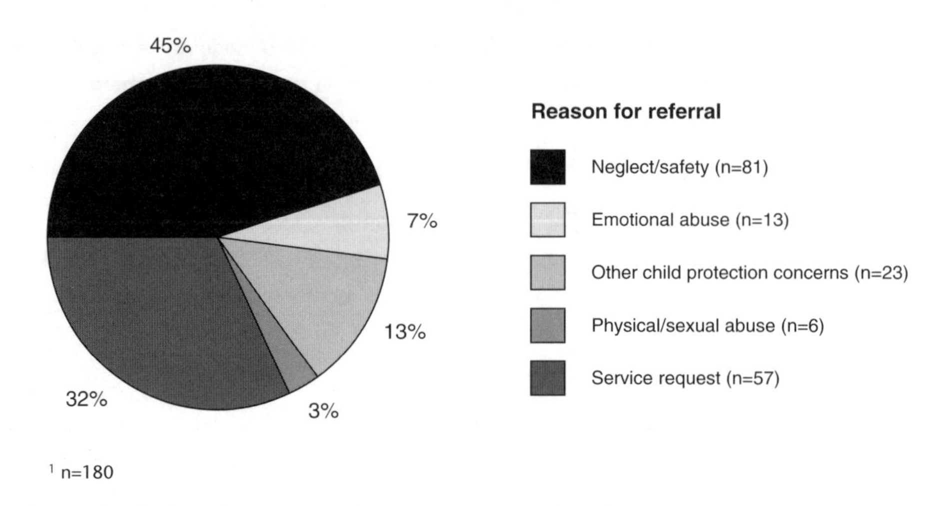

[1] n=180

Figure 3.6 ***Reason for referral by area (intensive sample)***[1]

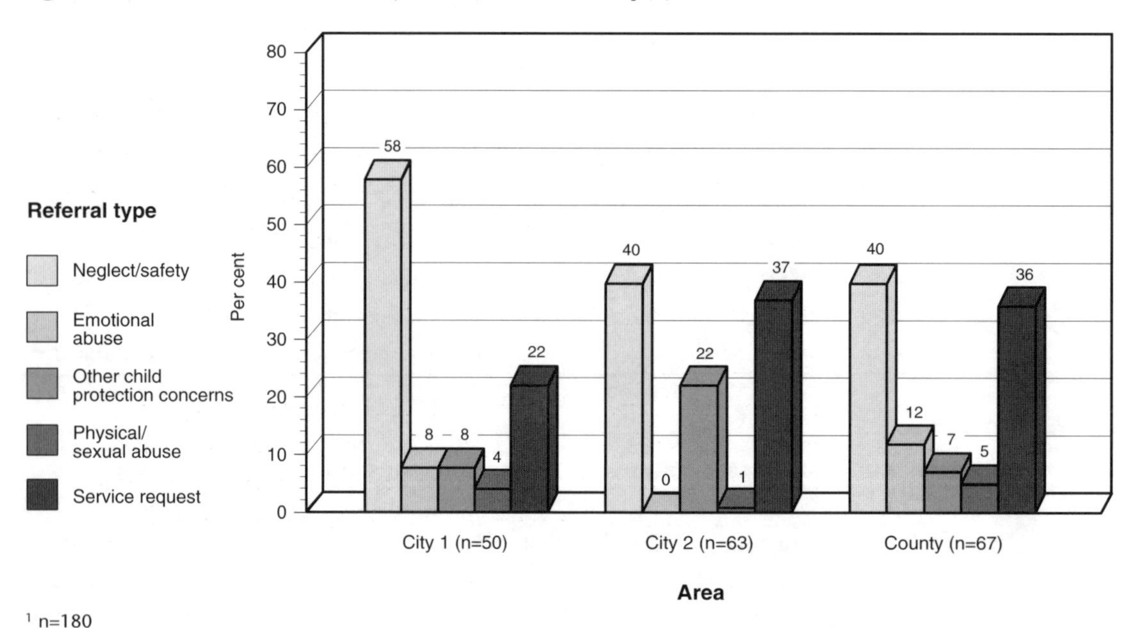

[1] n=180

the 29 referred because of concerns about neglect, there were also concerns about possible emotional maltreatment (four cases), safety (six cases), possible physical abuse (three cases), as well as specific services having been requested (two cases). Whilst several reasons for referral were mentioned on the referral forms, it was unusual for there to be a specific request for a service alongside a child protection referral (only six cases). As we shall see in Chapter 6, concerns about possible neglect or maltreatment emerged in respect of an important minority of the 'service request' cases. Figure 3.6 shows that more of those in the intensive sample in City 1 were referred because of concerns about neglect or child safety than was the case for City 2 or County. This should be borne in mind when considering our findings.

After the first file scrutiny and interviews, more complex patterns emerged. Table 3.8 lists the forms of maltreatment or neglect about which concern had been expressed using the NIPCAN categories developed by the US Department of Health and Human Services (1988). Although cases where sexual abuse was mentioned on the monitoring form had been specifically excluded from the intensive sample, it emerged that there were three cases in which there were concerns about sexual abuse. The pattern for the three areas in terms of the types of maltreatment was broadly similar. However, more City 2 cases came under the 'physical neglect' category (55% of the City 2 'neglect or emotional maltreatment' referrals) than was the case in City 1 (39%) and County (37%). (This trend did not reach statistical significance.) In contrast, there was a significant difference in respect of referrals under the 'emotional abuse' groupings, there being none in City 2, 18% in City 1 and 15% in County.

The high proportion in the 'inadequate supervision' category is flagged up here as it was within this group of referrals that there was most variation in terms of the needs of the parents and children, either for a high-level service or for none at all. This case was at one end of the spectrum:

> The school phoned that the child had not been collected from school by 4.45 p.m. The duty officer collected the child and returned him to the parents. The father spoke little English. He tried to explain that his wife was ill. A duty visit was made later and it was concluded that failure to collect was a 'one-off' due to mother's hospital appointment. The mother was advised through an interpreter of her legal responsibilities.

At the other end of the 'inadequate supervision' continuum:

A 4-year-old child of African descent was found wandering alone on the main road in the afternoon. She had several near misses with cars. The shopworker took her inside and called police as she would not communicate with her. The police took the child home following pointed directions. They found her 22-year-old brother with parental responsibility and six other children under 14. The sister aged 19 and the brother were looking after their brothers and sisters. Three years ago the 19-year-old saw her mother killed with a machine gun. The father died in a refugee camp.

Table 3.8 ***Frequency of types of maltreatment[1] (intensive sample, Stage 1)***

Types of maltreatment[1]	Neglect/emotional abuse/other child protection concerns		Service request	
	% with behaviour[2]			
Emotional abuse	**15**		**2**	
Close confinement		3		–
Verbal assault		5		2
Other emotional abuse		7		–
Emotional neglect	**23**		**10**	
Inadequate affection		3		–
Extreme spouse abuse		17		6
Permitted substance abuse		1		–
Permitted other maladaptive behaviour		1		–
Other emotional neglect		2		4
Physical neglect	**63**		**9**	
Refusal/delay health care		3		–
Abandonment		3		2
Other custody issue		2		–
Inadequate supervision		34		2
Other physical neglect		26		6
Unspecified neglect		5		4
Educational neglect	–		–	
Physical abuse	**12**		**2**	
Sexual abuse	**3**		–	
None of the above	**7**		**77**	
Base n=100%	**123**		**57**	

[1] The categories of maltreatment are based on those developed by the US Department of Health and Human Services (1988) in its study of the national incidence and prevalence of child abuse and neglect (NIPCAN).

[2] The percentages do not add to 100 as more than one type of behaviour could apply.

Not surprisingly, there was a difference between the 'service request' and the 'neglect' referrals when the more detailed information on causes for concern is considered.

Physical neglect was the largest sub-group (63% of the 'neglect' referrals and 9% of the 'service request' referrals). This was a 'service request' case which could equally well have been framed as a child protection referral:

> A friend from church referred a young mother who had recently had her third child and suffered from post-natal depression. The child was recently 'dropped' and taken to hospital. The mother was allegedly not coping and the father had a demanding job and was away from home for long hours.

Physical neglect cases were sometimes associated with parental substance abuse. This referral came from a paternal grandmother:

> The grandmother had received a phone call from the mother. The mother was very abusive and her speech was slurred – she was apparently under the influence of alcohol or drugs. The grandmother phoned the police because she was worried the young children could have accidents and was advised to phone the social services department. The mother had previous convictions for possession of drugs, drunkenness and theft.

Emotional neglect cases were often associated with traumatic events in the lives of the parents such as the death of a child or close relative, or marriage breakdown. This was a 'service request' case.

> GP referred a 'distressed single parent'. The mother of an 18-month-old-child was recently separated. She was struggling to overcome the trauma of marriage breakdown. There were financial problems relating to the separation and she was not coping well with her child.

This physical and emotional neglect referral was made by a neighbour who wished to remain anonymous:

The mother needed help because of miscarriages and depression. The two sisters went to school looking very unkempt. They were never properly dressed for bad weather. They had holes in their shoes and no change of clothing. They went to school in wet things from the day before. Their hair was uncombed and the other children bullied them because of their appearance.

Extreme spouse abuse which was considered likely to cause impairment to a child's emotional development was the third largest sub-category.

A neighbour referred a mother and children who had been subjected to domestic violence. The referrer said the mother was worried because the father from whom she was separated had been rehoused in the same area and could now find and physically abuse them.

These cases indicate that some referrers (including family members themselves) sometimes chose to frame concerns about neglect in 'family support' terms. In 10% of the 'service request' cases there were concerns about emotional neglect, and in 2% there were concerns about inadequate supervision. There was one 'verbal assault' referral, four 'extreme spouse abuse' referrals but no 'close confinement' or 'inadequate affection' referrals amongst the 'service request' group.

The social and environmental context

We attempted to locate the interviewed families within their social and environmental context by collecting data on ethnicity, household structure, employment status, housing and neighbourhood. A number of social factors were examined to identify the level of social disadvantage among the interviewed families. These were:

- having five or more children in the household;
- living in crowded accommodation (more than one person per room);
- having insecure accommodation (neither an owner occupier, nor a council or housing association tenant nor living in privately rented unfurnished accommodation);

- no wage-earner in the household;
- lacking exclusive use of three or more basic amenities or consumer items (a cooker with an oven, a fixed bath or shower, running hot water, indoor flush toilet, a car, a television, a fridge, a washing machine or a phone); and
- lacking one or more basic utilities (water, gas, electricity).

These data, along with other indicators of disadvantage, are summarised in Tables 3.9 and 3.10. Table 3.11 gives summary information about disabilities and mental or physical health problems or addictions of parents or children.

Although County was a much more prosperous area than City 1 or, especially, City 2, most of the respondents in all three research areas appeared to share a common poverty. In this respect, respondents in County were

Table 3.9 ***Indicators of housing and economic disadvantage of family (interview sample, Stage 1)***

Indicators of housing and economic disadvantage at first interview	No.[1]	%[2]
Housing stability		
Five or more house moves in previous five years	12	10
Insecure accommodation[3]	6	5
Housing conditions		
Crowded – more than 1 person per room	72	59
Crowded – more than 1.5 persons per room	18	15
Five or more children under 16 years of age in household	4	3
Three or more children under 5 years of age in household	4	3
Lacks exclusive use of one or more utilities[4]	22	18
Lacks exclusive use of one or more basic amenities[5]	4	3
Respondents' views of housing situation		
Dissatisfied with current housing	43	36
Would like to move	82	68
Economic situation		
No wage earner in household	69	57
Lacking consumer items		
Lacks two or more consumer items[6]	20	17
Lacks telephone	29	24

1 Number of cases per indicator varied between 118 and 122
2 Percentages calculated separately for each indicator
3 Insecure accommodation = not owner occupier; council or housing association tenant or in privately rented unfurnished accommodation
4 Utilities = water, electricity and gas
5 Basic amenities = cooker with oven, fixed bath or shower, running hot water and indoor flush toilet
6 Consumer items = colour television, refrigerator, washing machine and car

Table 3.10 ***Other indicators of disadvantage of family (interview sample, Stage 1)***

Indicators of disadvantage at first interview	No.[1]	%[2]
Household structure		
Lone parent	57	47
Reconstituted family	14	12
Type of family		
Family with long-term social, emotional and environmental problems	33	27
Disability		
Parent in the household with physical disability, learning difficulties or long-term/serious physical illness	32	26
Any child in the household with physical disability, learning difficulties or long-term/serious physical illness	29	24
Social support		
Mother of respondent no longer alive or not living in the UK	34	28
Father of respondent no longer alive or not living in the UK	47	39
No relatives seen or spoken to in last four weeks	16	13
No one available to help with:		
Advice	17	14
Material help	30	25
Help with the children	22	18
Private feelings	14	12
Problems reported by the respondent		
Very many problems with:		
Social contact	42	35
Finances	47	40
Health	36	30
Parenting	29	24
Relationship with partner in household (n=66)	8	12
Personal stress level as reported by the respondent		
Marked or high levels of emotional stress	68	56

[1] Number of cases per indicator varied between 119 and 122
[2] Percentages calculated separately for each indicator

Table 3.11 ***Disability and serious ill health of family members***[1] ***(interview sample, Stage 1)***

Index child	**No.**	**%**
Physical disability	10	8
Learning disability	7	6
Undiagnosed problem	2	2
Behavioural/emotional problems	15	12
Chronic ill health/asthma	20	16
None	68	56
Any sibling with a disability (main problem)		
Physical disability	4	3
Learning disability	5	4
Behavioural/emotional problems	14	11
Chronic ill health/asthma	7	6
No disability	63	52
No sibling	29	24
Adult in household (most serious problem)		
Physical disability	11	9
Learning disability	3	2
Mental ill health (including alcohol and substance abuse)	37	30
Violent behaviour	19	16
None	52	43
Base n=100%	**122**	

[1] Main disability. Twenty-three of the index children, 18 of the siblings and 19 of the parents had more than one health problem or disability. Percentages calculated separately for each indicator.

probably more like their fellow users of social services in Cities 1 and 2 than the generality of families living in County (see Table 3.12).

Family structure and support

There were no significant differences between families in the different research areas in terms of *household structure*. Mothers were the main care-givers (and hence the respondents) in 109 (89%) of the families. Respondents' mean age was between 29 and 30 in all areas. Table 3.13 shows that very young mothers were quite uncommon. Between 28% (in City 1) and 51% (in County) identified themselves as married or co-habiting. Between 24% (in County) and 36% (in City 2) had no current partner, but between 41% (City 2) and 64% (City 1) were in lone-parent households, in the sense that there was either no current partner or there was a partner who did not live with them on a full-time basis. (We learned from the interviews that 'live-out' partners were involved in the lives of some of these families.)

Table 3.12 ***Indicators of social disadvantage by research areas***[1] ***(interview sample, Stage 1)***

Disadvantage indicator	City 1 %	City 2 %	County %	All %
5+ children	4	–	5	3
Crowded	46	62	64	59
Insecure accommodation	7	5	4	5
No wage earner	57	54	58	57
Lacked 3+ basic items	11	13	7	10
Base n=100%	**28**	**39**	**55**	**122**

[1] Percentages calculated separately for each indicator

Table 3.13 ***Age of respondents***[1] ***(interview sample, Stage 1)***

Age group	No.	%
17–19 years	5	4
20–24 years	25	21
25–29 years	37	30
30–34 years	26	21
35–39 years	20	16
40+	9	7
Total	**122**	**100**

[1] Mean age 29.5 years; age range 19–45

Table 3.14 summarises the data on available support in the three areas and shows that City 2 families were particularly likely to lack people to whom they could turn.

There were no differences in *employment status*, with roughly equal numbers in each area reporting that no one in the household was economically active.

There were some differences in *housing*. Families in City 1 tended to be more often renting from the local authority or a housing association and less often buying their houses. Respondents in County generally felt more satisfied with their neighbourhoods and had more garden space. They were significantly more likely to have cars. However, County respondents moved house as much

Table 3.14 ***Mean number of people available for support in research areas (interview sample, Stage 1)***

Type of support	City 1 (28)	City 2 (39)	County (55)	Significance[1]
	Mean number			
Advice	2.6	1.1	3.2	p<.001
Loans, material help	2.3	0.8	3.2	p<.001
Help with children	2.2	0.8	3.1	p<.001
Intimate confiding	1.7	1.0	2.3	p<.001

[1] One-way analysis of variance

or more often: 42% had lived at their present address for less than a year, compared with 41% in City 2 and 32% in City 1. County families were more likely to lack exclusive use of one or more utilities, this being sometimes explained by their living in shared accommodation, but also because there was no gas supply in some parts of the area. There was a trend, which did not reach statistical significance, towards city families being dissatisfied with their housing and wanting to move. More city families lacked three or more consumer items.

On relationship-related or personal aspects of disadvantage there were statistically significant differences in that County children were more likely to live in reconstituted families and to have a parent who had a physical or learning disability of a long-term illness (38% of County families in this group). Children in City 1 and City 2 were more likely to have a grandparent who was either dead or living abroad, and City 2 families were less likely to have spoken to a relative in the last four weeks and less likely to be able to turn to friends or neighbours for advice. We will return to data on social support in Chapter 5.

There were no statistically significant differences on these broad indicators of social disadvantage between those who referred themselves, or were referred, for a service and those who came into contact with Social Services because of concerns about neglect or emotional maltreatment (Table 3.15).

Personal and relationship difficulties

As well as being asked about their material and social circumstances, parents completed the Rutter 'malaise' schedule (Rutter et al. 1981; Robins and Rutter 1990) and also a checklist on family problems (adapted from Gibbons 1990). Table 3.16 gives the scores on the six dimensions. Respondents in City 2 scored significantly higher on perceived lack of social contact. This was consistent with their comparative lack of people to turn to for social support.

Table 3.15 ***Indicators of social disadvantage by type of referral (interview sample, Stage 1)***

Disadvantage indicator	Neglect/emotional abuse/ other child protection concerns		Service request		All	
	No.	**%**	**No.**	**%**	**No.**	**%**[1]
Five or more children in household	4	5	–	–	4	3
Crowded	48	59	24	60	72	59
Insecure accommodation	4	5	2	5	6	5
No wage earner	47	57	22	55	69	57
Lacked three or more consumer items	10	12	3	8	13	11
Base n=	**82**		**40**		**122**	

[1] Percentages calculated separately for each indicator; no statistically significant differences for any of the five indicators

Table 3.16 ***Family problem scores in research areas and comparison area***[1] ***(interview sample, Stage 1)***[1]

Type of problem	City 1	City 2	County	Comparison
	Mean scores			
Social contact[2]	13.2 sd 3.6	15.1 sd 3.7	12.2 sd 4.6	10.9 sd 4.4
Money	16.2 sd 6.5	17.3 sd 5.3	16.5 sd 6.2	8.6 sd 3.8
Health	7.6 sd 3.8	8.1 sd 3.9	6.6 sd 3.5	5.1 sd 2.5
Parenting	18.9 sd 7.2	20.2 sd 7.2	18.4 sd 6.3	13.9 sd 5.4
Partner relationship	8.2 sd 5.0	7.3 sd 4.5	7.8 sd 4.3	5.6 sd 2.3
Malaise[3]	9.1 sd 5.2	8.2 sd 4.8	6.6 sd 5.2	– –

[1] Scores of a random sample of 358 parents living on council estates in southern England (Gibbons 1990)
[2] One-way analysis of variance p<.01
[3] Rutter 'malaise' schedule (Rutter et al. 1981)

Otherwise there were no significant differences between the research areas. As would be expected, mean scores on all the scales were higher than those of a randomly drawn sample of parents living on council estates in two counties in the late 1980s (Gibbons 1990).

Far more parents in this present study rated themselves in the 'very many problems' group on the social contact dimension (35%) than was the case for a cohort of parents whose children were newly identified as 'suffering or likely to suffer significant harm' (7%; $p<.001$) (Brandon et al. 1999). Proportions saying they had financial problems were roughly similar in the two studies, although more in the 'significant harm' sample said they had 'no or few problems'. Similar proportions in both studies rated themselves as having no or few health problems, but proportions in the 'very many problems' group though high for this present study (36%), were even higher for the 'significant harm' study (48%; $p<.05$). Parents in the 'significant harm' group were also more likely to rate themselves more highly on the dimension of parenting problems and partner problems (with statistically significant differences at the $p<0.5$ level for parenting problems and $p<.0001$ for partner problems). These differences may in part be explained by the fact that the 'significant harm' study included children in all age groups. Comparisons do indicate that emotional and relationship problems in this referral group, though marked, had not yet reached levels at which it might be anticipated that positive change would be most difficult to achieve.

In the weeks after referral to social services departments, respondents were continuing to experience high levels of stress, as reflected in their scores on the 'malaise' schedule (Rutter et al. 1981). Table 3.17 shows that, although similar proportions had *low* levels of emotional stress, more in the 'significant

Table 3.17 *Social 'malaise' score (interview sample, Stage 1)*[1]

Social malaise score[2]	Family support study		Significant harm[3] study	
	No.	%	No.	%
Low emotional stress (score 0–6)	54	44	18	39
Marked emotional stress (score 7–14)	53	44	14	30
High emotional stress (score 15 or more)	15	12	14	30
Total	**122**	**100**	**46**	**100**

[1] x^2: 21.071 df:2 $p<.0001$
[2] Rutter et al. (1981)
[3] From Brandon et al. (1999)

harm' study than in this present study had high emotional stress levels ($p<.0001$). However, in both city areas the mean 'malaise' score was above the conventional cut-off for possible psychiatric disorder, and it approached this level in County. There was a trend (which did not reach statistical significance) in the direction of 'service request' families reporting *higher* levels of emotional stress and more social contact and health problems, and towards those referred because of concerns about neglect or emotional maltreatment reporting more financial and marital or partner problems.

In the light of all the data available, each family was allocated to one of the categories that emerged from a study by Cleaver and Freeman (1995) (subsequently used by Brandon et al. (1999) in their study of significant harm cases). This 'researcher rating' was based on separate ratings and discussion between two of the researchers after reading all the available data. In using this 'categorisation' we are aware of the dangers inherent in any 'labelling' process. However, assessment, as we shall see in Chapters 6 and 7, is of central importance to the provision of a sensitive, appropriate and cost-effective service. There is an urgent need for assessment tools to be developed for planners, service managers and practitioners, and this involves some attempt at categorisation if appropriate services are to be developed to prevent further impairment of the health and development of children living in different circumstances. However, with individual families, there is no substitute for a thorough assessment, carefully recorded on each dimension of functioning of each family member. The *depth* of the assessment will depend on the reason for seeking help or being referred, and the extent and likelihood of any harm to each child in the family.

Families were allocated to the '*multiple and long-standing problems*' category, either because the problems were already long-standing or because (for younger parents) one or other had a history of difficulties as a young adult which continued after the birth of the index child. An example of families with multiple and long-term problems was:

The referral was made via the NSPCC. The anonymous caller said that the mother threw a 5-year-old across the room and tried to strangle him. The caller said that the mother was on heavy medication, and that tablets were littered about and dangerous to the child. The home was described as filthy. The child appeared underweight and there was no food in the cupboard. The mother told the anonymous caller that she was not bothered about the children. A Section 47 enquiry was undertaken and the police investigated the possibility of criminal neglect. There was no child protection conference or registration, and the family was allocated to the long-term child and family team. A careful assessment concluded that the mother suffered from recurrent bouts of depression. Family support plans were put in place including short-term accommodation for the children, help with cash to clear off debts, practical help with the cleaning of the house, and referral to NEWPIN. There was liaison with the adult psychiatrist.

Whilst most of the families with multiple and long-standing problems also lived in circumstances of poverty and poor housing, this was not always the case:

A father who was separated from his wife and children told the school that he was very concerned about the care they were being given. He thought his ex-wife was often drunk and he was worried that the new partner might be drinking also and possibly maltreating the children in some unspecified way. The mother, when interviewed by the social worker and by the researcher, said that there were no problems, and that her ex-husband was trying to make things difficult for her. The house was clean and tidy and mother and children well-spoken and friendly. There were eight further referrals in this case, including some from the mother asking for financial help and from the father because of his continuing concerns. Nine months later the mother with her children went to a women's refuge after a violent attack from the partner. She left the children there for two days without saying where she was going, and an Emergency Protection Order was sought. It later became clear that the partner had been sexually abusing one of the girls and that the mother had been drinking heavily for several years, this being one of the reasons for the breakdown of the first marriage. At the end of the year the children were placed on a permanent basis with their uncle and aunt, but the mother was again pregnant. A pre-birth child protection conference was to be held.

'*Acute distress*' families were, at the time of referral, in a state of actual or near collapse. They differed from the first group in that there was information to suggest that past problems had been dealt with until one overwhelming incident or sequence of events precipitated child maltreatment or the exposure of a child to actual or likely impairment of physical, emotional or educational development (Section 17(b) of the Children Act 1989). Some of the refugee families came into this group, as did some of the parents with a disability or serious illness and some of those who experienced serious marital or partner conflict. Examples of 'acute distress' families are:

The hospital referred a mother and her 10-day-old baby, the youngest in a family of four children under five. They were Vietnamese refugees who had come to the UK after surviving the hazards and trauma of being 'boat people'. The mother was reported to drink heavily and told the social worker she was planning to leave the family. The case was referred immediately for long-term work because of its complexity and the vulnerability of the children. The school said that the father hit the older children and there were allegations of the children being left on their own. The baby had quite bad eczema which was not being properly treated The father was clearly attached to the children and was the main carer. His depression and emotional problems were compounded by a further sense of loss and isolation when his wife left. The poverty of the living conditions was described as appalling. The social worker said that she 'assessed straightaway that this was a family in need because they didn't have quite basic things that they needed'. When the most basic problems had been sorted out and help with day care and a family aide provided, the social worker provided a longer-term counselling service as well as advice on child care and discipline. At the end of the year there were signs that the acute problems were diminishing and that the children were receiving good enough emotional and physical care. The risk to the children as well as the needs of the family as a whole were kept constantly under review, but it was concluded that the formal child protection system would be unhelpful in this case.

A young Asian mother was referred because the playgroup noted scratches on the face of a 3-year-old. The mother was asthmatic and lived on the eighteenth floor of a tower block with her four children. Her husband had recently left her, and although she expressed relief at this as the relationship had been conflictual, she was depressed, apathetic and extremely isolated. One of the children had serious behaviour problems and his sister was described as shy and withdrawn. At both interviews on the family problem questionnaire checklist she scored as having very many social contact problems, considerable money problems, and very many health and parent–child problems. This case was originally treated as a child protection referral, and on realising that the scratches on the child's face were almost certainly caused by a sibling, the social worker gave advice about local groups and closed the case. The mother told our interviewer that she was surprised to get a letter from Social Services and was angry at first. She said the social worker was quite friendly and easy to talk to, but that she did not offer anything. The mother herself subsequently applied for subsidised playgroup places and at this stage her extreme isolation and inability to respond fully to the emotional needs of her children was picked up. The case was more carefully assessed, and subsidised playgroup places provided. The mother said at the second interview: 'I would like to know what is available and how to get the help when I need it. They should tell people what is on offer. They should be there to help you when you need them.'

In families who were allocated by the researchers to the '*specific issue*' group there was at least one parent who was usually able to provide adequate physical and emotional care to the child but was impeded at the time of the referral by a particular type of problem. This may then have led on to other difficulties which would be clarified if the main problem could be adequately resolved. Most of the refugee families came into this group, having apparently managed well until thrown off balance by the traumatic events that caused them to leave their countries of origin and the stresses of life as asylum seekers in a strange country with very different customs. The normal coping and parenting strategies of others were disrupted by illness or disability, an increase in the misuse of drugs or alcohol by either parent, or an escalation of marital conflict. Although they needed help, they were not yet at collapse point.

A request was made by the mother of a 3-year-old for financial assistance to pay for a private helper and for winter clothing for her daughter. A Social Fund request had been refused. The family was of Iranian descent. Although there was a cousin living in another part of the city, the disability led to considerable isolation for mother and daughter. The mother was epileptic. She was awaiting hospital treatment as an in-patient and would have difficulty financing care of her child. Her bedroom, kitchen and bathroom were damp. The mother and child were both assessed as 'at risk' because of the mother's ill health and physical incapacity. The mother was assessed as needing help with domestic tasks and child care, and the child was assessed as needing more stimulation because she was indoors with the mother most of the time. The family support plan included the offer of home care services; help to apply for the disability living allowance; the provision of a nursery place for the child on three days a week, plus escort to and from the nursery; liaison with the welfare benefits unit; and contact with the housing department about the mother's claim of harassment and noise from the upstairs neighbour and regarding damp in the house. Although this mother was living in very depressing circumstances, she was a resourceful and emotionally resilient person who, when provided with the help necessary because of her disability, could provide for her child's emotional and physical needs.

Whilst some families in which domestic violence figured were categorised as families with long-standing and multiple problems, other cases were allocated by the researchers to the 'specific issue' group because one or other parent, usually the mother, appeared able to provide good emotional and physical care to the child if the partner problems could be resolved or reduced.

The police referred a case to Social Services because a mother had reported that their father, from whom she was separated, had taken the child to another part of the country without her permission. There were counter-allegations about violence between mother and father. During private law proceedings, following an application for a Residence Order, it became clear that the father had seriously assaulted the mother on several occasions. A strategy meeting discussed the impact the domestic violence had had on the child, who appeared fearful and upset. The father was imprisoned and the mother was rehoused at an address that was kept secret from him. The mother requested counselling for the child, who was still fearful and anxious even though the mother was able to provide adequate parenting once the threat of violence to herself had diminished.

The '*short-term problems*' group consisted of families where at least one child was 'in need' (Section 17 of the Children Act 1989), but the difficulties could be resolved by practical help, advice, counselling or casework to meet a short-term problem or to help the child receive more appropriate help from the mainstream services.

The '*no serious problem*' group consisted of families in which after assessment it appeared that no child in the family was 'in need' as defined by the Children Act 1989. Some might have been experiencing problems that were real enough to them, but they were able to protect their children from adverse consequences. Advice and referral elsewhere was often appreciated, but others were angry or disappointed that their request for a service (mostly practical help such as day care) was turned down. Others in this group had been referred because of child protection concerns that proved to be without substance.

Figure 3.7 gives the numbers in each group and shows that just over a quarter were categorised as having long-standing or chronic and multiple problems. The largest group (41%) were in the 'specific issue' group. More of the families in County were rated as having multiple and long-standing or acute problems; more in City 1 were in the 'acute distress' group and more in City 2 were in the 'specific issue' group. Fewer in County had short-term problems, but more in County than in the city areas (20%) were experiencing

Figure 3.7 ***Type of family (interview sample)***[1]

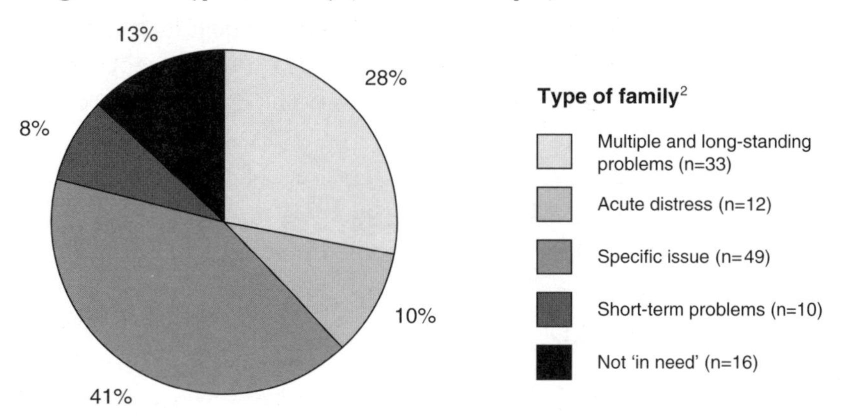

[1] n=120

[2] Typology adapted from Cleaver and Freeman (1995) and Brandon et al. (1999); two families did not fit into this typology.

only minor problems such that the child was not considered to be 'in need'. These differences between the areas did not reach statistical significance.

Table 3.18 serves as a reminder that the type of maltreatment is *not necessarily* associated with any one cluster of family problems, and is thus not a reliable guide to the sort of service that is most likely to be helpful. It shows that families in the 'acute distress' group were more likely to be referred because of concerns about physical neglect ($p<.01$) (in six of these nine cases the reason was 'inadequate supervision'). This was also the case with those about whom it was concluded that concerns were unfounded (ten of the 16 in this group were

Table 3.18 ***Family type by main type of alleged abuse (interview sample, Stage 1)***

Family type	Physical neglect		Emotional neglect		Emotional abuse		None		Total	
	No.	%	No.	%	No.	%	No.	%	No.	%
Long-standing problems	15	47	8	25	5	16	4	12	32	100
Acute distress	9	75	1	8	1	8	1	8	12	100
Specific issue	16	33	11	23	5	10	16	33	48	100
Short-term problems	1	10	1	10	–	–	8	80	10	100
Not 'in need'	10	62	1	6	1	6	4	25	16	100
Total	**51**	**43**	**22**	**19**	**12**	**10**	**33**	**28**	**118**	**100**

[1] Missing=4

referred because of concerns about physical neglect, including six cases where the reason for referral was concern about inadequate supervision). The largest proportion of referrals because of concerns about emotional abuse were in the 'multiple and long-standing problems' group (16%).

All four of those referred because of concerns about close confinement were in the 'multiple and long-standing problems' group. The verbal abuse referrals were in respect of an 'acute distress' family and two 'specific issue' families.

Ethnic origin

As with the referral cohort, there were major differences in the ethnic and cultural backgrounds of the children in the three research areas (Table 3.19). One child in County was of mixed-race parentage (2%). However, half of those in City 1 and nearly 80% in City 2 were of minority ethnic origin. Whereas all respondents in County had English as their main language, this was the case for 75% in City 1 and only 55% in City 2 (Table 3.20). There were also big differences in religion: 40% of respondents in County had no intention of bringing up their child in any religious faith, compared with 22% in City 1 and only 13% in City 2. Muslim, Hindu or Sikh affiliations were reported by 14% of respondents in City 1, 29% in City 2 and none in County.

The need for support, and the types of support required, might also be influenced by length of stay in the UK and by any trauma or stress resulting from the reasons for coming to the UK. White families were headed by parent(s) known to be not born in the UK or Ireland in only two cases. One or both parents in 12 families were of minority ethnic origin but born in the UK. Twenty-eight of the parents were of minority ethnic origin and came to this country – in 19 cases as immigrants and in at least nine cases as refugees. In nine cases it is not clear whether parents of minority ethnic origin were born in the UK or came to the UK as immigrants. Thus, at least 30 of the 122 families in the interview sample were refugees or immigrants (over a third, and almost a half if only the city authorities are included). The place of birth of nine of the parents of minority ethnic origin was not known.

On environmental and economic indicators, there were no statistically significant differences between white families and those of minority ethnic origin in the city areas (where white and ethnic minority families lived side-by-side in very similar circumstances).

When less tangible indicators are used there are more differences. More of the white families had long-term social, environmental *and* emotional prob-

Table 3.19 ***Ethnic backgrounds of children by area (interview sample, Stage 1)***

Ethnic background	City 1		City 2		County		All	
	No.	%	No.	%	No.	%	No.	%
White	14	50	8	20.5	54	98	76	62
Asian	2	7	13	33	–	–	15	12
Black African	4	14	8	20.5	–	–	12	10
African–Caribbean	1	4	3	8	–	–	4	3
Black other	3	11	2	5	–	–	5	4
Mixed-race parentage/ other	4	14	5	13	1	2	10	8
Total	**28**	**100**	**39**	**100**	**55**	**100**	**122**	**100**

Table 3.20 ***First language of respondents in research areas (interview sample, Stage 1)***

Language	City 1 %	City 2 %	County %
English	75	55	100
Punjabi	–	11	–
Gujerati	–	8	–
Bengali	–	8	–
Urdu	4	5	–
Portuguese	–	5	–
Somali	4	–	–
Twi	3	–	–
French	4	3	–
Other European	7	–	–
Other non-European	3	5	–
Base n=100%	**28**	**39**	**55**

lems than the families of minority ethnic origin. More of the white parents had a physical, learning or mental disability. The parents of minority ethnic origin were less likely to be in touch with family members and had fewer sources of support. They were also more likely than white parents to report high levels of emotional stress as indicated by the Rutter's 'malaise' schedule (Rutter et al. 1981; Robins and Rutter 1990) and to report more problems with parenting.

When the detailed reasons for referral (NIPCAN categories of neglect) are considered, the only statistically significant difference between the white families and those of minority ethnic origin is that, although over 50% of the families in the two city areas were black, 86% of those in the 'emotional abuse' referral group were white ($p<.05$). There was a trend, which did not reach statistical significance, for more of the minority ethnic families to be referred because of concerns about physical neglect (53%) than was the case for the white families (40%). This was mainly accounted for by the larger proportion of black or Asian families in the 'inadequate supervision' sub-category (39%, compared with 21% of the white families). Equal proportions of the white and the black families (17%) were referred because of concerns about emotional neglect.

Looking at the smaller categories, four of the five in the 'verbal assault' and three of the four in the 'close confinement' categories were white families. The 'extreme spouse abuse' referrals were more evenly balanced: these cases concerned 15% of the white children and 12% of the children of minority ethnic origin.

There was a statistically significant difference between the families of minority ethnic origin and the white families in respect of the types of families, (using the Cleaver and Freeman (1995) categorisation (see Table 3.21). Since most of the white families were in County, this difference is probably interacting with area differences. (However, the differences were still there, if less marked, when only city families were included.) White families were more likely to be in the 'multiple and long-standing problem' group, and those of minority ethnic origin were more likely to have characteristics which led to allocation to the 'acute distress' or 'specific issue' groups. More of the white families were in the 'no serious problems/ child not 'in need' group, and more

Table 3.21 ***Type of family by ethnicity (interview sample, Stage 1)***[1]

Type of family[2]	**White**		**Minority ethnic origin**		**All**	
	No.	**%**	**No.**	**%**	**No.**	**%**
Long-standing problems	27	40	4	9	31	28
Acute distress	4	6	7	16	11	10
Specific issue	24	36	20	46	44	40
Short-term problems	2	3	8	19	10	9
Not 'in need'	10	15	4	9	14	13
Total	**67**	**100**	**43**	**100**	**110**	**100**

[1] Missing cases=12; x^2=20.14 df:4 $p<.001$

[2] Adapted from Cleaver and Freeman (1995) and Brandon et al. (1999)

families of minority ethnic origin were in the 'short-term problems' group. This is probably explained in large part by the lower levels of support from relatives.

Did neglect and emotional abuse characterise a particular type of family?

The literature on emotional maltreatment and neglect reviewed in Chapter 1 would lead one to predict that parents of children referred to social services departments because of these concerns would form a distinctive group – more socially disadvantaged, younger and also more socially isolated. In this chapter we have compared the referrals where concerns were expressed about neglectful or emotionally abusive behaviour with those where a family support or a specific service was requested. In fact, there were few statistically significant differences. In spite of the large differences in racial and cultural background – which were reflected in relative lack of social support and feelings of isolation – there were few differences between the respondents in the three research areas. They were similar in their experience of poverty and crowded living conditions, in their housing mobility and in the structure of their households.

There were, however, significant differences between the two groups in respect of less tangible indicators of emotional well-being and family cohesion. These would become apparent only if one were to undertake a fuller social work assessment of the reasons for referral, including risks and needs, vulnerability and resilience factors, sources of support, and patterns of relationships and attachments, as discussed by Howe et al. (1999). Table 3.22 shows that differences between the 'neglect' and the 'service request' families are in the expected direction: proportionately, almost twice as many of the families referred because of concerns about neglect or emotional maltreatment were rated as having multiple and long-standing problems. However 18% of the 'service request' families also came into this group. As one might expect, more of the 'service request' families had 'short-term problems' or were allocated to the 'specific issue' group (most often because of the disability of a parent or child). However, 19% of those referred because of concerns about 'neglect' did not, on further enquiry appear to have serious problems that would lead to the conclusion that the child was 'in need', as defined by Section 17 of the Children Act 1989.

Our interview data suggest that, even among families in respect of whom concerns about emotional maltreatment or neglect were substantiated, most were aware of the needs of their children. For much of the time (as, for

Table 3.22 ***Type of family by referral (interview sample, Stage 1)***[1]

Type of family[2]	Type of referral					
	Neglect/ emotional abuse		Service request		All	
	No.	%	No.	%	No.	%
Long-standing problems	26	32	7	18	33	28
Acute distress	11	14	1	2	12	10
Specific issue	24	30	25	63	49	41
Short-term problem	4	5	6	15	10	8
Not 'in need'	15	19	1	2	16	13
Total	**80**	**100**	**40**	**100**	**120**	**100**

[1] Missing cases=2; x^2:20.94 df:4 p<.001
[2] Adapted from Cleaver and Freeman (1995) and Brandon et al. (1999)

example, with those with a recurrent mental illness) they met their children's needs to a 'good enough standard'. Others, despite the limitations of multiple difficulties, met many of their children's needs when appropriate packages of help and support were provided.

There is evidence in our interview data that *some* of the families referred because of concerns about emotional maltreatment or neglect were behaving in such a way as to cause – or, if services were not provided, be *likely* to cause – significant impairment to their children's long-term development. However, a larger proportion of those referred because of concerns about neglect were concerned parents who had a strong work ethic and were determined to do their best for their children in very difficult circumstances. In most cases they needed practical services, including transport, better housing and especially access to pre-school and after-school care.

As part of the Stage 2 interview, the parents were asked four questions in order to ascertain how they viewed the parenting task:

- What sort of behaviour do you think most people would consider is neglecting the needs of children?
- What sort of behaviour do you think causes Social Services or health visitors or doctors to say that somebody is neglecting the needs of their children?
- What do *you* consider is neglecting the needs of children?

- Social workers sometimes talk about emotional abuse – what do you think that means?

At a different point in the interview parents were asked for their general views about the nature of parenting and the challenges presented to parents in the neighbourhood in which they lived:

- What do you think are the most important things needed to bring up children so that they are healthy and safe?
- What do you think are the most important things to provide for a child of [name's] age?
- What do you think is the hardest thing about being a parent for most people?
- What do you think you have done really well as a parent?

Whilst some parents had very little to say on these more general questions, others appeared to appreciate the opportunity to share their thoughts with the interviewers. There was little in their responses that would be out of place if voiced by a professional involved in leading a parent training group. From the files, it was clear that some of the families were unable to live up to their aspirations and beliefs about good parenting – and, indeed, they were well aware of the extent to which they sometimes fell below their own expectations. Our findings in this respect replicate the conclusions of Wilson and Herbert (1978) in a seminal work on parenting and child neglect in the inner cities. The responses of the parents on *emotional abuse* are particularly interesting and mirror the definitions of Glaser and Prior (1997). Some said: 'I'm not sure what that means' – but then went on to think through what it might mean. Brief responses included: 'no loving'; 'bullying them or pushing them away'; 'not loving them or talking to them'; 'if you are constantly insulting them, abusing them or whatever'; 'bullying them and forcing them to be frightened of you'. Others talked of less extreme behaviour that they often saw in those around them and realised, as they sometimes regretfully reported, that this characterised their own parenting when things were not going well for them:

> If you feel upset you could take it out on the other person by talking to them harshly or aggressively.

> They are not being hit, but nobody is taking time to listen to their feelings. They are just being ignored, basically, and passed on from 'hand-to-hand'.

> Verbal abuse, perhaps; telling the children off without actually hitting them; unnecessarily telling them off.

> Not showing children that you care for them, not showing them any affection or giving them any praise.
>
> Constantly telling them 'in a minute', 'shut up' and never listening to them; never having any time for them – I see that a lot – more than anything.
>
> Yes, when – I can't explain it – you're not abusing your child – well, you are, but by your voice and that – mentally.

Some responded in terms of racial harassment:

> Ignoring one's way of thinking, racial discrimination; children being discriminated against because they come from another country.

For others this was a new concept: for those, perhaps, who had referred themselves because they had a child with a disability, but also for those who had been referred because of concerns about neglect or lack of supervision that proved to be unfounded:

> I can't really think of it. It's hard when you don't know anyone who's been abused.

Several of the parents commented on the emotionally abusive nature of conflictual relationships played out in front of children, mostly with partners but sometimes with relatives or neighbours:

> Fighting and arguing with other people in the same room as the children.
>
> Being put down or upset by your parents' attitude to each other if they row a lot; emotional blackmail from parent to parent; lack of confidence and security could create a situation when they see what other children get.
>
> When a child has been subjected to rows and stuff like that – not actually physical but mental trauma.
>
> That would be if partners are rowing all the time, if you are abusing them by shouting at them all the time, and calling them names, or if they're seeing violence.
>
> I suppose that's like emotional blackmail, if a child was being torn between mother and father, being made to choose.
>
> [Name] has witnessed his father being violent to me and talked about this at nursery – that was seen by Social Services as emotional abuse.

Other definitions could be grouped under the heading of emotional blackmail or consistently making the child's needs subservient to their own wishes:

When a parent says to a child, 'I'm going out tonight'. If you're upset about this, I'll take this from you tomorrow, or you won't get this or that. Emotional blackmail. A parent gets to do what he wants. A child keeps quiet.
Saying if you don't do this, I'll cry; if you don't do this, I'll do this, etc.

When they might say to a child: 'Oh you are stupid'; or: 'Because of you this happened'. Lay all the blame on the child.

Some of the parents clearly knew what was meant by emotional abuse because they themselves had experienced it as children or adults:

I've suffered a lot of this from my husband, so I know all about it.

Saying unkind things to you, so that you lose your confidence, and you grow up with this. That's why I tell my son he's clever, he's so good. He believes in himself.

I suppose that's not giving your kid any love. Mum was like that, saying 'I wish you weren't born – I'd had an abortion' – that's really cruel.

Some told the interviewers that this label had been given to them or someone they knew:

I had that with [my son]. The school said that. Not really cared for, not looked after, not being there for them, not interested, I suppose.

I am not going to answer that one because I was involved with a friend who was accused of that and I wasn't happy with the way it was handled. I don't see how they can prove that – I think everybody emotionally abuses people to some degree – either intentionally or unintentionally.

I suppose, like, threatening behaviour to them, like me: I've got a loud voice.

Some families understood the inter-relationship of different forms of maltreatment, and their definition encompassed the range of, potentially, emotionally harmful behaviour:

Hitting a child; sexual abuse; having problems is a form of emotional abuse.

These quotes, along with those about neglect, indicate that the families interviewed understood – very much in the same way as professionals – that children can be harmed not only by more dramatic acts of abuse but by day-to-day unthoughtful parenting. However, what also came through in the other parts of the interviews was that when the 'label' was applied to them, they found it extremely distressing as they considered those applying it often failed to understand the stresses in their lives that led them to behave in ways of which they themselves did not approve.

If one takes the 'multiple and long-standing problems' group to be broadly similar to the 'high criticism and low warmth' families – identified by the researchers whose work is summarised in *Child Protection: Messages from Research* (Dartington Social Research Unit 1995a) – or the neglectful or emotionally abusive families who have the potential to do so much harm to their children – as identified in the USA by Polansky (1981) and, more recently, in the UK by O'Hagan (1993), Stevenson (1996; 1998), Glaser and Prior (1997), Iwaniec (1997) – less than a third of those referred because of concerns about emotional maltreatment or neglect came into this group.

Our findings, therefore, point to the conclusion that a proportion of those re-referred because of concerns about emotional maltreatment or neglect will have been inappropriately referred. If, therefore, they are included in the statistics as 'neglect' referrals, this may distort perceptions as to the numbers of 'neglectful' or 'emotionally abusive' families in the population. On further enquiry, 'home alone' or 'child safety' cases were more likely to come into the not 'in need' group than the other 'neglect' referrals. But our more general conclusion is that a substantial proportion of the children referred under the child protection *and* the service request categories have parents who are struggling and not quite managing to cope with the serious practical problems of rural or urban deprivation or with those resulting from trauma or disability. They are, as our interview data reveal, far removed from the neglectful families of much of the child abuse literature.

Viewed in this light, the resources needed to provide a good enough service to the children likely to suffer most harm in neglectful and emotionally harmful families are less than might be assumed if one looks at the child protection statistics for neglect and emotional abuse referrals. However, we are mindful of the fact that a proportion of the physical and sexual abuse referrals concern families who are also neglecting or emotionally maltreating their children. The challenge is to provide those longer-term, comprehensive and cost-effective services that must be available to families who are most likely to be most harmful to their children. Alongside this, it is necessary to provide an appropriate short-term service that will prevent deterioration of the situation for parents who, despite their best intentions, may otherwise fail to meet the needs of their children when faced with the problems that brought them to seek help or be referred for it.

Summary

Seven hundred and twelve children under 8 years of age from 555 families were referred to the child and family teams during the monitoring period. Children of minority ethnic origin or cultural heritage appeared to be over-represented in the city areas – 61% of the children in City 1 and 76% in City 2. Data on ethnicity were unreliable for County; County families are, therefore, omitted from the analysis when ethnicity is considered.

More than half of the referrals of children in each area involved a request for general support or a specific service. Thirteen per cent involved concerns about child safety or a child left alone; concerns about the possibility of other forms of neglect or of physical abuse were each recorded in 12% of cases; the possibility of sexual abuse was the reason for referral in 7% of cases, and emotional abuse in 5% of cases. When only child protection referrals are considered (337 cases), those where the main concern was about sexual or physical abuse comprised just over a third of the referrals, while neglect, child safety or emotional maltreatment as the main cause for concern accounted for 63%. The reasons for referral often overlapped.

The balance between child protection referrals and more general child welfare concerns was similar in the three areas despite their very different socio-demographic characteristics. However, there were significant differences between the areas in respect of the more detailed profile of child protection concerns. In City 2, fewer referrals were categorised as involving neglect or emotional abuse, and there were more 'other child protection' cases – no doubt reflecting the very complex range of difficulties experienced by families in this very deprived urban area.

When those of minority ethnic origin were compared with white children, there was a statistically significant difference between the two groups, with the black children less likely to be referred because of concerns about sexual abuse, emotional maltreatment or neglect.

The 'intensive sample' comprised 180 'index' children randomly selected from neglect or emotional abuse referrals and from those referred for a service. The sample was weighted towards neglect and emotional abuse cases because the focus of this study was primarily on this group of children. One hundred and twenty-three of the 180 were child safety, neglect or emotional maltreatment referrals; 57 families were 'service request' cases.

Interviews were completed with parents in 52% of all families (who could be traced) referred because of concerns about neglect or emotional maltreatment, and in 14% of all 'service request' referrals.

Just over half of those interviewed lived in one of the city areas. There were slightly fewer 'service request' cases in City 1 than in the other two areas, and more of those interviewed in the City 1 sample were referred because of concerns about neglect or child safety.

The families referred in all three areas were almost all living in socially deprived communities, or in pockets of social deprivation within more prosperous communities. Though most could be described as coming from a 'working class' background, some parents had been brought up in middle class or professional families. For the white families, there was evidence of downward social mobility, sometimes associated with marriage breakdown or substance abuse. Some of the refugee or immigrant families had a professional background and had left behind a more comfortable way of life.

On broad indicators of social disadvantage, there were few differences between the 'neglect' and 'service request' families.

Families in all three areas reported many family problems and their responses to a 'malaise' schedule indicated high levels of stress. However, levels of stress were not, on average, as high as for a cohort of families whose children were suffering, or likely to suffer, 'significant harm'. This suggests that, for most of the families referred, emotional and relationship problems had not yet reached levels at which it might be anticipated that positive change would be most difficult to achieve.

There was a trend towards more of the 'service request' families reporting higher levels of stress than was the case for 'neglect' referrals, and towards more of those referred because of concerns about emotional maltreatment or neglect reporting financial and partner problems.

A typology developed by Cleaver and Freeman (1995) that considered the full range of child abuse referrals was adapted to make it more relevant to family support referrals. Just over a quarter were characterised as having multiple and long-standing problems. The largest group (41% of the interviewed families) had a 'specific issue', the alleviation of which would be likely to result in improved well-being. Eight per cent had short-term problems.

More of the white families were in the 'multiple and long-standing problems' group and more of the families of minority ethnic origin were in the 'acute distress' or 'specific issue' groups.

It was concluded from this part of the analysis that neither the reason for referral ('neglect' or 'service request') nor the different categories of maltreatment were associated with any particular cluster of family difficulties, and were thus not a reliable guide to the type of service that was most likely to be effective.

The chapter concludes with quotations from the parents interviewed on their perceptions of 'need', 'harm', 'neglect' and 'emotional abuse' as well as on the tasks of parenting in the areas in which they lived and the type of services they might find helpful.

From the detailed analysis of the characteristics of the families and their responses to these questions, it was concluded that fewer than a third of the 'neglect' referrals and a small minority of the 'service request' families came into the 'high criticism and low warmth' category of families in the *Child Protection: Messages from Research* studies (Dartington Social Research Unit 1995a).

A proportion of those not coming into this group had been inappropriately referred; others had temporarily succumbed to emotional or environmental pressures but appeared to have the resources to meet their children's needs if appropriate short-term or episodic help were provided.

4 The children: 'in need' or 'in need of protection'?

Chapter 3 provided much background information about the children in the context of their families. In this chapter we focus on them as individuals, on their specific problems and (from the interview data and reports in the files) on their strengths and coping strategies as well as their vulnerabilities.

The referral sample

There were 712 children under 8 years of age, 337 of whom were referred because of child protection concerns and 375 for whom help was sought because of other concerns.

Over 200 children were in each of the two oldest age groups (3–4 years and 5–7 years), 158 were between 1 and 2 years of age and 117 were less than 1 year old (Figure 4.1). Figure 4.2 shows that the children in City 1 were younger, with 79% being under 5, compared with 66% in City 2 and 67% in County ($p<.01$). Similar numbers of male and female children were referred (49% and 51%, respectively) and this pattern was the same in the three areas.

Figure 4.1 ***Age of children (referral sample)***[1]

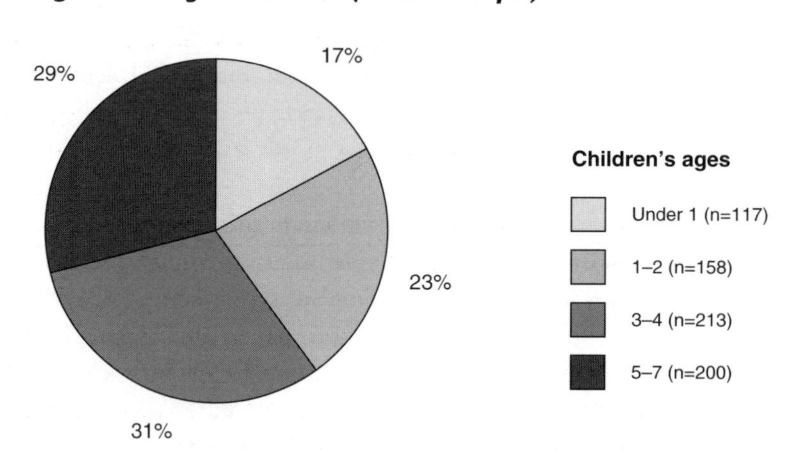

[1] n=688; missing data=24; in some cases age of child not known by referrer

Figure 4.2 ***Age of child by area (referral sample)***

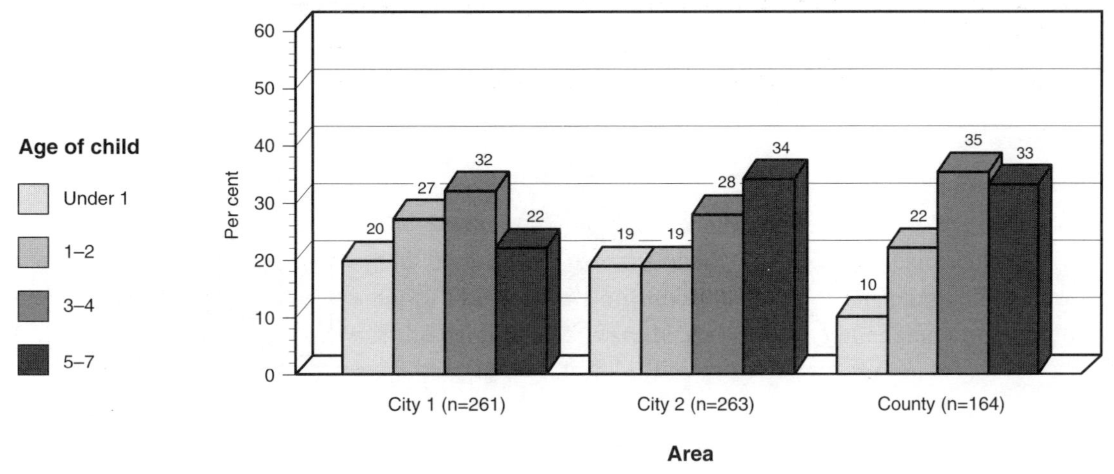

[1] n=688; missing data=24; x^2:18.469 df:6 p<.01

Reasons for referral

In Chapter 3 we noted that 53% of the referrals involved a request for general support or a specific service, or included other matters not seen as coming within the framework of child protection. It was noted that, when 'service request' cases were omitted, those where the main concern was about sexual or physical abuse comprised just over a third of the referrals whilst neglect, child safety or emotional maltreatment as the main cause for concern accounted for 63%.

Ethnicity

Although the monitoring form requested information on the child's ethnic group, this information was not provided for over 40% of cases (see Chapter 3 for a fuller discussion of how this was handled in the study). Figures 3.1 and 4.3 show the ethnic diversity of the children referred and point to the need for policy and practice to take this into account. Figure 4.3 shows that a high proportion of the children in City 2 were of Asian origin and that there were more in City 1 of African–Caribbean descent. This study, therefore, provides an important opportunity to learn about those children 'in need' or 'in need of protection' who are of minority ethnic origin and come into contact with social services departments. This is especially important since attention has appropriately been drawn to the under-representation of such families among research samples (Dartington Social Research Unit 1995a; Butt and Mirza 1996; Barn et al. 1997). Figure 4.4 shows that there is a trend (which does not reach statistical significance) for more children of minority ethnic origin to be in the youngest age group.

Figure 4.3 ***Child's ethnicity by area, city areas only (referral sample)***[1]

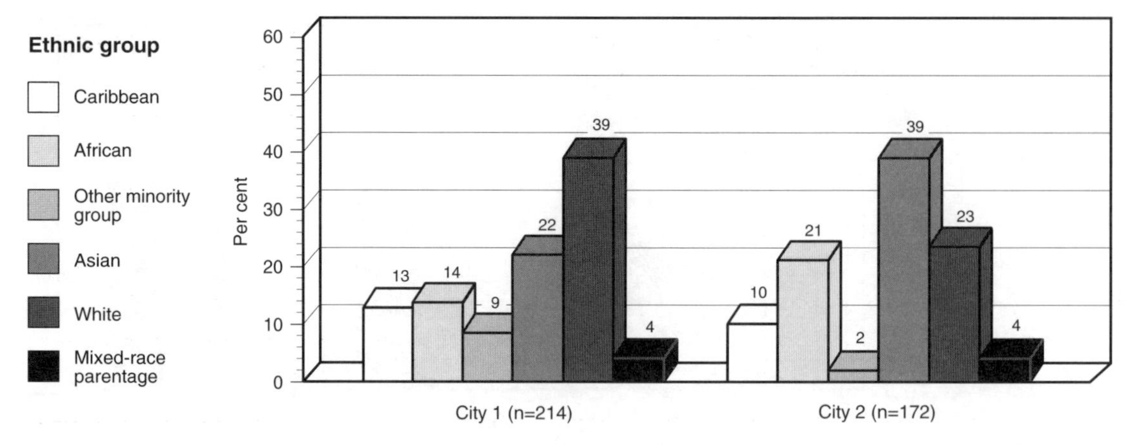

[1] n=386 children for whom data on ethnicity available; x^2:25.06 df:5 p<.001

Figure 4.4 ***Child's ethnicity by age, city areas only (referral sample)***

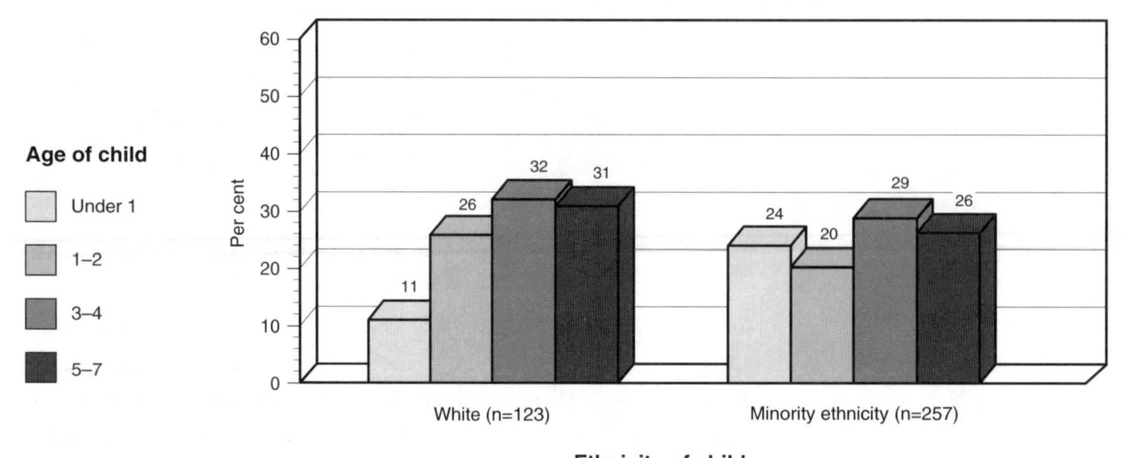

[1] n=380 where age and ethnicity known; x^2:10.21 df:3 p<.05

Perhaps as a result of the complex situations in which many families of minority ethnic origin were living, these families were more likely to be referred because of child protection concerns that could not easily be categorised at the early stage when the monitoring form was completed. When the different ethnic groups are considered separately, numbers for some groups are too small for separate analysis. However Table 4.1 shows that neglect was a more frequent reason for referral of children who were of Asian descent (33% referred for this reason) and those of mixed-race parentage (29%) than was the case for those of African–Caribbean, African or white British or Irish descent (20%, 21% and 21%, respectively). White children

Table 4.1 ***Reason for referral and ethnic background, city cases only (referral sample)***[1]

	African–Caribbean %	Black African %	Black other %	Asian %	White %	Mixed-race parentage %	Other %
Physical/sexual abuse	11	12	30	11	24	14	9
Neglect	20	21	–	33	21	29	18
Emotional abuse	2	–	–	–	4	–	–
Other child protection	15	15	–	5	7	–	9
Other service	51	52	69	50	43	57	64
Total	**45**	**66**	**13**	**114**	**123**	**14**	**11**

[1] n=386 children whose ethnic origin was stated on monitoring form

and those described as 'black other' were more likely to be referred because of concerns about physical or sexual abuse (24% and 30%) than African–Caribbean children (11%), African children (12%) or Asian children (11%). African–Caribbean children and African children were more likely than Asian or white children to be referred because of less specific child protection concerns (15% and 15% compared with 5% and 7%, respectively).

The children in the intensive sample

Further details about the children and the reasons for referral were not available for the total cohort. They were, however, obtained from the social services' records for the 180 families in the intensive sample and from interviews with the main parent or carer of 122 of the children. These data were supplemented by information from the health visitor on at least one occasion in respect of 109 children.

As with the referral sample as a whole, there were equal numbers of male and female children, and no differences of note were found on any of the variables. It may be that the gender differences in terms of behaviour and types of maltreatment that have been found by other researchers begin to emerge as the children get older (i.e., over 8 years of age). Figure 4.5 gives the ages of the children in the intensive sample. The proportions in the different age groups were broadly similar for the referral sample and the intensive sample. However, fewer interviews were completed with parents of children in the youngest age group and more with parents of children aged 1–2. Seventeen of the children lived with a single parent, but 30% lived in households with five

Figure 4.5 ***Age groups of index children (intensive sample)***[1]

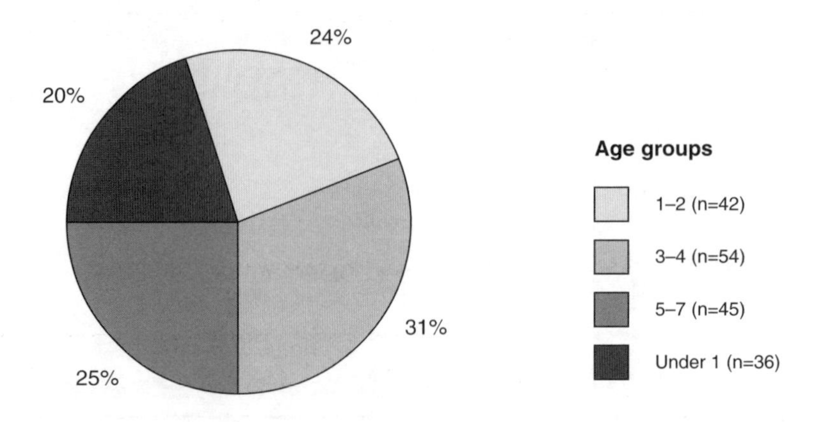

[1] n=177; missing data=3

or more members. Just over a quarter were lone children, 29% had one sibling, 27% had two siblings and 17% had three or more siblings (Figure 4.6).

As noted in the introduction to Chapter 3, there were no marked differences between the referral and the intensive samples except that those where there was a specific referral because of concerns about sexual or physical abuse alone were omitted from this purposive sample which specifically focused on neglect and emotional maltreatment.

Table 4.2 shows that physical neglect was the main concern in respect of the 180 'intensive sample' children. This was especially so for those aged 5 and

Figure 4.6 ***Number of children in family (intensive sample)***[1]

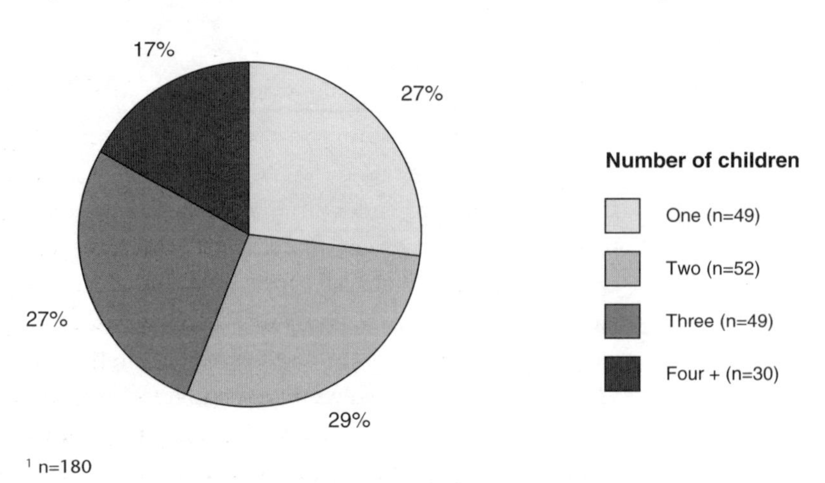

[1] n=180

Table 4.2 ***Age of child by type of neglect or emotional maltreatment (intensive sample)***[1]

Age of child	Physical neglect		Emotional neglect		Emotional abuse		None		All	
	No.	**%**	**No.**	**%**	**No.**	**%**	**No.**	**%**	**No.**	**%**
<1	15	43	4	11	3	9	13	37	35	100
1–2	17	40	8	19	5	12	12	29	42	100
3–4	17	33	11	22	6	12	17	33	51	100
5+	25	60	9	21	4	9	4	9	42	100
Total	**74**	**44**	**32**	**19**	**18**	**11**	**46**	**27**	**170**	**100**

[1] Missing=10; not statistically significant

over. Emotional neglect was more likely to be a cause for concern with children over 1 year of age. Emotional abuse, 'verbal assault' and extreme spouse abuse were reasons for concern in respect of children in all age groups. Inadequate affection was noted in respect of one child under 1, a 1-year-old and one child over 5 years of age.

It should be noted that concerns about 'educational neglect' were not recorded in any of these cases, even though it was clear from our interviews that there were serious educational difficulties in respect of an important minority of these children.

As with the referral sample, the majority of children were white British or Irish (62%). However, when only the city areas are included 69% of the children in the intensive sample of 180 were of minority ethnic origin (58% of those in City 1 and 79% of those in City 2).

Difficulties and special needs of the children

We have already noted (in Chapter 3) the many problems experienced by the families as a whole. Tables 4.3 to 4.6 list the problems of the index children themselves, as identified by their parents during the first interviews. Table 4.7 shows that health visitors or school nurses had identified concerns about the health, development or safety of the children in an important minority of cases, and were also concerned about environmental hazards and lack of parental care. Concerns about the child's growth were noted in respect of 33% of the 'service request' and 28% of the 'neglect' cases. Completed health forms noted delays in walking and speech in 19% and 28% of the 'service request' cases and 9% and 13% of the 'neglect' cases. When all sources of data

Table 4.3 ***Details of concerns about child's health and development as identified by respondent (interview sample, Stage 1)***

Concerns	No.
Not growing normally	3
Not developing normally	4
Asthma	12
Other chest problems	1
Eye problems	6
Speech problems	6
Overweight	2
Underweight	3
Walking problems	4
Skin problems, including eczema and dermatitis	3
Sleeping problems	3
Worry about getting infections/bugs	3
Diarrhoea	1
Other bowel problems	2
Eating problems	2
Ear/hearing problems	1
Teeth problems	1
Nose-bleeds	1
Iron deficiency	1
Blood problems	1
Hypertonia	1
Dislocated hip	1
Twisted spine	1
Ankle problems	1
Cystic fibrosis	1
Kidney failure	2
Liver failure/problem	1
Too weak to eat or do anything	1
Disabled – bone problem	1
Heart murmur	1
Learning difficulties	2
Premature birth	2
Allergic to milk	1
Has a virus	1
No pain threshold	1
Autistic	1

Table 4.4 ***Number of days unwell in the past six months (parent's report, Stage 1)***

	City 1 %	City 2 %	County %	Neglect/ emotional abuse group %	Service request group %	All cases %
0–7 days	68	62	71	69	63	67
8–14 days	21	15	9	13	15	14
15+ days	7	15	20	13	20	16
Not known	4	8	–	4	3	3
n=	**28**	**39**	**55**	**82**	**40**	**122**

Table 4.5 ***Child's growth and development (parent's report, Stage 1)***

	City 1 %	City 2 %	County %	Neglect/ emotional abuse group %	Service request group %	All cases %
Satisfactory	89	67	89	85	75	82
Some concerns	7	18	9	12	10	11
Serious concerns	4	13	2	1	15	6
Not known	–	3	–	1	–	1
n=	**28**	**39**	**55**	**82**	**40**	**122**

Table 4.6 ***Total accidents in last six months (parent's report, Stage 1)***

	City 1 %	City 2 %	County %	Neglect/ emotional abuse group %	Service request group %	All cases %
None	75	85	85	83	82	83
1 accident	18	13	9	11	15	12
2 accidents	–	–	–	–	–	–
3 accidents	4	–	–	1	–	1
4 or more accidents	4	3	6	5	3	4
n=	**28**	**39**	**55**	**82**	**40**	**122**

Table 4.7 *Community nurse concerns (interview sample, Stage 1)*

Health concern	Neglect/ emotional abuse %	Service request %[1]
Child's growth	28	33
Parent not complying with preventive health	11	16
Parent failing to protect against environmental hazards	35	40
Delay in child's walking	9	19
Delay in child's speech	13	28
Parental care rated generally inadequate	5	–
n=100%	**53**	**24**

[1] Percentages do not add up to 100% because more than one concern indicated in some cases.

were included, asthma was the most frequently mentioned child problem, followed by behaviour difficulties.

Although an important minority did have problems, it is perhaps more important to note that there were no significant differences among the children in the different areas, nor between those referred because of child protection concerns and those requesting a service. No concerns about the child's health or development were expressed by the parents interviewed in respect of almost half of the children in both the 'service request' and the 'neglect' groups. Whilst a proportion (13% of those interviewed) were considered, in the light of all the information, not to cross the 'in need' threshold as they were likely to achieve 'a reasonable standard of health or development without the provision of services under the Act', these data show that a substantial proportion of children crossing the Children Act 1989 'in need' threshold do so solely because of environmental and relationship difficulties for the whole family. At this young age, these debilitating circumstances have not yet had a serious impact on the physical, emotional, behavioural or educational development of most of the children.

In some cases it was abundantly clear from our interviews that stresses and problems of the parents were sometimes contributing to the health and behaviour problems of the children. In other cases the disabilities and health and behavioural problems of the children were the reason for or added to stresses on the parents. There were some differences between the 'service request' and 'neglect' groups in that it was more likely that the parents of those in the neglect group would express more than one concern than it was for parents of those in the 'service request' group. Parents in the two city areas were more likely to identify more than one health or behavioural problem in the child than was the case for County parents. Children in City 2 were more likely to be in the 'serious concerns' category than those in City 1 or County.

While the research was being undertaken there was interest in ascertaining whether the *Looking After Children* schedules (Ward 1995) (developed for use with 'looked after' populations of children) could be adapted for use with parents in the community, and especially those referred to social services departments because of concerns about neglect or impairment to health or development. The sections on emotional and behavioural difficulties were used with the parents in this study. As with an earlier study of children suffering or likely to suffer 'significant harm' (Brandon et al. 1999), our interviewers found that most parents were willing to provide this information and generally saw its relevance. It was at this point in the interviews that the strengths and resilience of some of the children also became apparent.

As the responses to these schedules have not been standardised on general populations, it is not possible to use them for comparative purposes other than within the sample. The mean number of problems was under two for the under-threes but rose to six for those aged 3–4 and 5.8 for those aged 5–7.

The problems most likely to be noted were: being fearful; unwilling to share; demanding of parental attention; restless, fidgety and lacking concentration; often disobedient or disruptive. For the older children problems most often noted were: unable to talk about personal feelings; often irritable and bad tempered; having no close friends; getting involved with fighting and bullying. These characteristics were likely to be aggravated by the negative impact on parenting of the stresses that led to the referral to the social services department.

In conclusion, although some of these children referred to a social services department when under 8 years of age had health, learning or behavioural problems, these made up a minority of the cohort. Only six of the 48 children under 3 years of age and six of the 42 3–4-year-olds were described by their parent as having multiple health or behavioural difficulties. However, 14 of the 31 children aged 5–7 (almost half) were described as having six or more of the problem behaviours listed. The difficulties that led to the approach to the social services department were in most cases difficulties for the family as a whole. However, if appropriate and timely assistance and support is not made available it may be predicted that the family stresses will begin to show through in the behaviour of the children.

Summary

There were 712 children under eight in the 'referral' sample; 180 in the 'intensive' sample and 122 in the 'interview' sample. The children themselves were not interviewed but much information about them was gained from the social services department records, the health forms and interviews with parents and social workers.

Over 200 children were in each of the 3–4 and 5–7 age groups; 158 were aged between 1 and 2, and 117 were aged under 12 months at the time of referral. More of the children referred in City 1 were in the youngest age group.

Similar numbers of male and female children were referred in each area.

Differences in the *type* of maltreatment were noted for the different minority ethnic groups, with more Asian children and children of mixed-race parentage referred because of concerns about neglect (including child safety); and African–Caribbean and African children more likely than Asian or white children to be referred because of less specific child protection concerns.

With the intensive sample of 180 families, if more than one child in a family was referred, the 'index' child was the youngest in the family about whom concerns had been expressed. A quarter were lone children; there were two children in 29% of the families; three children in 27% and four or more in 17% of the families.

Physical neglect was the main reason for referral of 44% of the children in the intensive sample; the possibility of emotional neglect was mentioned in 19% of cases and emotional abuse in 11% of cases. Twenty-seven per cent of the children lived in the 'service request' families.

There were concerns about the health or development of almost half of the children in each of the 'service request' and 'neglect' groups. In this respect city and County cases were similar.

In the light of available information, it appeared that 13% were not 'in need' as defined by the Children Act 1989. These were families in which a concern about maltreatment, neglect or child safety proved to be without substance, or was the result of a one-off event that was not likely to be repeated.

In some cases where the children did not themselves have difficulties, they were considered to be 'in need' because their health or development was *likely* to be impaired or their needs not met because of hazards in their environment or the problems of the parents, including difficulty in relationships between partners or between the partners and their children.

In some of the families where the index children did not themselves have problems of health or development, there were older children in the family who did.

The emotional and behavioural sections of the *Looking After Children* schedules (Ward 1995) were used with the parents. The mean number of problems was under two for the under-threes, but rose to six for those in the 3–4 age group and 5.8 for those aged 5–7.

These data show that the children and the parents in the 'service request' and 'neglect' referral groups shared many of the same problems.

5 Support available to the parents and children

Support from relatives and friends

As was noted in Chapter 1, research and professional writing on the relationship between maternal depression and family support has recently been extended into the area of child maltreatment. The families interviewed for this study varied very considerably in terms of the extent to which they could call on support from family and friends during the stressful periods, that led to their contact with the social services departments. As Table 5.1 shows, whilst 19% could be with their mothers within ten minutes, 28% either did not have a mother living in the UK or their mother was dead. Fifty-five per cent had had direct or telephone contact with their mother within the last week, but 31% either had no contact or had not had contact within the

Table 5.1 ***Respondent's personal support system – contact with mother (interview sample, Stage 1)***

Contact with mother	No.	%
Respondent's distance from mother		
Lives with me	2	2
Up to 10 minutes away	21	17
10 minutes up to and including 1 hour away	37	30
Over 1 hour away, but in UK	27	22
Not in the UK	21	17
No longer alive/no contact	13	11
Not known	1	1
Total	**122**	**100**
Last contact with mother		
Within last 7 days	67	55
Over 7 days up to and including 1 month	9	7
Over 1 month	24	20
No contact/no longer alive	13	11
Not known	9	7
Total	**122**	**100**

previous month. Table 5.2 shows that almost half had had contact with their fathers within the last month, but 28% had no contact at all with their fathers or their father was dead. However, only 13% had had no contact at all with a relative during the previous month. Although the data were collected slightly differently, these proportions appear similar to those found by McGlone et al. (1998) in their report of the social contacts of families surveyed for the *British Social Attitudes* survey. In that survey 51% of parents of a child under 5 years of age saw their mother at least once a week and 62% had telephone contact.

Table 5.3 includes all sources of help or support. In order to avoid generalisations, respondents were asked to name the person to whom they were referring when responding to these questions. They were asked about those available to provide support and those who had actually provided it during the previous month.

A quarter of the families were unable to turn to others for financial or material help. This compares unfavourably with the 2% in McGlone et al. (1998). Almost one in five had no one to turn to for help with the children, but only 11% had no one to whom they could talk about their private feelings. (The

Table 5.2 ***Respondent's personal support system – contact with father (interview sample, Stage 1)***

Contact with father	No.	%
Respondent's distance from father		
Lives with me	1	1
Up to 10 minutes away	16	13
10 minutes up to and including 1 hour away	34	28
Over 1 hour away, but in the UK	21	17
Not in UK	13	11
No longer alive/no contact	34	28
Not known	3	2
Total	**122**	**100**
Last contact with father		
Within last 7 days	47	39
Over 7 days up to and including 1 month	10	8
Over 1 month	24	20
No contact/no longer alive	34	28
Not known	7	6
Total	**122**	**100**

Table 5.3 ***Number of people in respondent's personal support system (interview sample, Stage 1)***

Type of support	Number of people available to provide support		Number of people who gave support in past month	
	No.	%	No.	%
Advice				
No one	17	14	29	24
1 or 2 people	59	48	61	50
3 or 4 people	28	23	22	18
5 or more people	18	15	10	8
Total	**122**	**100**	**122**	**100**
Material aid				
No one	30	25	46	38
1 or 2 people	48	39	46	38
3 or 4 people	25	20	23	19
5 or more people	19	16	7	6
Total	**122**	**100**	**122**	**100**
Help with the children				
No one	22	18	26	21
1 or 2 people	53	43	61	50
3 or 4 people	32	26	29	24
5 or more people	15	12	6	5
Total	**122**	**100**	**122**	**100**
Private feelings				
No one	14	11	24	20
1 or 2 people	84	69	79	65
3 or 4 people	18	15	15	12
5 or more people	6	5	4	3
Total	**122**	**100**	**122**	**100**

General Household Survey (1993) reported that only 5% had no one to turn to for help with marital problems.) However, Table 5.4 shows a considerable amount of conflict: less than a third having had no disagreements in the previous month and 14% having had disagreements with three or more people.

As we saw in Chapter 3 (Table 3.16) the main caregivers in City 2 appeared particularly socially isolated. Less than 3% of these respondents lived within a ten-minute journey of their mothers, compared with 11% in City 1 and

Table 5.4 ***Number of people respondent expects to have disagreements with (interview sample, Stage 1)***

Number of people	Likely to have disagreements with		Disagreements in past month	
	No.	%	No.	%
No one	34	28	40	33
1 or 2 people	66	54	65	53
3 or 4 people	20	16	15	12
5 or more people	2	2	2	2
Total	**122**	**100**	**122**	**100**

31% in County (p<.001). In City 2 about half the respondents could not turn to their mothers for support, either because they had died (13%) or lived abroad (37%). This was the case for only about a third in City 1 and about a tenth in County. In City 2 respondents had seen or spoken on the telephone to an average of 2.8 relatives in the previous four weeks, but in City 1 the mean number was 4.7 and in County it was 5.6. The lack of relatives within a reasonable distance, as well as the fact that English was often not their first language, must have reduced the availability of personal support for respondents in City 2. Table 5.5 shows significant differences between parents in City 2 and parents in the other areas in respect of the *numbers* of people they could turn to for advice, practical help, help with children and intimate talk. This reflects the degree of mobility and instability in the lives of a high proportion of young families living in this area.

Table 5.5 ***Number of people available to give support, by area (interview sample, Stage 2)***[1]

Number available	City 1		City 2		County		All	
	No.	%	No.	%	No.	%	No.	%
0	–	–	3	9	1	2	4	4
1–3	5	23	20	61	7	13	32	30
4–6	10	45	8	24	30	57	48	44
7–9	4	18	2	6	12	23	18	17
10+	3	14	–	–	3	6	6	6
Total	**22**	**100**	**33**	**100**	**53**	**100**	**108**	**100**

[1] n=108; x^2:32.349 df:8 p<.0001

Support from professionals

The nature of the social work service will be considered in more detail in Chapter 6. When parents were asked, during the second interview, about the people to whom they had turned for support during the year, they did not often refer spontaneously to social workers and other professionals. They were more likely to mention family and friends; advice workers and health and social services personnel came a long way behind. Social services staff were mentioned spontaneously only once as sources of conflict, and health service staff four times.

When asked if any of a list of professionals had been either helpful or unhelpful to them in the bringing up of their children in the past year, a different picture emerges (Table 5.6). For example, although only 15% spontaneously mentioned health service staff as being helpful, when specifically asked if they had found their GP helpful, 74% said 'yes'. The professionals most frequently ticked as being either helpful or unhelpful by the 108 families interviewed at the 12-month stage were, not surprisingly, those employed by 'universalist'

Table 5.6 ***Professional sources of support or services (interview sample, Stage 2)***[1]

Professional/agency	Proportion of cases where service was used			
	Times mentioned	% of cases[2]	% helpful	% unhelpful
Main social worker	45	42	71	11
Other social services staff	38	35	46	29
Day nursery	19	18	80	13
Nursery class	28	26	65	4
Playgroup	24	22	71	4
Playscheme (holidays or after school)	15	14	80	13
Child-minder	18	17	94	6
Health visitor	68	63	69	4
GP	100	93	74	8
Hospital staff	61	56	77	13
Other health personnel	28	26	93	4
Teacher	78	72	68	9
Other school staff	40	37	53	12
Psychiatrist/psychologist	15	14	67	13
Family therapist	7	6	57	–
Police	28	26	39	35
Solicitor	36	33	81	8
Probation officer	2	2	50	–

n=108

[1] Thirty-seven others who did not fit into any of the above groupings were mentioned: 89% of cases were helpful and 11% unhelpful

[2] Does not total 100% as some referred to more than one source of professional support

services. Ninety-three per cent mentioned the GP and 63% the health visitor. The fact that 56% mentioned hospital staff is confirmation of the extent of illness and disability among the parents and children in these families. The 42% who mentioned a social worker is close to the total who had had anything other than a very brief contact with a social worker at the time of the referral.

Child-minders were most frequently mentioned as helpful, and they were never 'neutral' (94% helpful; 6% unhelpful). They were closely followed in the 'helpful' rankings by day nursery and playscheme staff, solicitors and hospital staff or health service staff other than GPs and health visitors. The main social workers, the health visitors, playgroup leaders, GPs and psychiatrists or psychologists were found helpful by around 70% of those who had contact with them.

In view of the fact that the main social worker often intervened initially in order to make enquiries about neglect or emotional maltreatment, this finding is worth noting. Social services staff other than the main social worker and the day nursery staff (including workers with under-eights, home care managers or social work managers) were less often seen as helpful. Together with the police, they were most often regarded as unhelpful.

Community and neighbourhood services and supports

In order to help us ascertain the extent to which the families were making use of neighbourhood support facilities, a survey was undertaken in the three areas. During the second interview families were specifically asked whether they had heard about, and whether they had used, a list of neighbourhood children and family support services that were either within easy reach or were particularly relevant (because they sought to provide a service for the same ethnic group as the family being interviewed, or for children with a similar disability to a child in the family). All three areas were relatively well provided with neighbourhood and community resources, although distance and lack of transport presented problems for County families.

Thirty-seven groups, centres or advice agencies serving the local communities in these three areas were listed. One in five of the families had used none of these local groups during the previous year, even though most knew of at least one that was available to them. Thirteen of the 15 South Asian families knew of at least one of the eight community resources for South Asian families that were listed, but only two had used any of them during the year.

Fifteen of the 23 African–Caribbean or African families interviewed knew of a group or centre that was specifically for their community, but only four families had used one of these during the year.

Eleven of the 16 parents who had a child with a chronic illness or disability knew of a group or resource that provided support to families who had a child with a similar disability. Seven had made use of such a facility.

Thus, although all three of these areas were fairly well catered for by neighbourhood, community or cultural group facilities – and it appeared that a substantial proportion of these families knew about them – they were underutilised. Four out of five families had had some contact – usually to seek a specific service or advice – but few turned to these groups for support when under stress unless they provided specific services such as day care:

> I only went once, but didn't bother again

was a typical response. The reasons most frequently given for not using services were waiting lists and shortage of places, cost, distance or lack of transport:

> Some play groups you have to pay for. It's difficult when you are on social security.

For some, the facilities had been tried but found to be inadequate:

> I was not impressed with the local playscheme. They were not rigorous enough in the way they chose to run it. They were a very rough lot of children and there were not many looking after them.

Others, in one way or another, reported that they felt some stigma attached to using a particular service:

> I see it as a 'way out' for parents and not really for children; when parents can't be bothered.

More personal reasons were given by others:

> Just not getting round to it. There are lots of things I won't go and do by myself.

A minority had not heard of any local resources:

> Respondent said she had not heard of any of them. She wanted the list as a reference so I left it with her.

Table 5.7 summarises the data on the use made of the main child care and neighbourhood support groups as reported by the families.

Table 5.7 ***Extent to which available resources used by any member of household during previous year (interview sample, Stage 2)***[1]

Resource	Used in last 12 months		Using now	
	No.	%	No.	%
Day nursery	19	18	9	8
Nursery class	28	26	10	9
Religious group or church school	26	24	23	21
Child-minder	18	17	7	6
Mother and toddler group	22	20	14	13
Playgroup	27	25	14	13
After-school club	10	9	6	6
Women's group	6	6	3	3
Neighbourhood centre	2	2	2	2
NEWPIN (parent support)	1	1	1	1
Family centre	5	5	–	–
Home start (volunteer visiting)	2	2	1	1
Telephone helpline	7	6	–	–
NSPCC centre	2	2	1	1
Citizen's Advice Bureau (CAB)	32	30	6	6
Law centre	8	7	4	4
Other advice centre	9	8	3	3

n=108

[1] Thirty-four per cent said there was a resource that they would like to use, but were unable to access – most often because there was a waiting list (for church schools or day care facilities), because they couldn't afford it or because the distance was too great and they did not have transport

Subjective views of support

As well as asking factual questions about actual contact with potential sources of support, parents were asked how much, over the past month, they 'needed' people to talk to in the four identified areas (advice, material aid, help with children, private feelings). General advice and help with the children had been 'needed a great deal' by almost a third of the parents, and financial help and 'opportunities to talk about feelings' by around one in five. Only one in ten had needed no help or advice with the children, and a similar proportion had not needed to talk about private feelings. Twenty per cent had needed no material help and 14% no general advice.

Since emotional support has been highlighted by the authors, whose work is discussed in Chapter 1 as a possibly protective factor in the prevention of maternal depression and child maltreatment, an analysis was made of the responses to questions about supportive relationships and opportunities to discuss private feelings. It may be argued that those willing to tell a research interviewer that they would have liked 'a lot more opportunities to talk to people about personal and private feelings' might be a particular sub-group of those perceiving themselves as lacking sources of emotional support. Indeed, they might be more willing to seek help from community and professional sources than those who responded differently to this question but were similarly isolated. Data were also therefore analysed on those who had a high score on the questions in the 'family problems checklist' (Gibbons 1990) which indicated difficulties with social contact. (Thirty-five per cent of the parents had a high score on this dimension in that they said they 'strongly agreed' or 'agreed' with negative statements, including 'I often feel lonely', and strongly disagreed with positive statements, including 'I feel I have a satisfying social life'.)

In order to consider those families who lacked emotional support as a group we combined the families who were rated as having very many problems in relation to social contact with those who had some social contact problems but who also said that they would like a lot more opportunity to talk to people about private feelings. This highlighted a group of 47 parents (26% of those interviewed in Stage 1) who indicated that they saw themselves as lacking sources of emotional support. Table 5.8 shows the proportion of interviewed families who reported a marked lack of emotional support at Stages 1 and 2.

Table 5.8 ***Availability of emotional support as reported by families (interview sample, Stage 1)***

Emotional support	Stage 1		Stage 2	
	No.	%	No.	%
Some emotional support	75	62	76	70
Poor emotional support	47	38	32	30
Total	**122**	**100**	**108**	**100**

Figure 5.1 shows a trend (which did not reach statistical significance) towards more of the city families lacking emotional support at the start of the study. Indeed, this was the case for over half of the City 2 families interviewed.

Figure 5.1 ***Social and emotional support by area (interview sample, Stage 1)***[1]

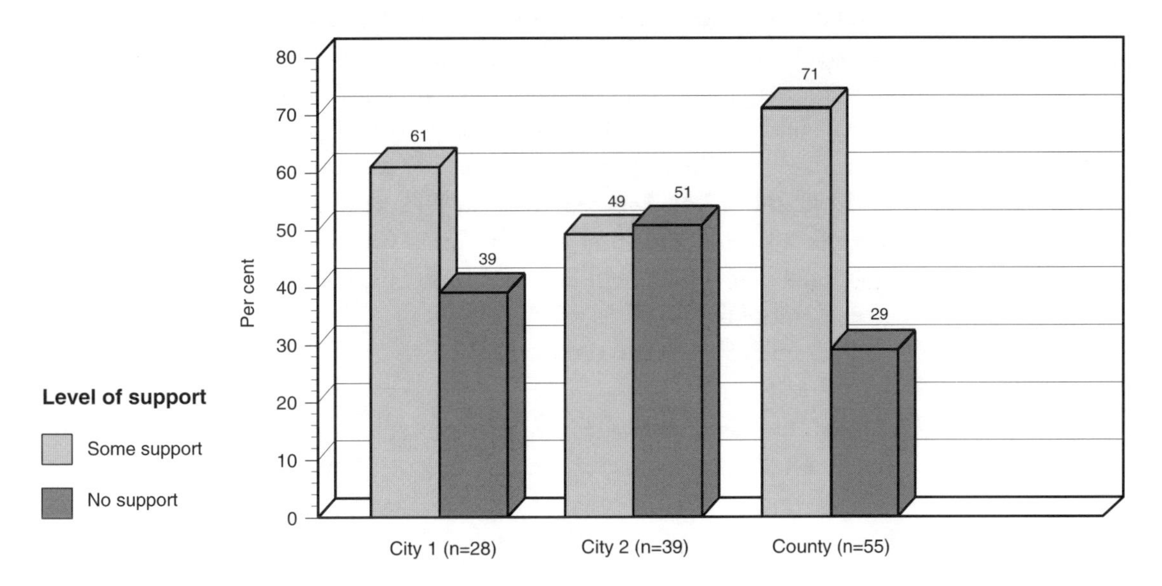

[1] n=122; not statistically significant

As shown in Table 5.9, there was no difference in the reported availability of emotional support at Stage 1 between the parents of white children and those of minority ethnic origin. Interview data suggest that this apparent similarity conceals a difference in the reason behind the lack of support. Whilst the black or Asian families were likely to be cut off from the emotional support that could have been provided by close relatives, they were more likely to get support from partners. With white families it was more likely to be the other way round.

Table 5.9 ***Availability of emotional support by ethnicity of child, city areas only (interview sample, Stage 1)***[1]

Emotional support	**White**		**Minority ethnic origin**		**All**	
	No.	**%**	**No.**	**%**	**No.**	**%**
Some emotional support	12	54	24	53	36	54
Poor emotional support	10	46	21	47	31	46
Total	**22**	**100**	**45**	**100**	**67**	**100**

[1] Not statistically significant

Figure 5.2 shows no difference between 'service request' families and 'neglect' referrals. However, within the 'neglect' groups, lack of emotional support was a characteristic of 48% of the 52 cases where *physical neglect* was a cause for concern, a trend that did not quite reach statistical significance. However, parents in families where there were concerns about emotional *abuse* were less likely than the others to report lack of emotional support (31% did so at Stage 1). It should be noted that numbers in this group are small – four out of 13 reported a lack of emotional support. Those where there were concerns about emotional *neglect* were neither more nor less likely than the others to report a lack of emotional support: 36% (eight out of 22) compared with 39% for the total sample of interviewed parents.

Turning to the pattern of family functioning, in Chapter 3 we described how families had been grouped in terms of the clusters of problems. Figure 5.3 shows a non-significant trend towards the 'acute distress' families being most likely to be lacking in emotional support, which may have been one of the factors that 'pushed them over' from generally coping to non-coping families. (This group was most likely to show improvement on the dimension of emotional support over the period of study.) Families with long-standing and multiple problems were more likely to report lack of emotional support (just over half did so, though the trend does not reach statistical significance).

Figure 5.2 ***Social and emotional support by type of referral (interview sample, Stage 1)***[1]

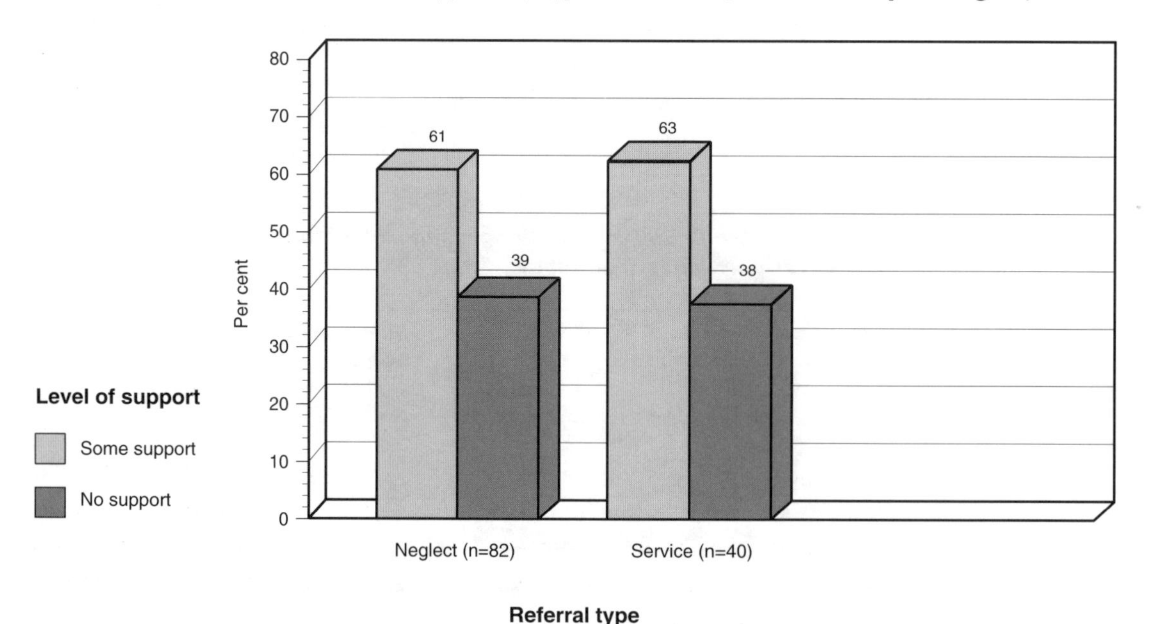

[1] n=122; not statistically significant

Figure 5.3 ***Social and emotional support by type of family (interview sample, Stage 1)***[1]

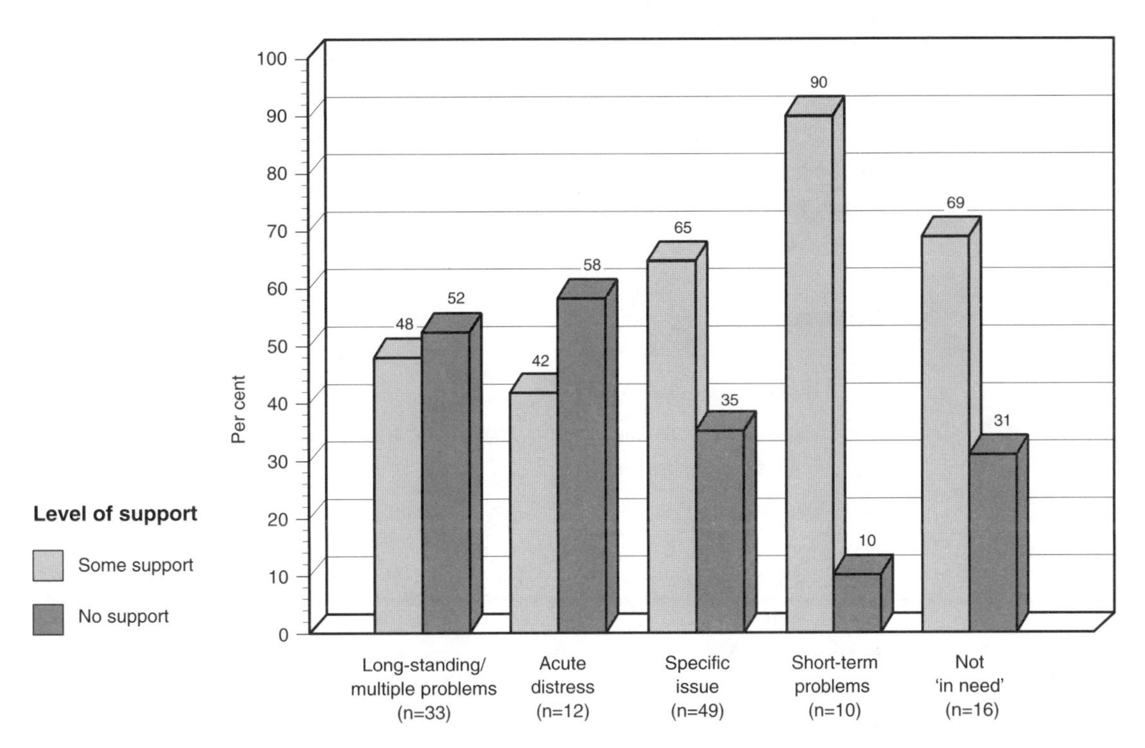

[1] n=120; missing data=2; not statistically significant

They were also less likely to report improvement than the 'acute distress' families, even though there was some change for the better. On a slightly different dimension, 46% of those who were seeking – or at least willing to accept – help reported a serious lack of emotional support compared with only one in five of those who were resistant to or refused help. This is probably explained to some extent by the fact that those referred because of concerns about unsubstantiated maltreatment were often resistant to receiving help.

Conclusion

In this chapter we have considered the extent to which families were actually able to get in touch with people and agencies who could offer a range of practical and emotional support services as well as the families' subjective accounts of their need for support and its availability. Whilst by no means all the families lacked support, a high proportion spoke of their isolation and the subjective experience of loneliness at the time they came into contact with the social services department at the start of our study. Although there was improvement for many of them, 12 months later the extent of isolation was still considerable, especially in the city areas. Yet in all three areas the social services departments were already seeking to put into place a network of neighbourhood agencies. A major challenge is presented to those drawing up Children's Service Plans, not only to encourage the voluntary, neighbourhood and self-help sectors to join them in providing family support services, but also to find ways of helping those who need them most to make use of them.

Summary

The families varied considerably in terms of the extent to which they could call on support from family and friends at times of stress. Thirteen per cent (mostly in City 2) had not had any contact with a relative during the previous month.

Families were asked whether they had anyone to turn to for material help, advice, help with the children, and help with private feelings. They were least likely to be able to turn to someone for material or financial help (a quarter had no one); about one in five had no one to turn to for help with the children, but a smaller proportion (12%) had no one they could talk to about private feelings.

Around 70% of those who had had contact with social workers said, at the Stage 2 interview, that they found them helpful, and roughly 70% said they found their GP, health visitor and playgroup leader helpful. Larger proportions found child-minders, day nursery and day care workers, solicitors and hospital staff helpful. Social services staff other than the allocated social worker (including managers and workers with under-eights) and police were described as 'helpful' by smaller proportions and were more likely than the other professional groups to be described as 'unhelpful'.

Although the families were aware of neighbourhood resources, most did not use them, except for day care facilities. If they used them, it tended to be for relatively brief periods.

Whilst by no means all the families lacked support, a high proportion spoke to the interviewers of their isolation and the subjective experience of loneliness when they came into contact with the social services department at the start of this study.

6 Social work and family support services

Before examining the social work service provided to these families, it is important to record that, in all three areas, major changes occurred between the time the cases were referred and the end of our study two years later. This change was most marked in County, which had reassessed and changed its initial response to referrals or requests for service. It seemed likely that this would result in a response that was more sensitive to differences between referrals, and certainly morale seemed higher among the workers taking part in the team interview and interviewed individually about their long-term cases. Changes in the two city areas were organisational and were likely to have less impact on the nature of the service as experienced by clients. In part they were made in response to encouragement by the Department of Health to refocus services away from a narrow concentration on child protection enquiries and towards considering different ways of assessing need (Rose 1994; Dartington Social Research Unit 1995b). However, the changes were also a consequence of decreasing resources and, especially, of the rising volume of new work required to meet the basic needs of asylum seekers following changes in their income support and housing benefit entitlements. These changes need to be borne in mind when reading this chapter.

The responses of the social services departments to the cases in the referral sample and in the intensive sample are considered in turn. For the full cohort of 712 referred children (555 families) we have only basic data about the individual case and the immediate response. These data were taken from the monitoring form completed by social services staff. For 176 of the 180 families in the random (intensive) sample, details of social work assessment, intervention and services are available in the main family file for the first 12 months after referral, or until case closure. As some of these records were not located at the 12-month stage, the totals of some of the tables are less than 180.

It should be noted here that data on the family file did not always give the full picture: additional service records were kept by the 'home care' or 'under-eights' sections and our research plan did not allow time for these files to be tracked down. We make this point here as it seemed to us that important service information was sometimes missing from the child or family file, and there did not appear to be a mechanism for summarising the most important contents of these other records for inclusion in the main file at case review or on case closure.

For 122 of the 180 randomly selected families who agreed to be interviewed we have the perspective of the main carer on the initial social services response. Opinions on the adequacy and appropriateness of the social work and other services provided either until case closure or for the first 12 months after the immediate post-referral period is available from the 108 families interviewed at the 12-month stage. The perspectives of the social workers and managers were obtained in the course of the discussions with individuals and groups that took place after the interviews with family members had been completed. Finally, for 18 of the more complex cases there were tape-recorded interviews with the social workers, as they looked back over the cases and reflected particularly on the processes of assessment and how decisions were made about the nature of the services to be provided.

Initial decisions on the 712 children referred

An important aim of the Children Act 1989, reasserted by ministerial statements and DoH guidance and inspection reports following the publication of *Child Protection: Messages from Research* (Dartington Social Research Unit 1995a), was that family members seeking or referred for help or protection services should be involved in the assessment of their needs and any threats to their future well-being and that services should be provided in a spirit of partnership (DoH 1995b). Where there was not total agreement about the needs of children and any risks to which they may be exposed, negotiation was to be preferred. Coercion through the courts or more formal procedures was to be avoided unless the child's welfare required their use.

Figure 6.1 shows that in around one in five of the cases that got beyond the reception system and were reviewed by a member of a child and family social work team, the initial response was either an immediate or a less urgent enquiry under Section 47 of the Children Act to ascertain whether the child might be in need of more formal protection measures. Just over a quarter were assessed immediately for the provision of a specific service – most often day care or home care – and in a further 14% of cases the service requested either by the family member or the referrer was provided without any further assessment than that gained from the first interview, phone call or referral letter.

Figure 6.1 ***Initial response of social services departments (referral sample)***[1]

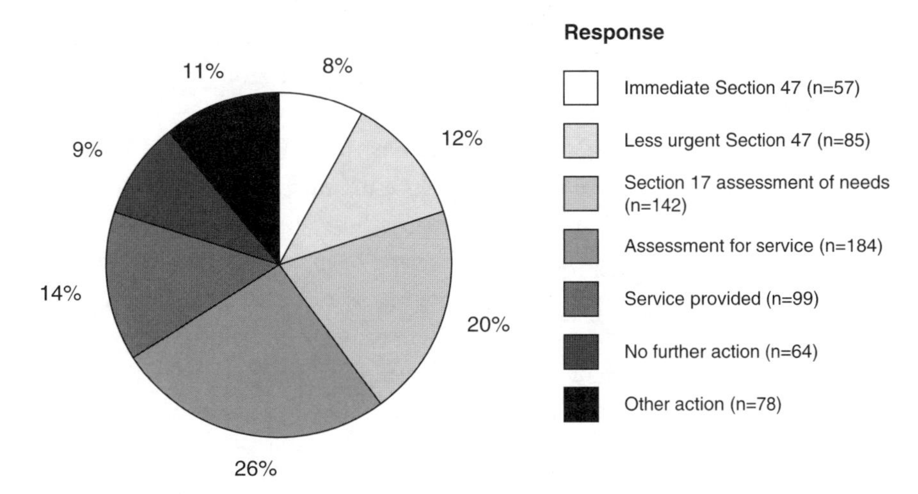

[1] n=709 children; missing data=3

In less than one case in ten no further action was taken at this stage. Other action was taken in 11% of cases, most often a phone call to aid referral to a more appropriate agency or an interview or extended phone call at which advice was given before immediate case closure. This pattern is generally in keeping with the aims of the Children Act 1989 *except that* opportunities may have been lost for more appropriate early preventive interventions. In only one case in five was there a more measured assessment of needs, under the provisions of Section 17 of the Act, before a decision was taken to close the case or to provide a specific service under the provisions of Section 17 or Section 47.

The *extent* of 'need' as defined by the Children Act 1989 may also be underestimated in our study in that not all referrals got as far as this level of initial assessment. Indeed it became clear from the family interviews that, in some cases, parents made one or more unrecorded visits to the 'initial contact', 'reception' or 'customer service' team, before or during the period of our research, because simple advice or redirection was the only action taken. From what we were told by the parents, such contacts – helpful or unhelpful – were on occasions seen to have an impact on subsequent attitudes towards contact with social workers. Realising that these 'gatekeepers' were an important first point of call, and had an impact on the services subsequently received, and also that many families might have several contacts before seeing a social worker or may never proceed beyond this point, it seems important to flag up that our research may be underestimating the volume of potentially 'in need' families who approach the social services departments.

The work of these receptionists and advice givers may be an important subject for future research, replicating an earlier study (Hall 1974).

It was noted in Chapter 3 that more than half the referrals that got through to the child and family teams were requests for a service. In a quarter of the cases there was some mention of physical or sexual abuse, and just under 30% were referred because of concerns about emotional maltreatment or neglect. As one might expect, there was a different pattern of initial decision-making depending on the type of referral. Figure 6.2 shows that more of the 'service request' cases were assessed for the provision of a specific service, and in only one in ten was there either a Section 47 assessment or a broader assessment of needs and risks of impairment of health or development (2% and 8%, respectively). For the intensive interview sample we were able to learn more about whether these levels of assessment were appropriate to the cases, or

Figure 6.2 ***Initial response by main reason for referral (referral sample)***[1]

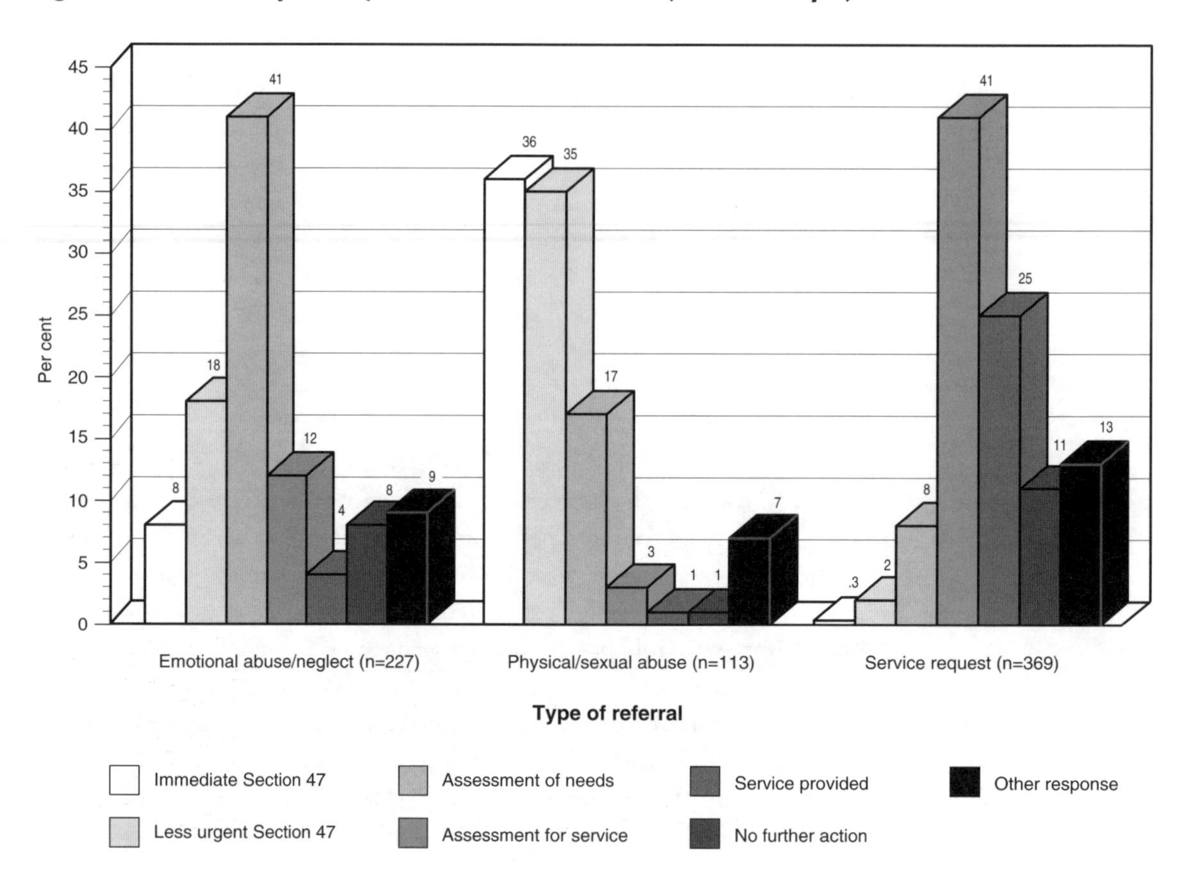

[1] n=709; missing data=3; x^2:448.15 df:12 p<.0001

whether opportunities were missed to gain more information about the families' needs and forestall more serious difficulties. These matters are discussed in Chapters 7 and 8, and in the concluding chapter.

Although Section 47 enquiries were more frequently found among those referrals where child protection concerns were mentioned, in 41% of the cases referred because of concerns about emotional maltreatment or neglect, 18% of physical abuse referrals and 13% of sexual abuse referrals the initial response was a Section 17 assessment of need, and not, at least at this early stage, a Section 47 child protection assessment. In 16% of emotional maltreatment or neglect cases and 4% of physical abuse referrals but in only one sexual abuse referral was there either an assessment for a specific service or the immediate provision of a specific service without a fuller assessment of need and risk of harm. There were 67 cases where rather vague child protection concerns were expressed by the referrers. These, and the 'home alone' cases, were more likely than other child protection cases to be initially assessed as children 'in need'. It was of note that over a quarter of these 'other child protection concerns' cases did not receive a more general assessment but were immediately assessed for or provided with a specific service. This would usually mean that the case was immediately passed to the specialist section allocating home care, day care or help with transport, without the possibility of a more general discussion of other needs and child welfare issues.

There were statistically significant differences in the initial responses made in the three areas (Figure 6.3). The proportions of referrals that resulted in a Section 47 enquiry were broadly similar. But in County fewer of the referrals resulted in a more general assessment of need, and the response to a larger

Figure 6.3 ***Initial response by area (referral sample)***[1]

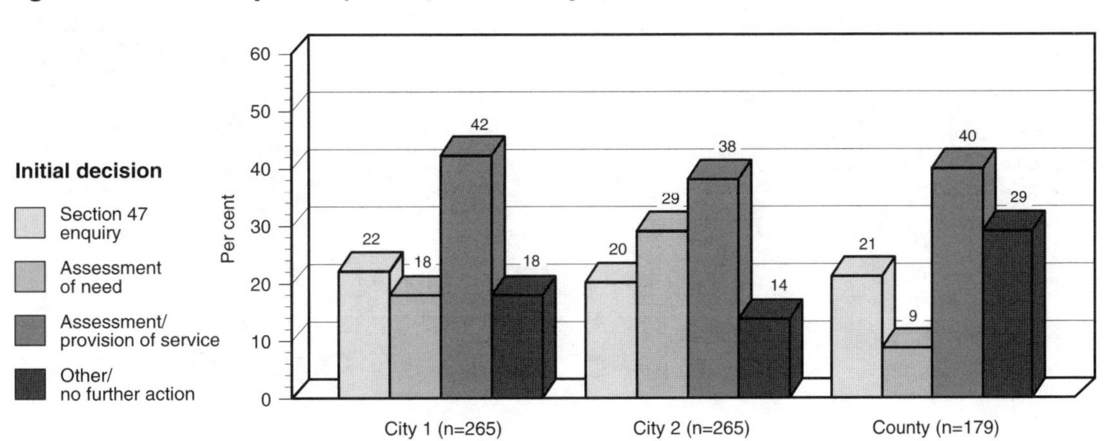

[1] n=709 children; missing data=3; x^2:34.39 df:6 p<.001

proportion was either no further action or some other response (such as referral to another agency) ($p<.0001$).

It was noted in Chapter 3 that there was a statistically significant difference between the reasons for referral of white families and those of minority ethnic origin in that the latter were less likely to be referred because of concerns about sexual abuse, emotional maltreatment or neglect. The proportion of those referred who came in the 'service request' group was roughly the same for black and for white families, but a statistically significant proportion of the black children ($p<.01$) were referred for 'other' concerns. As we have seen in Chapter 3, these concerns were usually complex and tended to be related to the extent of deprivation or disruption in their lives.

With this different pattern of reasons for referral, it is not surprising that the response from social services was different. Figure 6.4 shows that the response to the referral of a child of minority ethnic origin was less likely to be a Section 47 enquiry. Black or Asian families were more likely than the white families to be provided with a more general assessment of need or to be assessed for a specific service. (These differences were statistically significant at the $p<.001$ level.) Even when we consider only those families referred because of maltreatment, there was a statistically significant difference in the same direction, in that children of minority ethnic origin referred because of concerns about maltreatment or neglect were less likely to be the subjects of Section 47 enquiries and more likely to be provided with an assessment of need. This was most striking for those referred for reasons of child safety or being left alone. A Section 47 enquiry was the response in respect of 11 of the 14 white children in this group (79%) but for only eight of the 41 black children (19%), with 63%

Figure 6.4 ***Initial response by ethnicity, city cases only (referral sample)***[1]

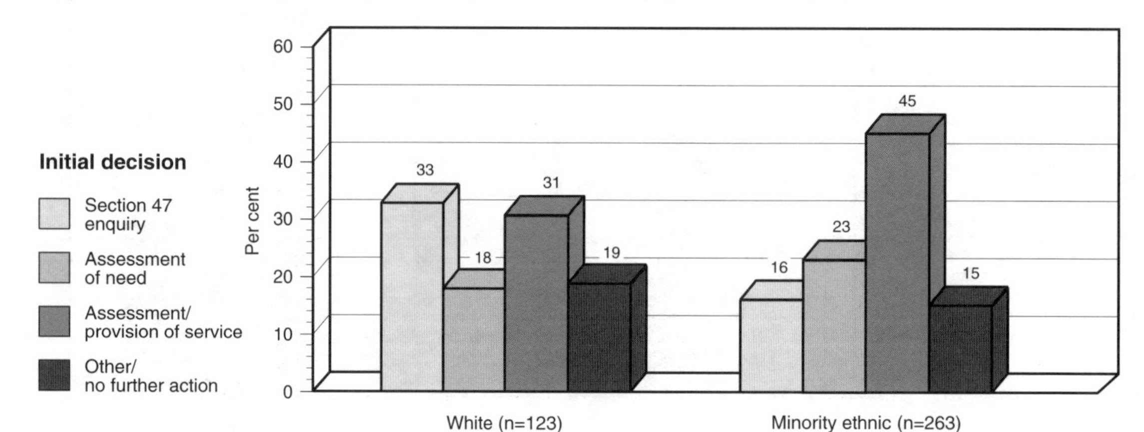

[1] n=386 cases where data on ethnicity available; x^2:40.29 df:15 $p<.001$

of the black children receiving a more general assessment of need as compared with 14% of the white children.

Initial decisions on the 180 intensive sample cases

For more detailed data on the service provided our sample size is either the 180 cases randomly identified and invited to take part in the research (the 'intensive sample' is often reduced to 176 as four files could not be found); the 122 who agreed to be interviewed at Stage 1, or the 108 interviewed at Stages 2 and 3.

Figure 6.5 gives the initial response of the team leader for 171 of the 180 families in the intensive sample. As with the referral sample, there was, as anticipated, a statistically significant difference in the initial response to those referred for a service and those referred because of concerns about neglect. More of the latter group received a Section 47 enquiry, but it should be noted that five of those referred for a service (9%) were also the subjects of a Section 47 enquiry very soon after the referral.

Figure 6.5 ***Initial response by type of referral (intensive sample)***[1]

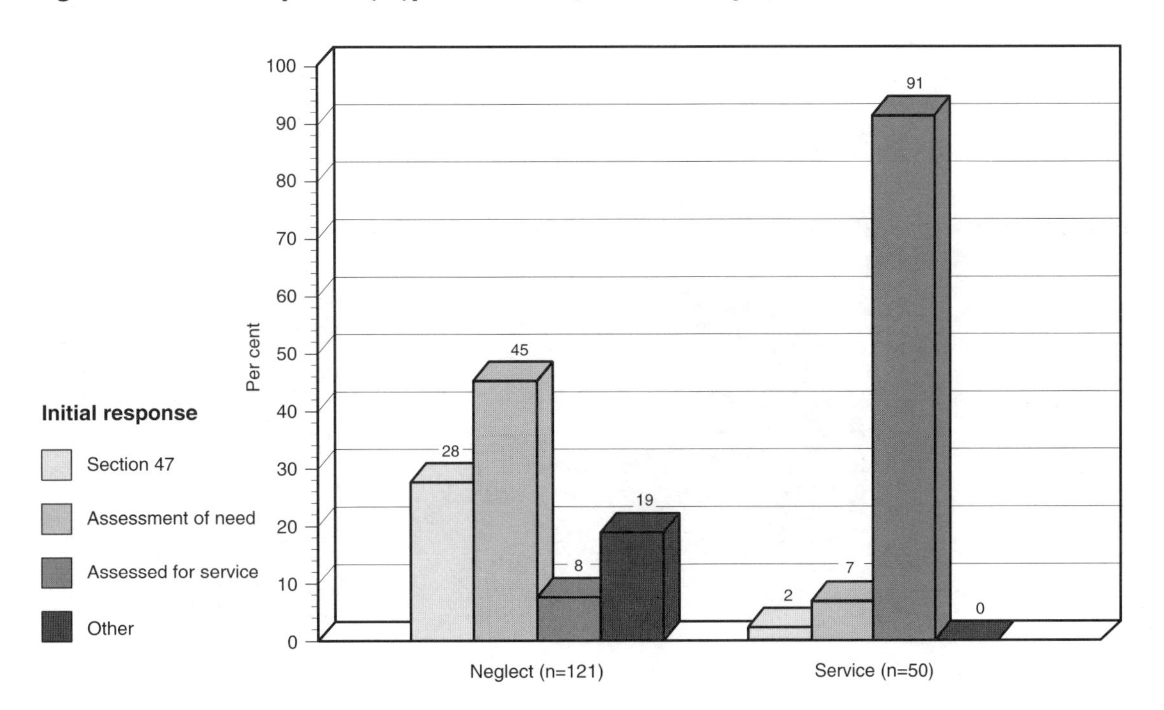

[1] n=171; missing data=9; x^2:119.15 df:3 p<.0001

In Chapter 3 the families were described using frameworks developed by Cleaver and Freeman (1995). There were some differences between the initial approach taken to the different types of families, but these did not reach statistical significance. 'Acute distress' families were most likely to receive either an assessment of need or a formal child protection assessment. The response to the families with multiple and long-standing problems was most varied, with 45% receiving neither an assessment of need nor an assessment of the need for protection.

Only two of the 23 families who were resistant to social work involvement received a formal child protection enquiry, compared with 18 (one in five) of those who either sought or welcomed the possibility of receiving social work help. Three of the 16 families whose children proved not to be 'in need' (as defined by the Children Act 1989) were assessed for a specific service; four of them experienced a child protection enquiry and five had their broader needs assessed.

Source of referral and previous contact with social services

Figure 6.6 shows that the largest proportions of referrals were made by health professionals or family members. More of the referrals made by the police were in the neglect or emotional maltreatment categories (32 of the 33 police referrals), and over a quarter of all the referrals in these categories were, in fact, made by the police. In contrast, 36% of the referrals requesting a service

Figure 6.6 ***Source of referral (intensive sample)***[1]

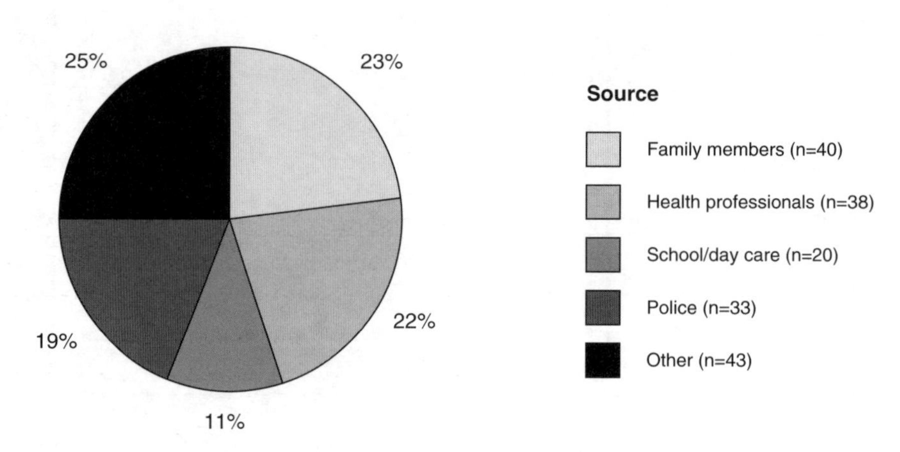

[1] n=174; missing data=6

came from health personnel, half of all referrals from this source being requests for service and half being referrals because of concerns about maltreatment or emotional neglect. Parents and family members were more likely to come to the office or pick up the phone as 'service request' cases, but nine of the 27 referrals made by a parent living in the household and 12 of the 13 referrals made by a non-resident parent or relative concerned emotional maltreatment or neglect. Ten of the 16 referrals from schools and six of the eight from social services personnel concerned emotional maltreatment or neglect.

The referral pattern for the three areas was broadly similar, except that a larger proportion of the City 1 referrals came from parents (20%) and a larger proportion of County's referrals came from health personnel (over a quarter), with fewer coming from the police and schools and more from a range of other sources. Roughly equal proportions of white parents and minority ethnic origin parents referred themselves. Seven children of minority ethnic origin were referred by a parent living outside the home or a relative, but no white children. More of the black or Asian families were referred by health or school personnel and roughly equal proportions were referred by the police. More of the white families were referred by 'other sources'. (These differences were not statistically significant.)

For just over half of the cases this was the first recorded referral, although some might have made one or more enquiries to the reception or customer service team and been redirected or told that no help was available in the circumstances described. Forty-five per cent had previously been referred to, or sought help from, the child and family team; in almost a quarter of the cases there had been an earlier Section 47 enquiry and in 12 cases (6%) a child had been registered on the Child Protection Register.

Taking into account overlaps in the above categories, 55% had previous contact with a child and family team social worker, and for 45% this was their first contact. There was a statistically significant difference between the three areas: re-referrals accounted for 70% of County's referrals but for only 50% of those of City 1 and 47% of those of City 2 ($p<.05$) (Figure 6.7). 'Service request' and 'neglect' cases were equally likely to be re-referrals. Four of the 51 service request cases had previously been the subjects of child protection enquiries, but none had resulted in the child's name being placed on the register.

Looking only at the city areas, more of the referrals of white than black or Asian families were re-referrals (Figure 6.8). Forty-six per cent of the white children but only 17% of those of minority ethnic origin had previously been the subjects of child protection enquiries ($p<.01$). Only two of the 64 children

Figure 6.7 ***Previous referrals by area (intensive sample)***[1]

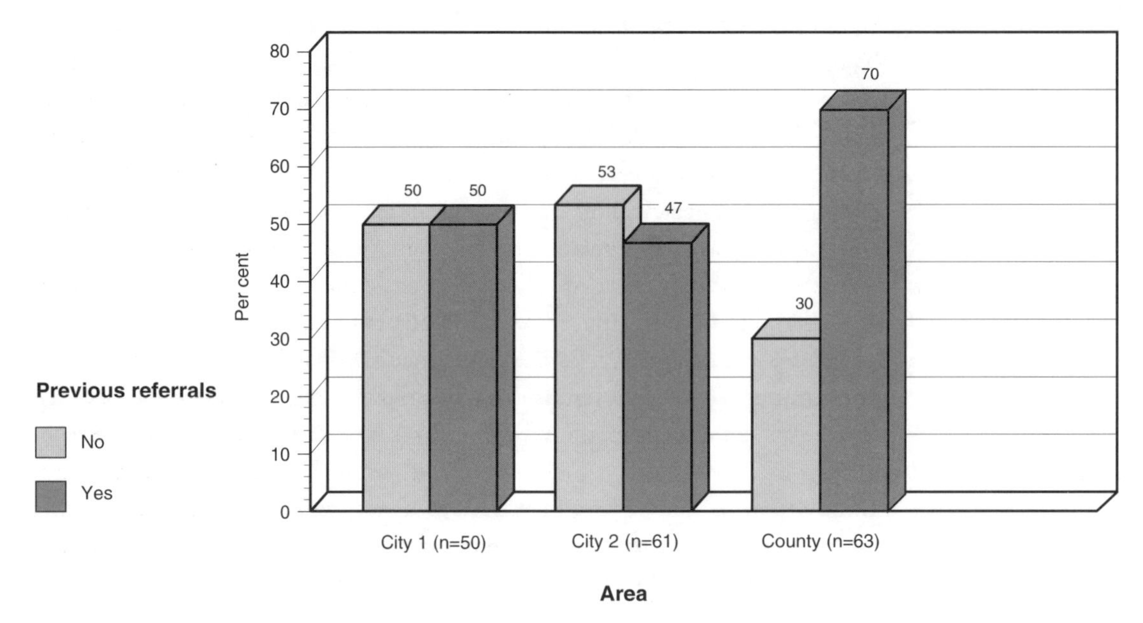

[1] n=174; missing data=6; x^2:6.725 df:2 p<.05

Figure 6.8 ***Previous referrals by ethnicity, city cases only (intensive sample)***[1]

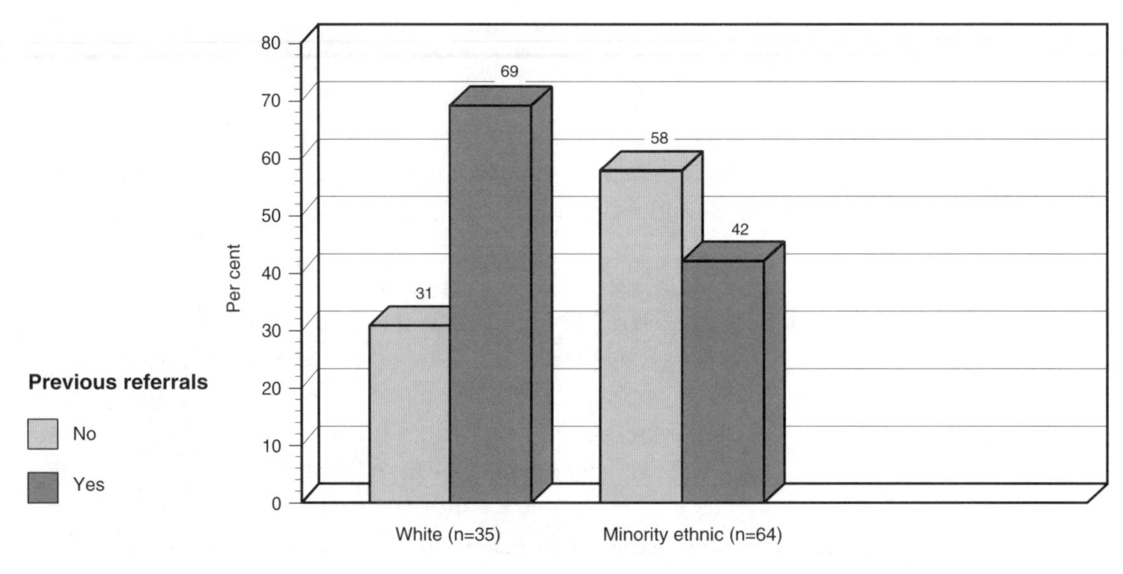

[1] n=99; missing data=14; x^2:6.40 df:2 p<.05

of minority ethnic origin (3%) but four of the 35 white children (11%) had previously been registered.

Since all of these were 'closed' cases at the start of the study, one can see that, before the referral that brought them into the research sample, many of these families had been on the receiving end of a 'revolving door' type of service. This was especially the case for the white families and for those in County. Not surprisingly, 83% of those with multiple and long-standing problems had already had contact with a social services department, as had 63% of the 'specific issue' families (compared with 45% of the 11 'acute distress' families and only 10% of the 'short-term problem' cases $p<.001$) (Figure 6.9). At least one child in almost half of the families with long-standing problems had been the subject of a child protection enquiry, as was the case for one in five of the 'specific issue' families and two of the 11 'acute distress' families. Five of the eight children whose names had previously been on the Child Protection Register were in the 'multiple and long-standing problems' group, one was a child in an 'acute distress' family and two of the previously registered children were in

Figure 6.9 *Previous referrals by type of family (interview sample, Stage 2)*[1]

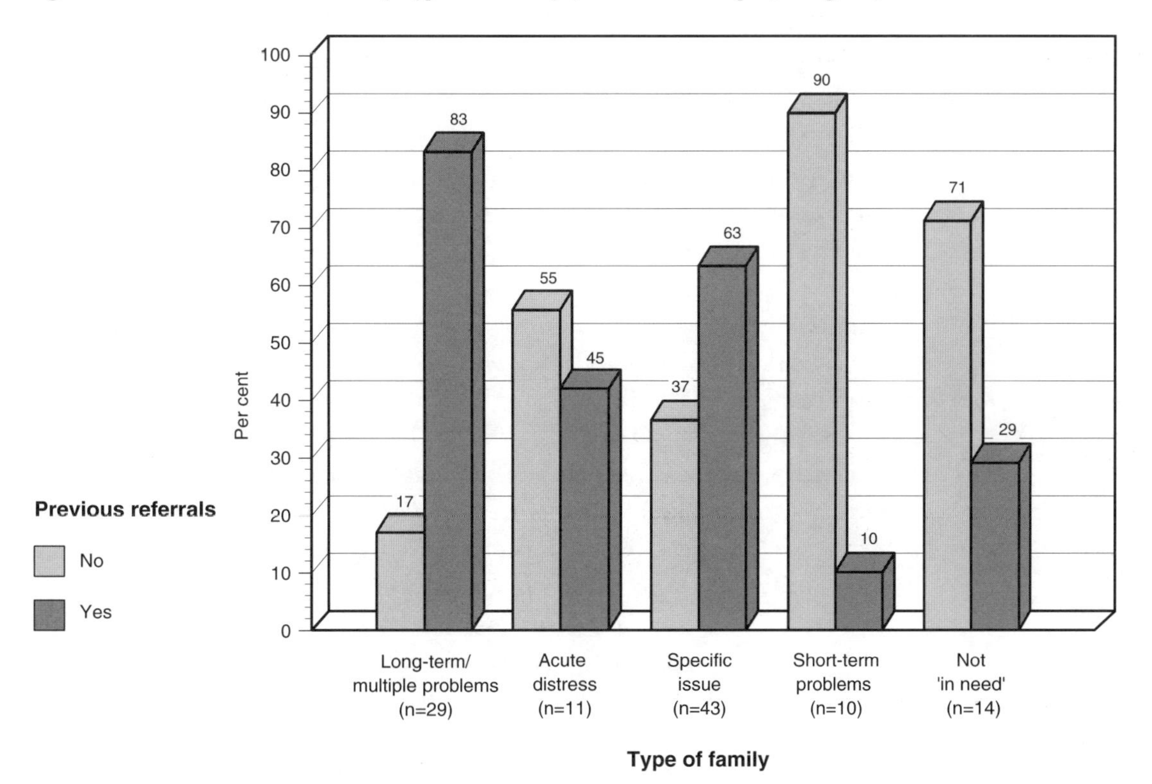

[1] n=107 families interviewed twice; missing=1; x^2:22.66 df:4 $p<.001$

'specific issue' families (17%, 9% and 5%, respectively, of these three groups of families). The main source of referrals for families in 'acute distress' was the police, and the main sources of referrals for 'specific issue' families were the families themselves, health visitors or the police. Combinations of health professionals were the main referrers of those with long-standing problems. Cases where there were concerns about physical neglect were most likely to involve families in which a child had previously been on the register (17% of 'physical neglect' referrals). A child had previously been registered in three of the 20 cases (15%) in which there were concerns about extreme spouse abuse. None of the four 'close confinement', the six 'verbal assault' or the three 'inadequate affection' cases had previously been registered.

The first four weeks

During the first four weeks, 37% of the families referred had no direct contact with a social worker. In these cases, social work activity was confined to letter writing, telephone contact or discussions with other professionals or within the department. In a quarter of cases a social worker had contact with a parent but not with the child, and in only a third of cases was there face-to-face contact with parents *and* child during the first four weeks. In summary, in 45% of cases there was no social work interview with any family member (though there may have been telephone contact), and in 45% of cases there was one interview during this period. In 14 cases (8%) there were two interviews and, at the other end of the spectrum, there were three families who had five or more office interviews with a social worker or were visited at home.

Families in the 'acute distress' group were most likely to be interviewed by a social worker during these early weeks (83%), followed by those with a short-term problem (70%). It was more likely that there would be contact with a social worker if this was a re-referral (81% were either phoned, visited or interviewed in the office) than if this was a first referral (69% had contact with a social worker), but this trend did not reach statistical significance. Those who had been the subjects of a previous child protection enquiry were more likely to have contact with a social worker during the first four weeks ($p<.05$). Only one of the 12 families whose child had previously been on the child protection register had no social work contact during this period. It should be noted that in some cases the social workers were slow to start, but, by the 12-month stage, only a quarter of the families had had no contact with a social worker. In some cases, however, the contact took place only after one or even several re-referrals.

Although not statistically significant, there was a trend towards fewer families having contact with a social worker during the first four weeks in County (51%) than in City 1 (66%) or City 2 (69%). When contact did occur, it was more likely to be an actual interview as opposed to phone contact in the two city areas. Figure 6.10 shows that 'service request' families were less likely to have a phone conversation or interview with a social worker during the first four weeks (only 49% had social work contact) than those referred because of concerns about emotional maltreatment or neglect (68% had contact). In the city areas, 76% of the families of minority ethnic origin and only 60% of white families had contact with a social worker during the first four weeks (a trend that did not reach statistical significance).

Figure 6.10 ***Contact with social worker within four weeks, by type of referral (intensive sample)***[1]

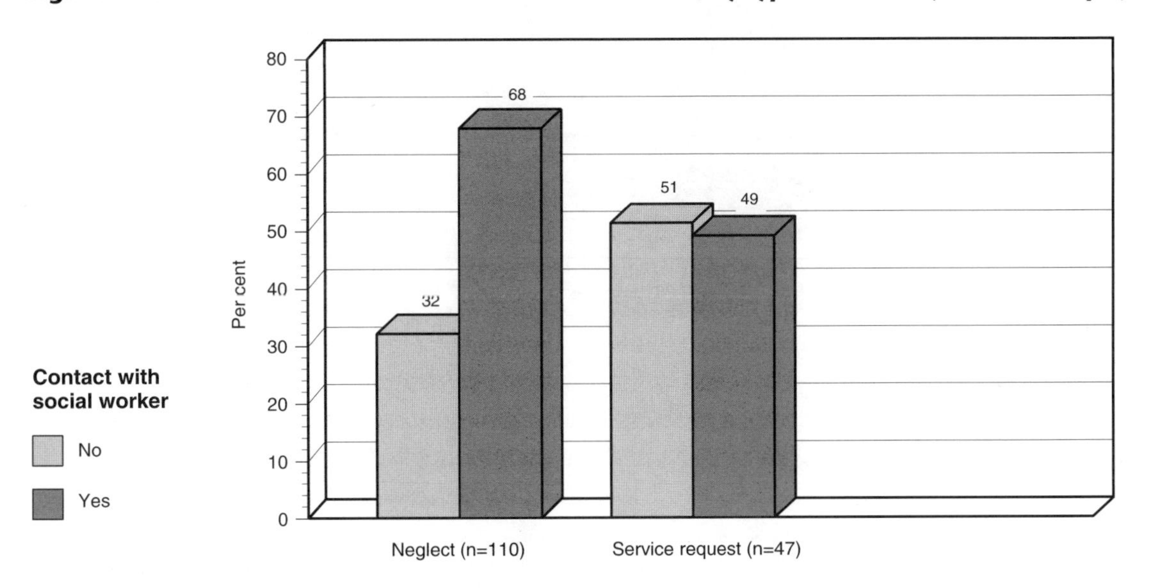

[1] n=157; missing data=23; x^2:5.199 df:1 p<.05

Initial assessments

Whilst the above information is likely to give an accurate picture of *contact* with a social worker, the following information about assessment tells us only what was recorded on file. From research interviews with social workers and families it is clear that some well-planned practice did occur, which was not fully recorded in a written assessment and plan. There was evidence that a manager had been consulted about the assessment in 82% of the cases.

During this early period no initial assessment was recorded on file for 42% of cases; there were some comments in the running record suggesting that an assessment had been made on 26% of the files; there was a separately recorded assessment of need in another 26% of the cases; and an assessment as part of a Section 47 enquiry for six (4%) of the cases (Figure 6.11). Almost equal proportions of those with multiple or long-standing problems (34%) and 'acute distress' and 'specific issue' families (33% for each group) had an assessment recorded on their files, compared with 20% of those with a short-term problem and those not 'in need'.

Figure 6.11 ***Assessments recorded (intensive sample)***[1]

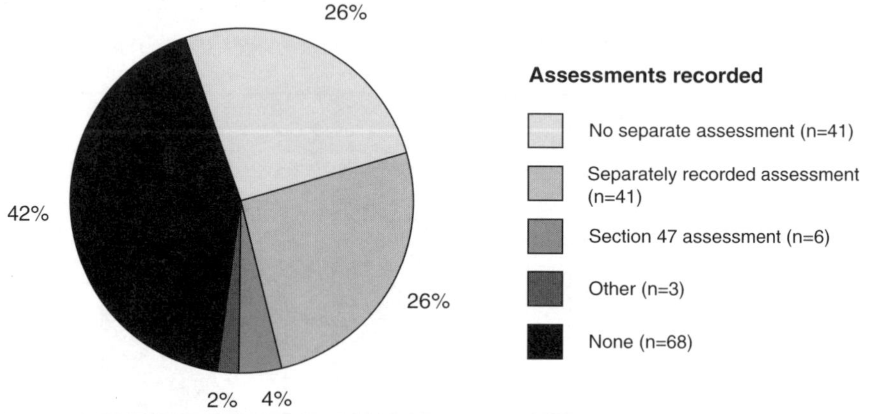

26%
42%
26%
2%
4%

Assessments recorded
No separate assessment (n=41)
Separately recorded assessment (n=41)
Section 47 assessment (n=6)
Other (n=3)
None (n=68)

[1] n=159; missing data=21

By the four-week stage there was no evidence on file of a *family support plan* in 48% of cases. There was mention of family support *services* in 45% of cases, but a coherent plan involving services and social work intervention was recorded in only 12 cases (7%).

It was more likely that there would be a recorded assessment if there had been a previous child protection enquiry (62% of such cases) ($p<.01$). Although a higher proportion of those who had previously been referred for any reason received an assessment (48%) than was the case for those being referred for the first time (37%), this difference was not statistically significant, and over half of those who had been referred before did not have an assessment of need or risk recorded on file. Since some came back yet again, these unrecorded assessments were neither cost-effective nor helpful to the family or the next social worker.

Families in County were less likely to have an assessment recorded (none recorded in the first four weeks in respect of 67%) than was the case for City 1

(28%) or City 2 (32%) (x^2:23.67; df:8; p<.01). Although there were more assessments on the 'neglect' referral files than the 'service request' files, the differences were not statistically significant. There was no difference between ethnic groups.

Re-referrals

By the four-week stage 86 cases (48% of the intensive sample cases) had been closed, with 19% of them being closed within a week. In 46% of the closed cases there had been no interview by a social worker.

From the evidence available to the researchers at the end of the study, it appeared that 19% of those children in the interview sample who had been referred because of concerns about emotional maltreatment or neglect were not at risk of maltreatment. Twenty-two per cent of the 'inadequate supervision' referrals required no further action or service, compared with 15% of the interview sample as a whole. Twenty per cent of the 'physical neglect' interview sample cases but only 1 of the 12 'emotional abuse' referrals (8%) and 1 of the 21 'emotional neglect' cases (5%) were also not in need of protective or other services.

Eighty cases were re-referred to the child and family or child protection social work teams during the following year. Some of these re-referrals were the result of new concerns about cases that had remained open, but just over half of the cases closed within four weeks were re-referred. Whilst 19% were re-referred only once, *29 of the 86 cases closed at four weeks were re-referred two or more times and four were re-referred six or more times.*

In addition to the 86 closed at the four-week stage (some of which later re-opened) a further 18 were closed at some stage during the year and were not re-referred. *Twelve months after the initial referral only 20 cases had remained open throughout the period.* A further five families were provided with a longer-term service at the time of the first referral, but the cases had been closed by the 12-month stage. Six received a long-term service after early delays but with the case remaining open throughout. Ten cases that had been closed during the first four weeks were re-referred and remained open to a social worker at the 12-month stage. *Thus 41 of these 180 cases were longer term and, sooner or later, were recognised as such, though in seven cases it took three or more referrals (with four of these being referred five or more times during the year) before such recognition.* Figure 6.12 shows that, in addition to these seven, there were 18 more 'revolving door' cases (i.e. in all 15%) that had been referred at least three times during the 12-month period. From the interviews and file data it was concluded that some of these ought to have been recognised as needing a longer-term social work service. Figure 6.13 gives the information on case closure in a slightly different way. Some of the cases that were closed only once were long-term cases that had remained open for some time before closure. Chapter 7 provides examples of the different patterns of service.

Figure 6.12 ***Pattern and duration of service (intensive sample)***[1]

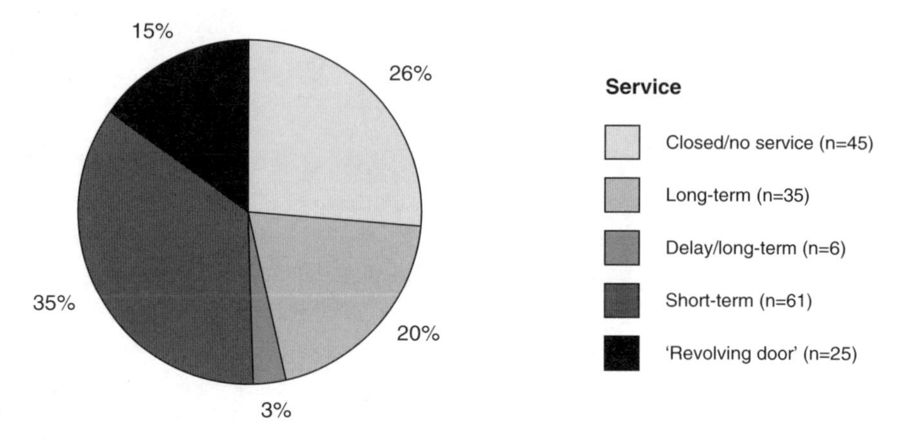

[1] n=172; missing data=8

Figure 6.13 ***Pattern of case closure (intensive sample)***[1]

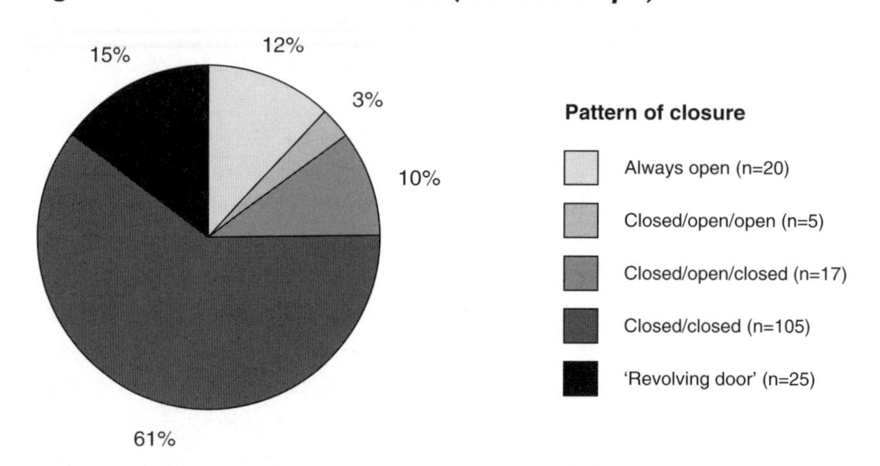

[1] n=172; missing data=8

There were different patterns of response in the three areas. Larger proportions of County and City 1 cases received a 'revolving door' service (in roughly equal proportions), but a larger proportion of City 2 cases received a short-term focused service. Families in City 1 were more likely to receive a longer-term service.

Figure 6.14 shows that in the two city areas (for which data on ethnicity were more reliable) there was a trend towards white families being more likely than those of minority ethnic origin to receive a longer-term service. A higher proportion of the families of minority ethnic origin received a short-term focused service (and any service was more likely to have ended within four weeks of referral). These differences were not statistically significant, and it seems likely that they were related to the different sorts of families and family problems being referred rather than to ethnic groups *per se*. Families with multiple and long-standing problems (who made up a larger proportion of the white families) were, not surprisingly, more likely to receive a long-term social work service.

Figure 6.14 ***Service type by ethnicity, city cases only (intensive sample)***[1]

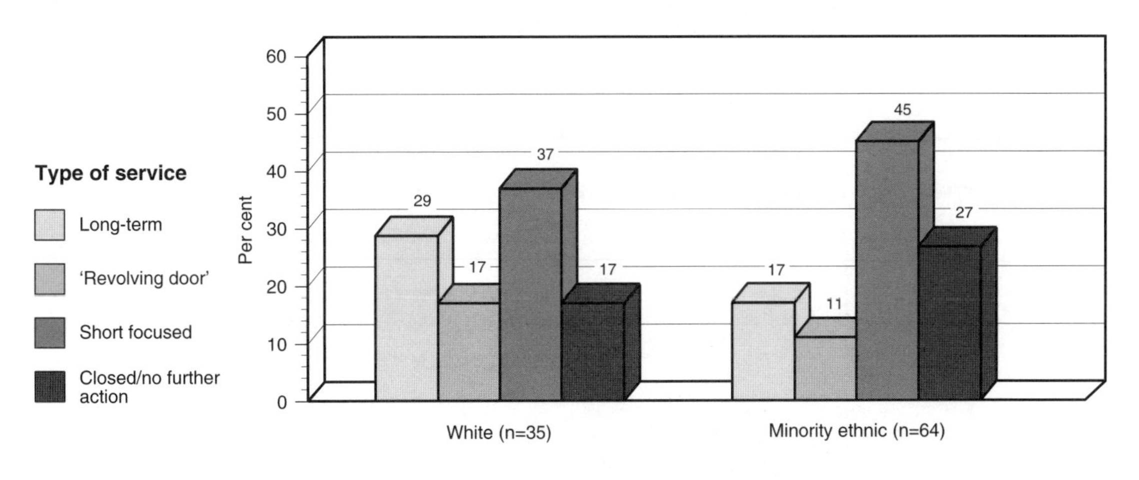

[1] n=99; missing data=14; not statistically significant

Families referred because of concerns about emotional maltreatment or neglect received a similar pattern of service to the 'service request' families, although there was a trend towards the service request families being more likely to receive a longer-term service (Figure 6.15). There was also a trend towards the emotional *abuse* referrals being among those who received a longer-term service (37%, compared with 20% for the sample as a whole). The 'extreme spouse abuse' cases made up only 14% of the whole sample but 22% of the 'always open' cases.

Families with multiple and long-term problems and 'specific issue' families were most likely to be provided with a long-term service, and those with multiple and long-term problems were also more likely to receive a 'revolving

Figure 6.15 ***Service type by type of referral (intensive sample)***[1]

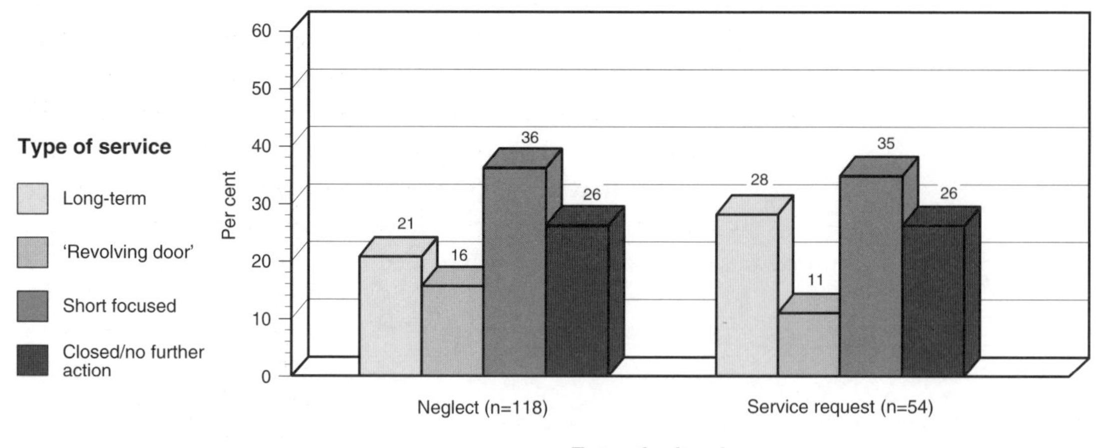

[1] n=172; missing data=8; not statistically significant

Figure 6.16 ***Service type by type of family (inteview sample, Stage 2)***[1]

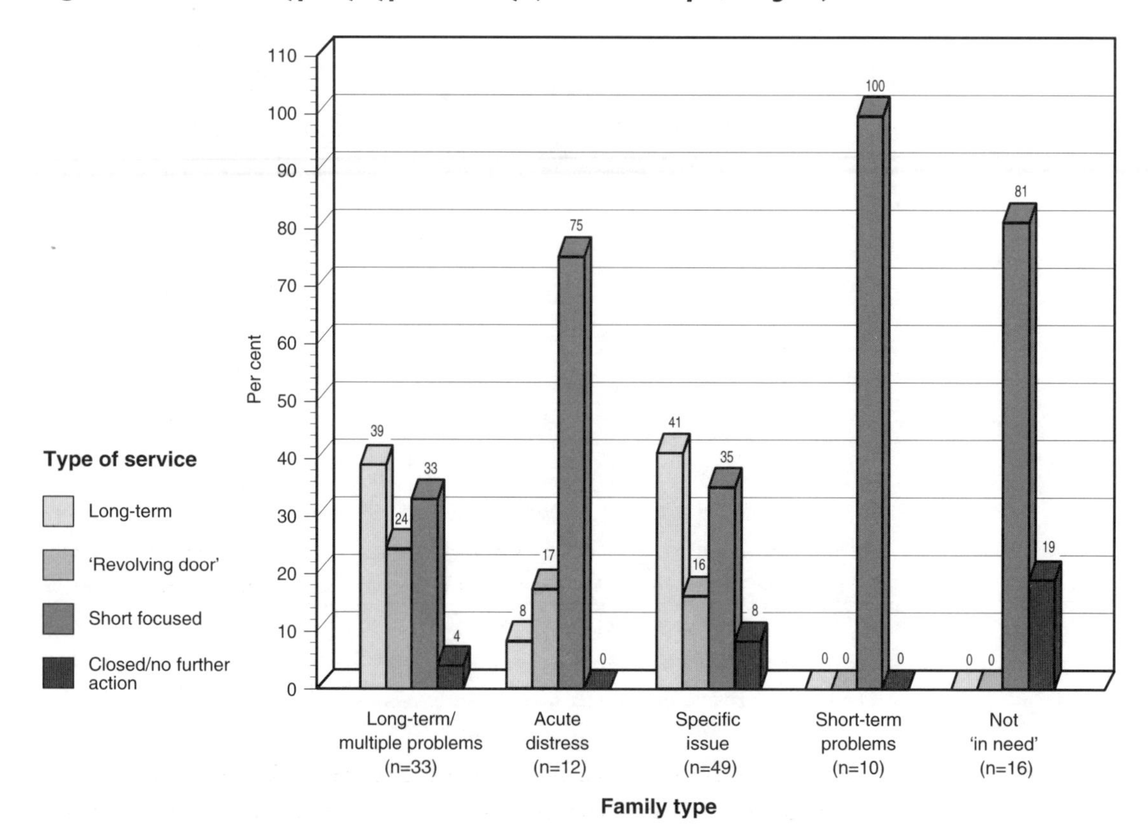

[1] n=120; missing data=2; x^2:28.58 df:12 p<.001

door' type of service (Figure 6.16). The 'acute distress' families and those with short-term problems were most likely to receive a short-term and focused service. Five of the 'specific issue' families and one family with long-standing problems received no service. It is interesting to note that some of the families in which the child was not 'in need' (as defined by the Children Act 1989 – which does not necessarily mean that they were totally problem free) received a short, focused service. From the interviews we know that some appreciated the advice given or the referral to a more appropriate service.

Table 6.1 shows that 29% of the re-referrals were made by parents in the household and almost a half by parents (within or without the household), relatives, friends or neighbours. These proportions relate only to direct referrals. We are aware from files and interviews that other professionals, especially health visitors, often made referrals at the request of parents. This indicates that, despite the possibility of stigmatisation, many families of children in need continue to seek help from social service departments.

Table 6.1 ***Source of referrals and re-referrals (intensive sample)***

Referrer	Stage 1		Stage 2	
	No.	%	No.	%
Parent in household	27	16	56	29
Parent not in household	9	5	7	4
Relative in household	3	2	5	3
Relative not in household	1	.5	8	4
Friend or neighbour	8	5	13	7
Health visitor	21	12	15	8
GP	4	2	9	5
Hospital	11	6	9	5
Other health professional	2	2	9	5
Education professional	16	9	14	7
Day care worker	4	1.5	6	3
Police	33	19	14	7
Other professional	8	5	12	6
Anonymous	8	5	13	7
Other	19	10	–	–
Total	**174**[1]	**100**	**190**[2]	**100**

[1] Missing data=6

[2] 163 families for whom data available. Total=190 because more than one re-referral in some cases

Table 6.2 lists the primary reasons given for all the referrals of the 163 families about whom we had adequate information from the second record search as well as any other reasons given. Needs were sometimes framed in terms of requests for services rather than the needs of children or parents. For example, concerns about neglect or marital problems might be framed *either* as a request for assessment *or* a request for the type of help that would be most appropriate (such as help with housing). The most frequently expressed needs were for help to care for a child (usually turned into a request for day care or after-school care) and for a service in respect of child neglect. It should be noted that among this group (originally selected to include referrals where there were concerns about emotional maltreatment or neglect but not about abuse alone or sexual abuse) 30 of the re-referrals mentioned physical abuse and 14 mentioned sexual abuse. Of cases closed early without an assessment of need, and often without a social work visit, 20 re-referrals were received concerning neglect, four concerning physical abuse and two concerning sexual abuse.

Table 6.2 ***Reasons recorded for referral or re-referral (all referrals, primary and secondary reasons, intensive sample)***

Problem/need leading to referral	Number of times given as main reason	Number of times given as primary or secondary reason
Need for day care	39	46
Respite care/accommodation for child	8	11
Need for home care/family aide	3	3
Financial advice/assistance	17	20
Transport for child or parent	4	6
Other practical/material help/advice	16	20
Housing/homelessness	1	5
Marital problems/violence	15	24
Conflict with neighbours/relatives	0	2
Illness/disability of child	9	29
Illness/disability of parent	7	19
Educational difficulties of child	5	10
Behaviour/problems of child	13	24
Behaviour of adults, e.g. substance abuse	9	27
Neglect of child	63	77
Emotional maltreatment	3	6
Physical abuse	17	30
Possible/actual sexual abuse	8	14
Criminal behaviour of a parent or older child	10	16
Need for an assessment of child	4	5

n=251

Table 6.3 lists the actions taken immediately after the initial consideration of the referrals. Space was left for the recording of up to three 'actions', and the total of 435 recognisable social work activities or decisions shows that there were on average 2.4 responses per case. There was no further action in respect of 99 referrals or re-referrals (involving 33 cases). The most frequently

Table 6.3 ***Initial actions taken in response to referral or re-referral (intensive sample)***

	Number of times mentioned
No further action	99
Liaison with or referral to other agencies	41
Home visit	39
Advice or information given	35
Allocated to social work caseload	31
Further assessment by assessment/duty team	30
Child protection enquiry	26
Information 'trawl'	22
Referral for day care assessment	19
Financial help given	18
Other practical help given	17
Child accommodated/Emergency Protection Order	13
Warning letter sent	12
Office interview	12
Links made with relatives	11
Refer for family aide/home help assessment	10

recorded actions were: liaison with or referral to other agencies; a home visit by a social worker; advice or information; referral for a fuller assessment or immediate allocation to a social worker's caseload for the provision of family support services; a child protection enquiry.

Longer-term services provided

As we saw earlier in this chapter, only a minority of the cases were allocated for a social work service after the initial referral. In a quarter of the longer-term cases there was at least one *re-assessment* within the year of the research. In response to the first referral 26 (16%) were allocated to the social worker who first assessed the referral and 33 (21%) were allocated to a different social worker. The remaining 20 were not allocated to a named worker. For half of those transferred the change of worker occurred within the first four weeks.

It has already been noted that a separate assessment of need, or a child protection assessment that included a broader assessment of need as well as risk, was to be found on only a minority of files. It was even more unusual to find a clear statement that an assessment had led to the conclusion that a child was (or was not) 'in need' as defined by the Children Act 1989. It would thus have been very difficult for families to gauge whether they might make representations if they disagreed with the decision as to whether they should be provided with services and about the sort of services to be provided. We saw little evidence that a record of the discussion about 'in need' services was shown to parents for checking or for them to retain, as recommended in texts on social work recording (Shemmings 1991; DoH 1995b). This may have happened and not been recorded on file. We know from interviews that eight of the 108 interviewees 'always' saw what social workers wrote about them and eight 'sometimes' saw this. Eight said they always contributed to the notes; five sometimes contributed.

During the second interview parents were asked two questions in an attempt to gauge their understanding of their rights and the agencies' duties under the family support and child protection aspects of the Children Act 1989. Interviewers also carried a copy of the DoH leaflet explaining the provisions of the Act (though rarely to be seen in social services department waiting areas) (DoH 1991b). Few parents recognised it, and they said it was unusual for them to be given any leaflets unless they became involved in formal child protection proceedings or a child had been accommodated. Only 11 of the 108 families said they had been given any leaflets detailing the services available. Only six answered yes to the question: 'Have you been told about or given information about whether you have a right to a service because your child is a child "in need" under the Children Act 1989?' Only three said they had been given a leaflet on this. Fourteen said they had been told about or received a leaflet about *services* for which they may be eligible. Slightly more were told about their right to know what was written about them and about the department's child protection responsibilities but few were aware of their own or their children's rights to be consulted or how they might make a complaint. Sixteen had been told about 'the possibility of having your child looked after to give you a break', but only two said they had been given a leaflet. No doubt others will have been told and forgotten, but these low numbers do fit with the picture given by the parents' more detailed responses in answer to the questions:

> Has anyone from Social Services told you whether they think that you are a family with a child 'in need' of services under the Children Act 1989?
>
> What do you think 'in need of services under the Children Act 1989' means?

These quotes indicate that, whether or not they tried, few social workers had succeeded in clarifying their rights under Section 17 of the Children Act. The most frequent response to the question about the meaning of 'in need' was 'don't know'. Or at a slightly greater length:

> I don't know because I don't know what is in the Children Act. It could mean anything from the needs [name] has to the needs of an abused child.

When they came up with their own definitions, some spoke of 'being needy':

> I don't know – without things.

Others spoke in terms of disability. Those who had sought help because their child had a disability were sometimes perplexed as to why services were either given or refused:

> They said we were NOT – I've told them that we are – why, and what part – as did the special needs adviser and the head of education welfare. I have a disabled child – I wanted them to offer me Link and any other services they can offer us as a family.

> I don't think it means, well really disabled – just that the child has got, like [name] has a hearing problem. My husband wouldn't think she was a child in need, but she does need the help.

This parent seemed to have a very good idea of the role of the Children Act 1989 in respect of children with disabilities:

> It means that they need a lot more help, basically. Help with schooling, physical stuff, wheelchairs, things to make things easier for you and the child. Things to make them independent.

The most frequent response after 'don't know' suggested that several saw the role of the social services departments simply in terms of child protection work:

> They feel that the child is in danger and they have constant visits to check.

> When there are allegations – knocking the children about – they'd put the children on the 'At Risk' list.

> No, because he said to me the child has to be abused. Was he really saying if I beat my children I would get help? I would say that my children *are* in need because of the small amount of money I get from Social Security.

> Haven't got a clue. Something to do with the child not being looked after.

Some, realistically, understood that a wide range of families might be eligible for help, but that the priority was with child protection cases:

> They have an 'At Risk' register – having a need or potentially at risk.

This mother understood why risk to her child led to a family support service. In response to the question as to what she thought 'in need' under the terms of the Children Act 1989 meant, she said:

> That I was in an extremely dangerous situation – when sitting down with people who were honest I realised it. They said we can take them but we don't want to, but the children must be safe.

Others understood the Children Act 1989 in terms of services to *children*:

> When she was in foster care – that was when she needed – in need of help of professional people – I could not give it to her.

The stepmother of a school-age child whose mother had died said:

> To help her with coping. Specifically her father was unable to tell her. We have a different aspect on this. I would tell the child; he just said she [mother] went away at first. That's where a lot of the problems came up. She thought her mother would return – after a very happy time; she became resentful because she thought her mother would come back; I would have explained it differently.

It was only a minority who arrived at a definition that covered the range of possible ways in which the 'in need' definition might lead to different sorts of services to different families. This parent clearly saw that, as intended, Section 17 of the Act facilitates the provision of additional help beyond what is available from the 'universalist' services:

> A parent – especially a single parent like me at the moment – needs to have *extra* help.

This mother's definition comes the closest to demonstrating an awareness of the potential of Section 17 and also stresses the importance of assessment – a point to which we return in more detail in Chapter 7:

> If a family comes to you and says we are having a problem, you should look at that – all families are different. You should take what parents say seriously because they know the child better than anybody else. All statements should be looked at without prejudice and without personal opinion.

These findings indicate that even among families who crossed their thresholds, these social services departments did not appear to be 'publish[ing] information about services provided by them' (Schedule 2 of the Children Act 1989). If they were, they did not appear, from what the families had to tell us, to be ensuring that social workers took 'such steps as are reasonably practicable to ensure that those who might benefit from the services receive the information relevant to them' (Schedule 2 of the Children Act 1989).

Despite the fairly low number of *recorded* assessments of need, it was possible to pick up from the files that some form of assessment of the reason for referral – and any services to be provided – must have been made, since a wide range of services was identified in respect of the families. Table 6.4 lists the

Table 6.4 ***Problems of families recorded on file (intensive sample)***

Problems	Number of cases in which mentioned
Financial problems/debts	45
Living on low or irregular income	41
Housing problems	41
Marital/partner violence	40
Difficulty in claiming benefit	34
Emotional/behavioural difficulties – child	31
Mental health problems – parent/carer or partner	25
Marital/partner discord	19
Significant member of household left home	18
Drug misuse by parent/carer	17
Emotional/behavioural difficulties – parent/carer	16
Alcohol misuse by parent/carer	16
Long-term illness – parent/carer	15
Physical disability – child	14
Criminality of parent/carer	14
Grandparent/s temporary or permanent carer of child/siblings	14
Inability to speak English	12
Physical disability – parent/carer	11
Alcohol misuse by partner	8
Drug misuse by partner	8
Other traumatic event – affecting child/family	8
Learning difficulties – child	8
Learning difficulties – parent/carer	7
Death of significant person – affecting parent/carer	7
Physical/sexual abuse – by parent or adult relative	7
Death of significant person – affecting child	6
Member of family in prison	6
Long-term illness – child	6
Significant adult addition to household	5
Miscarriage/abortion/termination of pregnancy	5
Racism/racial harassment	3
Contact with Schedule 1 offender (sexual abuse)	3
Contact with Schedule 1 offender (physical or neglect)	2
Physical/sexual abuse by sibling	2
Immigration issues	1

problems mentioned on file at any time since the referral. From this it can be seen that social workers recognised that these families experienced a wide range of practical, emotional and relationship difficulties. However, when compared with the list of difficulties given by the families, there is an under-recognition of the problems that characterised the daily lives of many of the families. The low proportion of families receiving a home visit from a social worker, and the tendency to concentrate on 'risk' at the expense of 'need', go some way towards explaining this difference.

Table 6.5 lists the number of cases in which services were suggested, offered, accepted or provided, and the number of cases in which the services were still being provided at the 12-month stage. That some services were offered and

Table 6.5 ***Services identified and provided (interview sample, Stage 2)***

Type of service	Number of times				
	Suggested in file	Offered to family	Accepted by family	Provided to family at any time	Still provided to family
Day nursery, playgroup or child-minding for child	46	38	32	29	21
Baby-sitting for child	3	2	1	1	1
Home help, a family aide or a family support worker to work with carer in the home	25	22	16	13	6
Welfare rights advice and help	23	22	21	20	4
Money, furniture or furnishings	26	22	22	21	4
Accommodation or respite care for child or sibling	20	16	13	14	5
Provided a holiday for carer or child	4	4	3	2	–
Transport for child or parent	11	8	7	7	1
Advice/advocacy *re* housing problems	10	9	9	9	2
Talking about parent's feelings or helping to sort out problems	49	47	40	39	14
Talking to child about feelings or helping him/her to sort out problems	11	9	9	9	4
Group work/support group for parent	4	4	2	2	–
Group work/support group for child	3	2	1	1	–
Family therapy	4	4	3	3	1
Individual therapy for child	9	7	6	5	2
Referred carer to a family centre	5	5	3	3	2
Referred carer to any other centre	14	11	9	8	3
Other	47	39	33	32	7

not taken up indicates that either the family found them unsuitable or that, in the light of the partnership requirements of the Children Act 1989, more than one service was offered and the family members opted for some but not others. There was evidence on file that just over one in five of the families (around a third of those offered a service) was given some choice about how their needs could best be met. Although this might not have resulted in the service they would ideally have wanted, they appreciated having some influence on the type of service provided. This mother would have liked a social casework service but appreciated that the allocated worker, who was providing a 'case management' overview, was doing the best she could:

> ***Mother:*** It is just we were looking to have a social worker but we never had. To have [name], – say – she's in charge of our case.
>
> ***Interviewer:*** Did you ask?
>
> ***Mother:*** Yes – they wanted to give me a different person but I was asking for the same person.
>
> ***Interviewer:*** Did you get that?
>
> ***Mother:*** Yes.

Of the 38 parents interviewed at Stage 2 who said they received a service from a social worker, ten (a quarter) said the services provided were definitely what they needed and a further 22 (over half of those receiving a social work service) said that what had been provided had to some extent been what they needed. Six said that the social work service provided had not been appropriate to their needs. At least one service was identified as needed in 102 of the cases (59% of those for which a parent was interviewed or the file was available at Stage 2) but half of those referred received no services. These data indicate that services identified as needed often failed to be provided. Sometimes families were offered a service that was not accepted, but in most cases there was no clarity about why a service, which was assessed as being needed, failed to materialise. Practical help was most likely to be accepted when offered. When it was not accepted, as in the case of day care, we know from parents that this was usually because the offer came too late or was considered to be the wrong sort or in the wrong place. The recommended services most likely to be provided were: welfare rights advice; assistance 'in cash or in kind'; help or advice with housing problems. Day care, help in the home and accommodation for the child were more likely to be suggested but not actually provided.

We have noted earlier in this chapter that even when cases were allocated to a social worker, the work tended to be short-term. Table 6.5 shows that a social casework service (defined broadly as 'talking about parent's feelings or helping them to sort out problems') was offered to only 47 of the 172 parents (27%) whose records were available (or the family was interviewed at the 12-month stage) and actually provided in only 39 cases (23%). Table 6.6 shows that only 10 of the 163 parents for whom records were available at the 12-month stage saw the main social worker more than 16 times during the year, whilst 11 saw him/her only once. There was no allocated social worker in 114 of these cases.

It should be noted that this does not give a picture of the *frequency* of contacts: some cases were open for a comparatively short period but there might have been daily contact with a social worker during a crisis. In longer-term cases frequency increased at times when, for example, a child protection enquiry was initiated or a child was accommodated. Table 6.7 lists the significant events that tended to increase the extent of social work involvement. In ten cases there were five or more such events during the year.

Table 6.6 ***Number of times family had face-to-face contact with main social worker (intensive sample, Stage 2)***[1]

Number of times	Number of families
Once	11
Twice	5
3–5 times	8
6–10 times	8
11–15 times	7
16+ times	10
Not allocated to a social worker	114
Total	**163**

[1] Missing data=17

Table 6.7 ***Specific events leading to increased social work contact (intensive sample, Stage 2)***[1]

Event	Number of times mentioned
Initial child protection conference	12
Review child protection conference	6
Index child accommodated	12
Sibling accommodated	4
Index child placed with relatives	12
Sibling placed with relatives	8
Child adopted	1
Other special events	7

Social work contacts (which might have been with one or a succession of duty social workers or long-term team workers) were most often in the family home (45 cases). Only in one case was the main setting for social work contact a family centre, and in two other cases contact took place variously in the office, the family home or a family centre.

The other setting for a meeting between family members, social workers, managers and other social services staff was a child protection conference or other such meeting. Meetings were held in respect of 32 of the families, two of these being convened by the education department or school and the others by social workers. Whilst no meetings were held in respect of 132 families, and only one in respect of 14 families, two or three meetings were held in respect of eight families, and in nine cases four or more meetings were held during the space of a year or an even shorter period (in three of these cases there were seven or more meetings). Most of these meetings were linked to formal child protection procedures. However, we learned from our interviews with social workers and managers that there was a trend towards more multi-disciplinary meetings being held outside these formal procedures and the 'looked after' review procedures. Various names were used for these meetings, the most frequent being 'planning' or 'network' meetings.

Services to those most in need of support

Since we are particularly concerned with the question of family support, the different aspects of the service were considered to see if there were any noticeable differences between the interventions with families who appeared to have community support and those who did not (see Chapter 5 for a fuller discussion of this variable). Although there was a trend towards families who perceived themselves as lacking in support being more likely to receive a long-term service, Table 6.8 shows that the only statistically significant association was that those lacking support were less likely to refer themselves or be referred by a family member ($p<.05$).

Table 6.8 ***Aspects of social work service related to parents' perceived emotional support (intensive sample, Stage 2)***

Service	Percentage receiving type of service		
	Some support	**No support**	**Significance**
Previous referral	60	40	ns
Children on Child Protection Register	8	7	ns
Referred by family member	20	9	p<.05
Referred by health professional	18	29	ns
Referred by police	17	24	ns
Assessment of need recorded	35	25	ns
Section 47 assessment	16	25	ns
No further action taken after referral	19	13	ns
Received a longer-term service	24	34	ns
Received a 'revolving door' service	15	15	ns
A social worker was allocated to the family	36	51	ns
Generally satisfied by service provided	40	28	ns

Looking at the case records in more detail, it appeared that the service to these more isolated families got off to a slower start and tended to be less well planned, though it was more likely, when it did get started, to be long-term.

Summary

For around one in five of the 555 families referred for a service or because of concerns about maltreatment, the initial response was either an immediate or less urgent Section 47 enquiry to ascertain whether the children might be in need of formal child protection measures. Just over a quarter were assessed for eligibility and prioritised for receipt of a specific service, and in a further 14% of cases a service was provided immediately without any further assessment than that which took place over the phone or at a single interview. In around one case in five no further action was taken or else the case was immediately referred elsewhere. In only one case in five was there a general assessment of need (including the need for protection).

Statistically significant differences were noted between the type of referral and the nature of the initial assessment. More of the physical, sexual and emotional abuse referrals were the subject of Section 47 enquiries than was the case for neglect referrals.

Those referred because of general neglect or more specifically because of concerns about lack of supervision were more likely (42% and 47%, respectively) to have an assessment of need. Sixty-eight per cent of those referred with a request for a service were either provided with the service without any further assessment or were assessed specifically for that service without their more general needs being assessed.

As a consequence of the higher proportion of white families being referred because of child protection concerns, a higher proportion of white families than families of minority ethnic origin experienced a Section 47 enquiry.

The largest proportions of referrals were made by health professionals and family members. Parents and family members were more likely to make 'service request' referrals.

In just over a half of the cases in the intensive sample this was the first recorded referral. 'Service request' and 'neglect' cases were equally likely to be re-referrals.

During the first four weeks, 37% of the families in the intensive sample had no face-to-face contact with a social worker. In these cases, social work activity was confined to letter writing or telephone contact.

By the four-week stage, just under half of the intensive sample cases had been closed, and half of these were re-referred at some point during the twelve months. Whilst 19% of cases were only re-referred once, 29 of the 86 cases closed at the four-week stage were re-referred two or more times, and four were re-referred six or more times. Only one in five of the intensive sample cases remained open throughout the twelve month period.

Forty-one of the 180 cases were provided with a longer-term service, although in seven cases it took three or more referrals before the need for a long-term service was recognised. Fifteen per cent of the cases received a 'revolving door' type service in that the case was opened and closed three or more times during the year without a long-term service ever being provided. The largest proportion (35%) received a short-term service, and 26% were closed quickly without the provision of a service other than, in some cases, referral to another agency.

Families referred because of concerns about emotional maltreatment or neglect received a similar pattern of service to the 'service request' families, although there was a trend towards more of the 'service request' families receiving a longer-term service and fewer receiving a 'revolving door' type service.

Assessment of needs, family strengths and problems were recorded on less than half of the files, and family support plans were even less likely to be spelled out. However, a wide range of services was provided to these families. Services most often provided involved practical assistance, such as the provision of day care or a family aide. In those cases that received a longer-term service, the allocated social worker provided a casework service that usually combined emotional support with the co-ordination of practical help.

Families were asked about their understanding of the 'in need' provisions of the Children Act 1989. They were rarely provided with leaflets to explain the family support provisions, and most families associated the term 'in need' with the need for child protection services.

7 Social workers' and parents' perceptions

The quantifiable aspects of the social work service were considered in Chapter 6. In this chapter we look in more detail at the interventions as they emerged from the records, and especially as they were described by the parents and the social workers interviewed or joining in group discussions. Throughout this report attention has been drawn to the crucial importance of assessment if the appropriate service is to be delivered at the right time to those families and children who most need it and can benefit from it. This chapter, therefore, starts with a consideration of the different levels of assessment.

Levels and types of assessment

In all three authorities a preliminary screening was undertaken by what was variously called the 'customer service team' or the 'reception team'. The importance of this first sifting stage became evident in the group interviews with social workers and managers, and our impressions of its importance were confirmed by the families. It became apparent that some of the families whose cases had been closed at an early stage returned on more than one occasion to the reception team and were given advice or referred elsewhere. When cases were closed, these contacts were not always recorded in the families' file, a significant omission if a full picture of family needs and requests for help is to be available in cases where more serious problems result in referral to the child care team.

The next sifting process occurred when decisions were taken by the intake or assessment teams as to whether the case should be responded to as a child protection referral or as a request for support under the provisions of Part III of the Children Act 1989. These were sometimes referred to as *first stage* assessments.

It has already been noted (Chapter 6) that neglect or emotional maltreatment referrals were more likely to lead to an assessment of need than those that mentioned sexual or physical abuse. One group of referrals stood out from the others: those that included concerns about inadequate supervision were less likely to result in any contact with a social worker. An opportunity to make a more considered assessment of any needs the children might have was missed in those cases in which the response was either a series of phone calls and case closure, or a letter to the parents warning of the dangers of not providing adequate supervision for their children. From our interviews it was clear that those assessing these cases generally made the appropriate decisions. However, considerable anger was aroused when letters were not followed up by any further contact. Few took up the invitation (usually included in the letter) to seek an appointment if it would be helpful, and the interview data suggest that parents in this situation were most likely to be deterred from seeking help even if they needed it. Reading through the research transcripts, one might be forgiven for calling this the 'deterrent model of prevention'. Yet we recognised the dilemma of hard-pressed social workers and team managers who were responding to the exhortation in Children Act guidance to be honest with families. They were uncomfortable about acting behind the backs of families by telephoning their GPs, health visitors or children's teachers and by opening a file on parents without telling them. There is no easy answer if there is insufficient time for a social worker to visit all these families, and such a visit would not be a high priority when cases of children who were being significantly harmed (including some already looked after) remained unallocated. Those who were visited by a social worker could at least express their anger and upset face-to-face and had the opportunity of learning in what ways the social services department might be able to help them. During those interviews the social workers, without delving into too many details, could at least satisfy themselves that neither the child nor the parents had serious health problems or disabilities. If, as sometimes happened, such problems did become apparent, the focus of the case changed to one of offering practical support.

An example of a 'no further action' case that led to anger and anxiety concerned a 3-year-old:

A neighbour who wished to remain anonymous rang to say that a mother was verbally abusing her 3-year-old child. A letter was sent warning her that this could be harmful to the child. The mother wrote back refuting the accusation, and a letter was sent acknowledging her response. There was no further contact, and from the responses to the family problem questionnaire and malaise schedule this did not appear to be a family of a child 'in need'. The mother told the interviewer that she was:

Very angry – it upset me a lot – I got the letter the day we were going on holiday. I wrote a letter the day I went on holiday, and I had another letter when I got back and that made me feel better.

Twelve months later she told the researcher that she still wanted to know if she was on a list at Social Services. The researcher's notes read: 'It is obviously not worrying her as much, but it still niggles.'

At the other end of the continuum, there were some cases in which a carefully undertaken assessment of referrals, which gave clear evidence that a child's health or development was being impaired or likely to be impaired (including cases in which it was clear that the 'significant harm' threshold had been crossed), led to the conclusion that the formal child protection system was not necessary and/or was likely to be counter-productive:

Paul, aged 4, was referred by the police after they had been called out by a neighbour. The house was extensively damaged by the mother's boyfriend and this was believed to be a regular occurrence. The mother had herself been in care, and there had been several previous referrals, including an – unsubstantiated – allegation of sexual abuse by the boyfriend. There were several referrals around this time, including one by the mother herself which did not result in a more thorough assessment. However, Paul's father instituted proceedings for a Residence Order, and an assessment was required as part of the private law court proceedings (Section 37 of the Children Act 1989).

At this point the case was referred to the long-term team and a comprehensive assessment was undertaken in order to write the court report. There was clear evidence of emotional neglect – possibly also emotional abuse in that the mother would sometimes ridicule Paul. The assessment led to the provision of a package of services. The social worker fulfilled a case management role but also provided a supportive casework service alongside the assessment to the mother and also to Paul.

The researcher's summary of the interview with the social worker notes: 'I asked the social worker if he saw Paul as a child 'in need' or a child 'at risk of harm?' His answer to this was that he didn't feel that Paul was at risk of *physical* harm from his mother. He outlined the needs that the family had – mainly for the mother to set up some routines and provide security for Paul and his sister, but also for more specialised therapeutic work. Although he did not use the words 'impairment of health or development', this is essentially what he went on to tell me. He said that at that point Paul did not appear to have problems with his development. Physically, emotionally and in his play, he was getting on fine. He mixed well with his peers, and the health visitor and the nursery did not have any serious concerns. However, the social worker said that without services he considered it was likely that Paul's development would be impaired in the future. The family support plan included provision of a family aide, attendance for Paul at the day care centre, and a referral to the family treatment centre (which was not followed up). A child protection conference was held after an incidence of bruising, but a decision was taken to continue with the support plan and Paul's name was not placed on the Child Protection Register.

An example of a 'middle-range assessment' was a referral made by a health visitor:

A mother of three children had suffered from depression after the birth of each child. A joint visit was made with a member of the mental health team. The mother admitted hitting her eldest child and said that she was worried that she may not be able to control her temper in her very depressed state. She spent much of the time crying and said she could not cope with the children. There were two further long interviews within a four-week period. She was assessed as needing counselling to deal with her feelings following an abortion several years earlier. To reduce the pressure, a part-time day care place was provided for the middle child. Discussions took place about how to avoid physical punishment and alternative ways of disciplining the children. The family support plan included six counselling sessions for the mother at the mental health unit in addition to the nursery place for the middle child. The case was then passed to the long-term team for further support and continuing assessment. However, this assessment did not take place and there were three further referrals during the year to the child care team. The third referral was made by the mother, requesting help with behaviour problems for her older son. A family aide was allocated but withdrawn three weeks later as the mother said she was managing. This was a not untypical 'revolving door' case in which an assessment was undertaken and family support plans drawn up but long-term social work input was not provided. The plans were ill-coordinated and the situation deteriorated.

In considering these 180 cases, most of which involved some degree of impairment or likely impairment to the health or development of a child, it was not clear why some cases were assessed under the formal child protection systems and some were not; why some resulted in a child protection conference and a further assessment, whilst others received similar services without being reviewed by a child protection meeting. Social workers were clearly giving some thought to these questions in light of the encouragement to provide services without necessarily going down the formal child protection route. Only 19% of those referred because there were concerns about maltreatment were the subject of Section 47 enquiries, and an initial child protection conference was held in only 12 cases during the 12-month research period. The social workers interviewed individually and in groups welcomed the opportunity to make a more flexible response in the light of individual circumstances. In response to the question about how she made a decision as to which route to follow, one worker said:

> We haven't got very clear statements of policy anywhere. Sometimes it [the formal child protection route] is the only way to get a detailed assessment. It is not using the system appropriately but – out of sheer desperation with children who have huge needs but are not necessarily at risk; when somebody needs to be involved just to co-ordinate services and put the care packages together – yes, I use the child protection system. If you are a good salesman you can sell anything as a CP child protection issue or sell anything as a child 'in need'. It's a case of how you present it. Sometimes in sheer desperation, if there is a lack of social workers to refer cases on to, then we take them to case conferences. And then it's almost like buying extra time by commissioning a risk assessment – they can bring other people in from outside because it becomes a CP issue and somebody *has* to be involved.

Others picked up on a point made by Sinclair et al. (1995) in the light of their research on the assessment of adolescents. They sought to avoid the formal child protection route because of the delay that often ensued between the decision to register and the start of the 'comprehensive assessment'. Since much work had already been put into involving family members in the first stage assessment, and the family were already engaged on working towards improving the situation, it was considered inappropriate to delay the continuation of the process of helping:

> I think I can do an assessment in two weeks and it is not going to improve an awful lot if I take two months. It is still only a snapshot. You really need an ongoing involvement. It may be different if I can do an assessment again in six months, or even in twelve months. But I think the nonsense of spending months and months on risk assessments holds things up.

Several social workers commented on the importance of *helping* at the same time as *assessing*. Describing her role with a family with very many practical and emotional problems, and where there was clear evidence that the child was being emotionally neglected, a social worker said that the case had been open in the duty system for some time but that she was the first person to actually work with the family. She said that with this kind of case it is not possible to assess quickly; it is necessary to put in help to see if the parents can make necessary changes.

> With the neglect factor it's not easy to get a clear picture. The physical environment you can see. Some people are poor and they cannot manage; sometimes it's because of health, you may find the house is untidy when the mother is sick; or it may be because of poverty that proper food cannot be provided for the children – but we should not say this is neglect. When we have to assess the real neglect factor, we have to see the mother's personality, how far she is capable, and if there is any mental health problem? Is she bonding with the children? What are her own needs?

Recording assessments and support plans

The interviews with the social workers and some of the families suggest that some records do not give a true indication of the extent of either the assessment or the provision of coherent services. Cases that were routed through the formal child protection system almost invariably had a recorded child protection or family support plan appended to the child protection conference records. However, these plans, although appearing to be well worked out, were not always put into effect. On the other hand, some families whose cases were not reviewed by the formal child protection system received well-planned family support services – though these were not always carefully spelled out in the case record.

Social workers and parents spoke of the importance of the co-ordination of services and the 'case management' role of the accountable worker. Sometimes this was an 'arms length' role with the main helping relationship and services provided by family aides, other professionals or day care workers. Most often, however, the 'key worker' or 'case manager' provided a supportive relationship to the parents and also to the children. The extent of physical and mental disability among parents and children has been noted, and in several of these cases it was necessary for the social worker to co-ordinate adult and child and family services within their own departments as well as across departmental boundaries.

The following examples of the different types of service provided indicate that deciding on the appropriate model of service provision is not simply a question of relating the service *either* to the reason for referral *or* to the needs of family members. The willingness or otherwise of parents to accept the service, or to accept one model of service over another, and environmental and relationship pressures all inform the decision. Finally, the availability of a social worker, therapist, support worker or community resource will dictate the nature of the service:

> They say we can purchase from outside agencies, but when we go for financial permission it takes a long time. Then sometimes they say: 'Use whatever is available from your own resources'. So you can understand it is not easy to find the appropriate resources in these financial circumstances. With everything you have to go for permission when a money matter comes up.

Case examples of assessments and service provision

No further action

Most of the cases that were closed after the minimal involvement of an assessment team worker were either of the 'inadequate supervision' type or 'service requests' such as a referral by a health visitor for payment of playgroup fees. Even though 'no further action' might be the appropriate response – since the family was functioning well enough not to need a support service – as already noted, a 'no further' action response could be a deterrent to any future contact if problems increased.

An Asian mother left the children alone while she went shopping. The neighbour across the landing in the tower block was supposed to be keeping an eye open. The children had been playing with the phone and dialled 999. The police took them to the police station from where they were collected by their parents. There were no further referrals during the year and this appeared to be a generally coping family. When asked if there were any problems at the first research interview, the mother said: 'No problems – leave us alone now. It was a mistake that my children dialled 999.'

The Asian research interviewer commented:

> The mother felt the contact with Social Services was all a mistake and did not want to be portrayed as a bad mother. She told me she would never neglect her children and that is why she was a housewife. She wanted to spend all her

time with her children. She was interviewed by the Social Services and she thought and felt afraid that her children would be taken away from her.

In similar cases there were examples of social workers who succeeded in reassuring the parents and also provided them with advice that was generally welcomed. This related particularly to mothers whose first language was not English and who were interviewed by a social worker who spoke the same language and conveyed an understanding of the everyday pressures of parenting.

'No further action' was the response to some families whose problems revolved around a specific issue, to some in acute distress and to some whose problems were long-term and multiple. Sometimes this was appropriate, or indeed the only response possible in those cases where the parents refused a service that was offered to them and concerns about the children were not sufficiently serious to warrant the use of coercion. In other cases, an opportunity was missed to provide services to families who were requesting or willing to accept a service and whose children were highly likely to suffer impairment of health or development without the provision of extra help:

The case was referred by a relative who found young children behaving in an inappropriate sexual way towards each other. Following a telephone call to the mother, the case was closed without any assessment. During the research interviews with these parents it became clear that the family was experiencing many difficulties that might well have had an adverse impact on the well-being of the children. One child in the family had a disability and the other had serious behaviour problems.

The following 'no further action' case concerned a family with long-standing multiple problems:

A single parent who had herself been in care was referred because her three young children were playing unsupervised close to a major road. She had very little support of either a practical or emotional nature and appeared overwhelmed with the struggle of coping with three children – the oldest of whom was already showing signs of disturbed behaviour. She told the first research interviewer: 'In the school holidays I would like some help because I know they can provide it. The official letter they sent was not very helpful. What was the point in sending a letter with no follow-up?' She asked for assistance with her oldest child shortly after the first referral but appears to have received no help other than advice in the course of a brief telephone conversation.

The interviewer concluded her notes of the second interview:

> As a parent, she is crying out for some support from Social Services. She knows what she needs to function better – a break, and help to pay for a play scheme.

Another family with similar stresses received a different, very 'short-term' service.

The family was reported by a neighbour when the children were left alone while the mother went shopping. They locked themselves out when they went into the garden. A social worker visited and recognised the potential stresses in a very impoverished family. The mother said she had found the talk with the social worker helpful but did not want any long-term help. However, she was given advice about how to request a housing transfer and also about how to claim housing benefit. The case was closed, but a note was made for toys to be provided for the children at Christmas. The toys were greatly appreciated. The mother said that she would approach Social Services for help if she felt she needed it.

Families who themselves requested help (either directly or via a health visitor, GP or teacher) because they had a child with a disability were more likely to receive a short-term service than a 'no further action' response. However, some did come into the 'no further action' group. Those who were told that their application for assistance was unsuccessful occasionally expressed resentment that families who maltreated their children got help. The combination of poverty and the high costs of caring for children with disabilities was particularly noted:

> My husband lost his job. I asked if they could help with playgroup as we are struggling with money. I didn't think I was asking for much. I would have paid for one day if they would pay for the other. How do you find out what you are entitled to? You shouldn't have to lie or beg or grovel.

One 'specific issue' case involved a young family. The mother was suffering from depression. The health visitor re-referred the case six weeks later when nothing had happened. Her letter said: 'Please help as this mother deserves a break before her depression gets worse.'

The case was allocated for assessment, but the mother then telephoned to say she did not need help, and the case was closed. From our interviews it was clear that this was another 'false negative' in that a visit from a social worker (preferably with a health visitor) might have found a way of providing the much-needed support.

Short-term interventions

Cases that led to short-term interventions ranged from families with long-term and multiple problems to those who coped well enough without the provision of additional services. Short-term help came in a variety of guises, from parcels of presents at Christmas to an 'acute distress' family who made it clear they did not want anything more than the arranging of short-term counselling with a voluntary agency. Where cash or furniture was provided under the terms of Section 17 of the Children Act 1989, this was particularly appreciated.

In some of these cases the formal child protection system was used in order to insist on parents accepting help that was clearly necessary to improve the living circumstances of the children as well as the parents. This was used to good effect, particularly in cases of marital violence and when the father refused to allow the mother to accept help. Whilst the majority of those interviewed appreciated the short-term service, others complained that it had ended too quickly. Families often spoke warmly of the support provided by the social worker who had helped them to work out what would be most useful, and sometimes differentiated between their *lack of satisfaction* with the resources available and their *appreciation* of the social worker's help: 'He is very sympathetic but they don't give them the money to help people' was the response of one mother suffering from post-natal depression. A nursery place had been provided for one of her children and help towards taxi fares to take her older children to school. The interviewer's notes said:

> Having received taxi fares to get the children to school for one month, the respondent was bemused as to why it had stopped. The interviewee said that she was completely unsatisfied with this service. 'However nice they are, it is no use if they cannot help. It is not what *they* should do – it is the government. The government does not give them the money to do the job.'

In other short-term cases the social work task consisted of identifying more appropriate family support services and helping the parents to link up with them:

A young woman with two young children returned from Bangladesh, where she had been nursing a sick relative, to find that her husband had left and she was homeless. The referral was made by a member of an Asian Women's Support Group and the social worker's main role was to link with the group and secure financial assistance under the provisions of Section 17. He also arranged for English classes in response to the mother's request. At the second interview, she said: 'Things have improved in some ways, and I do not need the help I needed then, although my brother-in-law gave me most help.'

Mostly, as one might expect with a study of services to children under 8 years of age, short-term social casework or counselling services were provided for the parents or relatives. In some cases short-term therapy was arranged for children who were suffering the effects of trauma; in others social workers spent time getting to know the children and giving them space to talk informally about any worries they may have.

Most of the cases that received a short-term service dealt with marital conflict (which sometimes continued after separation), disability of parents and/or children, extreme financial problems resulting from redundancy or marital breakdown, or depression. They were all very different and required a highly varied response. Considerable ingenuity was demonstrated by some of the social workers who worked with the families to find creative ways around the difficulties presented. Although some of the workers provided a short-term casework service for parents and children, the skills most frequently needed were 'signposting', advocacy, networking, and problem-solving in the face of the minimal resources of the families and of the agencies themselves.

In common with Gibbons (1990) we found that social workers did not spend much time linking families with community resources. Although some appeared particularly knowledgeable about what might be available within the communities in which these families lived, there were others who seemed to be ill-informed. It was the exception rather than the rule for the social worker to go beyond giving a contact name or making a referral by phone or letter. But there were some who took families to talk with workers and other families at community resources and stayed with them until they felt more at ease. African–Caribbean and Asian social workers appeared especially likely to recognise the importance of this for their white clients as well as for those of minority ethnic origin.

'Revolving door' cases

The service provided to the families in 'revolving door' cases was similar to that provided to the 'short-term service' group. However, these families differed in that they had longer-term problems that were not so easily resolved; they were less easily put off and were determined to seek and to get the help they needed; or they continued to behave in a way that raised the concerns of other services. Despite frequent referrals or requests for help, they had not, by the end of the 12-month period, been offered a planned service based on a full assessment of need and risk. There was clear evidence in most of these cases that either the health or the development of the children was already being or likely to be impaired. Marital problems – including violence, substance abuse, crime and imprisonment – featured in many of the cases. It was also noticeable that the referrers were often family members. Cases referred by absent fathers were least likely to be responded to by an assessment of need and risk to the child.

The separated father of a 3-year-old boy had been shown bruises on the boy's hand during an access visit. He complained to the social services department that the mother's boyfriend was hitting his son. The father also went to the police, who visited the child's home and found no cause for concern. A social worker paid a single visit to the mother and took no further action. There were referrals, but they were all presumed to be malicious. A planning meeting was held and the report stated: 'This is not a Section 47 investigation.' The conclusion was that the mother was a competent parent. A copy of the minutes was sent to the mother's solicitor. There was no full assessment of the needs of the mother and children. Social Services did not contact the father and he was not told of the meeting. He later complained that his concerns were not taken seriously. Two different social workers were involved. The mother was given advice about the marital dispute, contact issues, neighbour problems and housing. It was noted that she needed counselling about domestic violence, but nothing further was done about this. During the first research interview the mother said that her problems were mainly in terms of child care and the lack of opportunity to go back to work. However, there appeared to be quite serious emotional and relationship problems with her children, and the behaviour of the little boy appeared particularly disturbing. When asked during the second research interview what sort of help she had received, she said: 'Nothing – they haven't helped me and I need the help a lot. I feel very bad – it's terrible. They should help me so I can go back to work.'

Another 'revolving door' case was referred by the hospital social worker:

The third child in the family was born extremely prematurely, and the hospital social worker expressed concerns to the area team workers because of the parents' behaviour when they visited and the apparent lack of attachment between them and their new baby. Help with fares to visit the baby was offered but not taken up. Further referrals were received concerning marital violence; lack of money after the mother had been refused a crisis loan by the Social Fund; concerns about poor school attendance of the 5-year-old; the mother's bullying behaviour towards the 8-year-old; and unsuitable baby-sitting arrangements while the parents went out drinking. Each referral was responded to with the offer of practical help or advocacy, which was sometimes taken up. Six weeks after the referral, the case was closed without a proper assessment. A note said that the mother had assured the social worker that the older child was now going to school regularly. From the second research interview with the parent it was clear that the family had many difficulties and that the health of the children would be likely to be impaired without the provision of a more comprehensive package of services, co-ordinated by a social worker who could gain the confidence of the parents and also give practical help to improve the care given to the children.

This case fitted the 'low warmth and high criticism' pattern identified by the *Child Protection: Messages from Research* studies (Dartington Social Research Unit 1995a). It may have been a case that would have benefited from the use of the formal child protection procedures if the parents were unable to improve the quality of parenting without an element of coercion. A fuller assessment would have clarified the position.

Delayed long-term cases

These cases were similar to those that received a 'revolving door' type of service, except that at some point the needs were recognised and a more coherent longer-term service was provided. Sometimes this was after a slow start in responding to the initial referral; sometimes it took one or more re-referrals:

The four children in this family ranged between 11 and $1^1/_2$ years of age. The 3-year-old had learning disabilities. The parents requested help to keep him at the playgroup. The child was described as 'shy and doesn't mix'. The family were a middle-class African refugee family whose house had been repossessed two years earlier. They were in serious rent arrears and also in debt because of Social Fund repayments. In the first instance, there was no social work involvement, and the letter refusing help was signed by an administrator. The parents applied again and, after many phone calls and a formal complaint, a free nursery place was allocated five months later. The researcher's notes read: 'Poor communication between the two parts of the social services department – the under-8 team and the intake team – and with the mother.' The mother said that she thought the social worker who finally visited listened to what she said 'because we had a long talk about the problem. She could see there was a problem and she wanted to help, but she had no power to help.'

The following case study concerns another 'specific issue' family whose difficulties were alleviated when an appropriate service was provided:

The GP wrote with a request for assisted playgroup places for the youngest two of three children. The father had terminal cancer and was not willing to talk about it. The stresses were affecting the oldest child and the mother. The referral was marked as 'possible emotional abuse' on the monitoring form. The researcher scrutinising the file noted: 'It looked more like a service request to me.' After some delay the playgroup places were paid for jointly by the adult services team and the children's services team. There was an interruption in the payment of nursery fees when funding ran out towards the end of the year, but it was reinstated. Although this was a longer-term service, it was provided by different social workers on each occasion. However, the mother said, 'They were all pleasant and very helpful. The staff at the playgroup were brilliant, but they come up against policies which didn't help my case.'

This is an example of a family with long-standing and multiple problems for whom delay in providing a long-term service may have contributed to the need for long-term care:

A neighbour referred a father and his 5-year-old child for help. The wife had left him to go to live with a neighbour and he was apparently very depressed. The father had also been seen 'giving the child a puff of marijuana'. The case was closed after school checks revealed no concerns. The father was angry about the referral. Two months later a further referral was received from a neighbour alleging a chaotic pattern of life. The research interviewer's notes state:

> This respondent was a very lonely man and welcomed the opportunity to speak to me. He only spoke to his 5-year-old daughter and had no friends. He was very distressed and wanted to talk about his separation. He said he often turned to drink for comfort.

The father subsequently contacted the department, said he could not cope and requested accommodation for his daughter. The child was accommodated for two weeks. Despite the concerns expressed by the foster parents, there was no ongoing support plan after she returned to her father. The record stated that there had been the intention to allocate this case to the long-term team 'with a view to the child's and parent's needs being assessed, and the father being supported in meeting these'. There was no further action at that point until a further allegation was made regarding neglect and possible sexual harm from male visitors. Six months after the original referral the father requested long-term accommodation as he was unable to care for his daughter. At the end of the year the child was placed permanently with relatives and had very little contact with her father.

Longer-term services provided immediately

Lower intensity services provided immediately

There were three broad patterns of longer-term service provision that cut across differences between the type of referral and the type of family: services provided immediately; services provided episodically to 'open' cases; and longer duration and higher intensity services. The service to some families was essentially of the 'case manager' type, with a social worker putting together packages of service in consultation with the parents and essentially from then on monitoring the case and ensuring that the service was actually provided. This was the most likely response in cases where a child or a parent had a physical disability:

A health visitor requested help under Section 17 of the Children Act 1989. A baby born prematurely and now 1-year-old had been admitted to hospital on several occasions for investigation of failure to thrive and marked developmental delay. In the past the mother had refused input from Social Services but was now willing to consider it. Her partner was working abroad and unable to provide support. There was also an older child. A letter offering assistance was sent to the family, and the mother responded by requesting a home visit. An assessment recorded in the running record specifically emphasised that this was a child 'in need' and not at risk of abuse. Identified were the mother's need for help in caring for a sick baby and a lively toddler; her need for breaks from the children to get the housework done; and her need for a break just for herself – 'she is exhausted'. The service provided was a family aide for 2½ hours twice a week – mainly to look after the children and 'to offer emotional support, a listening ear and advice if required'. It became clear that the child did have a serious chronic illness that required long-term health supervision and frequent hospital appointments.

Despite the clear statement at the initial assessment that this was a family needing support, a child protection 'strategy meeting' (the convening of which did not fit the criteria described in *Working Together (*DoH 1991c)) was held without the parent being invited. The conclusion of this meeting, attended mainly by medical personnel and the social worker, was that respite care should be provided. However, after being introduced to the respite family the mother decided not to take up the offer at that stage. At the first interview the mother spoke very positively about the role played by the key worker, and her statement of what she needed coincided with the assessment made by the worker (who managed to reassure the mother that the purpose was to provide support):

> I was a bit worried at first – well, you don't know what the Social Services will do. There is always the worry they may see things they don't like and they may take the children away – but I am quite happy with them since my contact with them. I know that they are there basically when I need them. I can contact them whenever. But they need to improve their public image – definitely.

At the second interview she described how respite care had been provided for short periods. She found the family aide helpful for practical reasons but 'not really helpful – because it was general chatter'. As regards the social worker, who periodically reviewed the case and took time to listen to her views, the mother said she found her helpful because 'she's very supportive; you don't have to say too much to her and she understands'. However, she was more critical of the health authority personnel and to some extent also of the social worker: 'It would be nice to have some information about what was discussed about the child.' She did feel that she had some choice 'because she does what I ask her to do. Like, when I was wanting to restart the respite care, she acted on it and said OK there and then, and didn't judge me. She is a very caring person.' Although she felt she could contact the worker when needed, in some respects the 'case management' approach fell short of what she considered would be most helpful: 'I think they should have a lot more contact with the families and get to know exactly what the problems are and what can be done to help them, if possible.'

In another case the social worker's role was even more clearly that of a case manager rather than a social caseworker:

The single mother of children aged 2 and 5 was diabetic and had alcohol problems. She had originally been referred by the health visitor because of her poor health and the risk that she might pass out. Subsidised day care was provided, and the case was not allocated to a social worker until a review at the day care centre concluded that this might be helpful. A social worker visited for a general discussion with her about whether the day care was meeting her needs. The mother said at the first research interview:

> I've seen one woman. That's all. Nothing else. It might be different now my daughter is at the nursery. Yes, I'm satisfied; it's sort of what I wanted. But a bit late. You do have to be half dead before they do something. I spoke to someone before – they did nothing. When I passed out lots of times they did something. I was really ill – only then did they help you.

The social worker played a low-key role, reviewing the case with the staff at the children's centre and with the worker from the drugs and alcohol team. The recording from the children's centre, which, unusually, was on the main social services' file after the case closed, was described in the researcher's notes as 'excellent, with monthly summaries of the child's development'.

Services episodically provided to 'open' cases

The second type of long-term work involved the case remaining open, but with episodic periods of increased activity when there were crises. These cases often involved parents with mental health or addiction problems or children with behaviour difficulties. They might also involve parents who were reluctant to accept longer-term help, preferring to call upon it (or not to resist it if offered) at times of particular stress. Some refugee families and some families where there were serious marital problems also received this type of episodic longer-term service, which differed from the 'revolving door' type service in that the case was never formally closed and the same worker usually responded to the new request for assistance. In these cases a service such as a family aide or a supported playgroup or after-school service was often provided on a longer-term basis. Material aid and cash under the terms of Section 17 of the Children Act 1989 were sometimes made available in these cases:

A mother with a history of episodic psychiatric problems had a row with her own mother, who had been caring for her child. She went into bed and breakfast accommodation and then requested that her 5-year-old daughter be accommodated. She was advised to return the next day, but she went with her daughter to see the social worker at the psychiatric hospital and Section 20 accommodation was arranged for the child.

At the first placement review the needs identified were for the child to remain in foster care and for the mother to receive help regarding rehousing and with her mental health and relationship problems. The assessment clearly stated that the child was 'at risk of harm because of the separation from her mother and grandmother, and because of the mother's lack of parenting skills'. The foster care was provided as part of a family support plan, which also included help with the mother's mental health and parenting skills, help with housing and help for the mother in terms of her relationship with her own mother.

The first worker paid many visits to all members of the family. The case was then transferred to the long-term team when, in addition to the original needs, a need was identified to help the little girl with behaviour difficulties. Risks identified were: risk of harm resulting from mother's ambivalent relationship to the child; risk of harm because of two changes of main carer and because of mother's mental health problems and poor parenting skills. There was also risk from lack of supervision (neglect), as there had been episodes of the mother leaving the child briefly while she went to the launderette or the shops.

The mother complained to the research interviewer that the promised assistance did not materialise. She was referred to the family consultation centre, which she found helpful, but she did not get on with the area team social worker and eventually requested that she withdraw from the case. She continued to attend the family consultation centre. Given the pattern of difficulties, it seemed highly likely that when problems built up again this case would need to be re-opened within the area team and would require a co-ordinated package of services, possibly including respite care or longer-term accommodation of the child.

The social worker in the following case was extremely persistent about remaining involved in order to ensure that a 7-month-old child had 'good enough' parenting:

The referral was made by an anonymous caller who said that she had been worried about the safety of two young children after a conversation with their mother in a supermarket. The mother was described as 'dishevelled and wet' and said that she was pregnant and that the children had had nothing to eat since the previous day. The caller said that she believed that the mother was 'involved in the drugs scene'. There had been a previous child protection enquiry, which had not resulted in the children being registered.

After two interviews the social worker decided that this was a case calling for family support and that it was not necessary to use the formal child protection procedures as the mother was willing to accept help. The family was assessed as needing help with housing, day care to give the mother respite, and medical care, since the mother had not been keeping GP appointments during her pregnancy. At that point the case was referred to the long-term team for ongoing support. A further referral was received alleging physical abuse of one of the children by the father and also marital violence. A child protection enquiry resulted in a child protection conference and registration under the category of 'physical abuse'. The two children were temporarily accommodated while the mother had a brief period in hospital.

During the year there were strategy meetings and review conferences, resulting in informative assessment and re-assessment reports. It was concluded that the major problem was the violent relationship between the mother and her boyfriend. The mother was afraid to ask him to leave. The formality of the child protection system was helpful in this case in that it allowed the social worker to insist that the boyfriend should not have unsupervised contact with the children. It was difficult to do more than 'hang on in there' since the mother was afraid of the boyfriend who was unwilling to work with social services. A monitoring role was taken until problems mounted – when the grandmother looked after one child and the mother and youngest child went into a residential assessment unit. The family support plan at this point also included negotiation and advocacy re housing, cash and practical help, and attempts to work jointly with the young woman and her boyfriend. As well as a comprehensive assessment, which was fully recorded, the file included a 'partnership agreement', and consultation was provided by a senior practitioner.

There was evidence in this case that services changed as circumstances changed. Describing the nature of work in cases of marital violence that could not be resolved easily because the mother did not wish to end her relationship, the social worker said of this case:

> The difficult thing to work with was that the birth father, who allegedly caused the injury, would not work with us at all, and although he wouldn't work with us, his presence was always felt. His impact on the family and the consequences of that was always felt and had to be responded to by Social Services. He used to beat the mother, he stabbed her, he has broken her wrists, and the children saw a lot of that. He was an unquantifiable risk so, because we could not assess him with the children, we had to take the extreme view that he should not have contact with them unless there was an adult other than the mother present.

This case shows how use of the formal child protection system can be incorporated within a family support plan. The social worker said that initially he felt it was his priority to focus on the risks and it seemed that the best they could do at that stage was to give the mother the chance of a fresh start by helping her with housing. He therefore used Section 17 of the Children Act 1989 to provide a deposit on a new flat. Apart from this help, he said there was not much else in the way of support services that could be provided for some time. This was partly to do with the mobility of the family. Following another incident of violence, the pace changed and effort was put into helping the grandmother to supervise contact and providing additional support. The social worker tried to introduce the mother to a young women's group but 'access to those services requires a certain amount of stability. It is very hard to reach out to someone or to put in additional services when you don't know where they are going to be.' Subsequently the social worker persuaded the mother to agree to the children being accommodated for a period, and a further full assessment of the mother's ability to parent took place at the family centre. However, as the social worker put it:

> In their infinite wisdom the council decided to close down the children's centres, which meant that we had to change the day care arrangements. We paid the fares but she had to bring three children on two buses. This was impossible for her and their attendance tapered off. And obviously there was less monitoring of the children.

When asked what difference child protection registration had made, the social worker said he did not think it had made much difference:

> There was so much going on that all the other things seemed more important than whether the children were on the Child Protection Register or not.

However, the social worker did say that he thought he would not have been allowed to visit so frequently had the children not been on the Child Protection Register. Twelve months later episodic periods of more intensive help in the context of a longer-term casework relationship were being provided. On the question of marital violence, the social worker was clear that this often had an impact on the children's development:

> If the child is exhibiting extremely distressed behaviour, there is a likelihood they will be registered under the category of 'emotional abuse', but you do need to link it to some kind of consequence in the child, and sometimes that's a very simplistic way of looking at it. Sometimes an assessment by a psychotherapist is going to be necessary to find out what is going on for the child. But to get access to that sort of service normally does require some sort of formal framework – whether it is child protection registration, or court or whatever.

He concluded that for the first part of his work he saw the children as 'in need of protection' but that after the full assessment, when the mother realised she was in danger of losing the children into the care system, he saw them 'more as *children in need*' because he felt the mother had moved on and demonstrated during the assessment period at the family centre that she had good parenting skills.

The social worker concluded:

> Although we didn't always get on because of the issues that had to be faced, she felt that I was there and that I would listen and try to help if I could. I think she experienced me as supportive but sometimes meddling.

Longer duration and higher intensity services

The third pattern of long-term work involved complex cases where there was agreement between the parent(s) and the social worker about the many needs of the children and/or parents, and a longer-term package of relationship-based casework and support services could be negotiated and re-negotiated as appropriate. The following case study describes work in an 'acute distress' situation, the distress being caused by the ending of a violent relationship and the stresses of responding to the needs of a child with a disability, exacerbated by anxiety following a child protection referral.

A toddler with a serious disability and impaired sensation in her lower limbs was referred by the children's centre because of concerns about neglect following a burn that was accepted to be accidental. A long meeting between the mother and the intake worker was fully recorded. The needs identified included: the mother's problems from a previous relationship with a violent alcoholic man; the difficulty of keeping hospital appointments and looking after her other children; the need for incontinence pads (the previous authority had provided them free but they had to be paid for in this authority). Resources identified were: an application for supply of incontinence pads; applications to charities for financial help; referral to the occupational therapist to assess priority for rehousing because of the child's disabilities. The case was then transferred to the 'children with disabilities' team. The allocated worker undertook a more detailed assessment of the child's and family's needs. These were: help to move to more suitable housing; help to ensure that the child could attend hospital appointments by arranging transport; arranging visits to a special school; and organising a fuller assessment by the occupational therapist. The conclusion, clearly recorded, was that this was a child in need and that the parent was not a neglectful parent.

When interviewed for this research, the social worker said that, if children with disabilities were referred because of child protection concerns, the case was not passed to the disability team until the initial child protection assessment had been completed. There was a congruence between the description of the work given by the social worker and that given by the mother. The work can best be characterised as family casework, in that a relationship was built up in the context of which a combination of emotional support, counselling, financial and practical help, advocacy, networking with other agencies and the provision of day care were all provided at some point. The researcher's notes of her interview with the social worker included:

> The social worker told me that at the end of the six-month period she wrote the comprehensive assessment up as a discrete document which is now on the file. She said that this is standard procedure in her team for any case that looks as if it will continue beyond a six-month period. She said that she would not describe this assessment as an 'orange book' assessment (an assessment based on the Department of Health Guidance on undertaking comprehensive assessment in child protection work (DoH 1988) because it wasn't totally about child protection concerns and risk. The assessment did address the

original concerns about risk around the burn, but really it was more about 'need'. In terms of assessing the family and providing services the social worker worked very closely with education, housing and health, and especially the hospital. During this period the mother met a new boyfriend and had a child. The family moved several times and it was hard to keep in touch with them. 'It wasn't that she was not prepared to work with us, or that she didn't have her daughter's interests at heart, or that she was difficult or even that she was unable, it was just the physical circumstances that prevented her. As each problem got sorted out, the situation improved. In some ways, on reflection, it's one of the easiest cases I've ever had. It was so dire. If you like, in the beginning it went from a family who had so little, such little resources and the mother was so worn down – the children were really quite out of control with very little boundaries and very, very unsettled – to a family who, once all the practical things were put in place, functioned very well.'

Examples of counselling, advocacy, forceful advice, negotiation about how parents could meet their own needs without neglecting the needs of their children were all given in the interviews with the social workers. In the above case, the social worker described herself as originally using 'crisis intervention' models, but then moving on to 'task centred' work punctuated by 'psycho-dynamic style' casework. She also worked directly with the child who had the disability and had a great deal of informal contact with her since she sometimes helped with transport to school or hospital. This intensity of work continued for about twelve months and after a less intensive six-month period the case was closed.

At the first research interview after her discussion with the child protection team worker, the mother said:

> I don't want nothing to do with them. I just want them to stay out of my life. They are too nosy. They make you feel like they are thinking you are a bad parent. Stay away, just stay away. Social Services – the whole lot of them – I do not like them at all.

At the second interview she said:

> The previous social worker I had was basically coming in my house telling me that [the child] was at risk. It was like 'You have to look after her'. There was no help specifically, they only got her a playpen.

About the present social worker she said:

I think the social worker is really good and she has given me a lot of help. She doesn't come in and say 'You should do this'. She says, 'What do you think you need?' and I can relate to that. I think Social Services has got a lot to do with attitude. A lot of them tell you what you need. If they listened instead to what people need, people would have a different attitude to them.

Adequacy of the service and satisfaction of parents

Of the 122 families interviewed 47 (39%) said that they had received no help following the referral to the social services department, and 75 (61%) said they had received some help. In some of the 'no help' cases services or advice had been provided but had not been found to be helpful. Exactly the same proportion (39%) of those who were *without* community or family support and those who *did* have social and emotional support had received no help. It did not, therefore, appear that social workers were able to target their services to those who might be most in need of them because other supports were unavailable. It may also be, however, that those who were lacking in social support were more likely to perceive any services provided as 'no help'. Five of the 34 who had received a long-term service, five of the 18 'revolving door' cases, almost half of the short-term cases and nine out of the ten cases closed quickly with 'no further action' all said they had received 'no help'. Of those with long-standing and multiple problems 70% said they *had* received help, as did three-quarters of the 'specific issue' cases. However, only 42% of the families in 'acute distress' and 40% of those with a short-term problems said that they had been helped. Five of the 16 whose children were assessed as not 'in need' said that they had had some help (these differences are statistically significant: $p<.05$). The interaction between presenting problems, family characteristics and biography, service received and satisfaction is extremely complex. There is no quick and easy way to decide on the degree of priority and the type of service. In Chapter 9 we return to the importance of assessment and offer suggestions, drawn from our data, about how the high volume of referrals can be more effectively sifted.

Those scrutinising the files noted down examples of 'good practice' or 'bad practice' in the light of general guidance on family support work in social work texts and of Department of Health and Social Services Inspectorate Guidance documents. In this context they noted whether the practice was sensitive to the particular needs of families of minority ethnic origin. Specific examples of particularly good practice were noted in 21% of the cases and of bad practice in 15%. In 8% of the cases there were examples of both good and bad practice, and in 56% neither good nor bad practice stood out from the records or family interviews. However, from interviews with the parents and social workers it is clear that, in some cases, good practice was in evidence (sometimes against the odds) but that this was not apparent from the scrutiny of the records.

Table 7.1 gives the researchers' rating of the overall adequacy of the service provided by the social services departments. The rating was based on all sources of information. A 'good service' was one where there was evidence that family members were satisfied with the service and where the emotional support and services provided appeared appropriate to the identified needs of the family members. A generally adequate service with some deficits had some of the above characteristics but not all. Forty-six per cent of the cases fell into one or other of these categories. A 'poor service' was one of which family members were critical and in which services required to meet identified needs were not provided. Other cases were rated in the 'inappropriate service' group because the services provided were not those requested or needed. Over a third of the cases fell in one or other of these two categories. Some services were good after a slow start, sometimes requiring one or more re-referrals (six cases); others were delayed and generally good but with some deficits, whilst seven families experienced delay followed by an inadequate service, and a further eight families who needed a service received no service at all. If the 17 not needing a service are excluded, and the delayed categories are included in either the 'good' or the 'poor' service groups as appropriate, 55% were rated as receiving a good or adequate service and 45% a poor or inappropriate service. At first sight this may appear a disappointing finding.

Table 7.1 ***Overall adequacy of service provided by social services departments, researcher rating (interview sample, Stage 2)***

Adequacy of service	No.	%	
Generally good	22	18	46%
Service delayed – good	6	5	
Generally good with some deficits	23	20	
Service delayed – some deficits	4	3	
Poor service	21	18	39%
Inappropriate service	9	8	
Service delayed – poor	7	6	
Service needed but not provided	8	7	
No service needed	17	15	
Total	**117**	**100**	

However, if one considers that, at the time the research was undertaken, it was very common for social workers to say 'We only do child protection work. We have no time for family support work' and that Gibbons et al. (1995) found that a large proportion of neglect and emotional abuse cases received no services, it might be read as suggesting that 're-focusing' was already taking place and that more families were being offered a family support service outside the formal child protection system. Many of the families would come low down on the list of local authority priority groups identified by the early Section 17 (Children Act 1989) studies (Aldgate and Tunstill 1995).

When those not needing a service were omitted, more of the County families were rated as having received a generally adequate service (66%) than those in City 1 (54%) or City 2 (45%). More of the 'service request' families received a generally adequate service (62%) than was the case for neglect or emotional maltreatment referrals (50%). More of those with long-standing problems (73%) were rated as receiving a generally adequate service than was the case for the 'specific issue' families (49%), those with short-term problems (50%) or those in 'acute distress' (only four of the twelve families in 'acute distress' were rated as having received a generally adequate and appropriate service). These differences were statistically significant ($p<.05$).

Those who received a long-term service were most likely to be rated as receiving a generally good service (61% rated as good), but this was the case for only 47% of the 'revolving door' cases. Only 38% of the 'short-term service' cases were rated as receiving a 'good' service, with 58% receiving a service rated as poor or inappropriate. These differences were statistically significant ($p<.01$).

There was a trend, which did not quite reach statistical significance, for more of the white families to have a generally good service (68%) than the black families, whose service was only rated as generally good in 48% of cases. More of the services to black families appeared inappropriate to their needs.

Figure 7.1 shows that almost 40% of the parents interviewed were 'satisfied' with the service, 14% were undecided, nearly 38% were unsatisfied or dissatisfied, and for 9% contact was considered by the parent not to be necessary.

The alternatives given to the parents in the checklist included the word '*dis*-satisfied'. However, it became clear from the parents' accounts that, whilst some *were* dissatisfied, others spoke in positive terms of the attempts to help them but remained *un*satisfied because the resources requested were not available and their problems remained 'unsolved'. The way in which the data were

Figure 7.1 ***Parental satisfaction with service (interview sample, Stage 2)***[1]

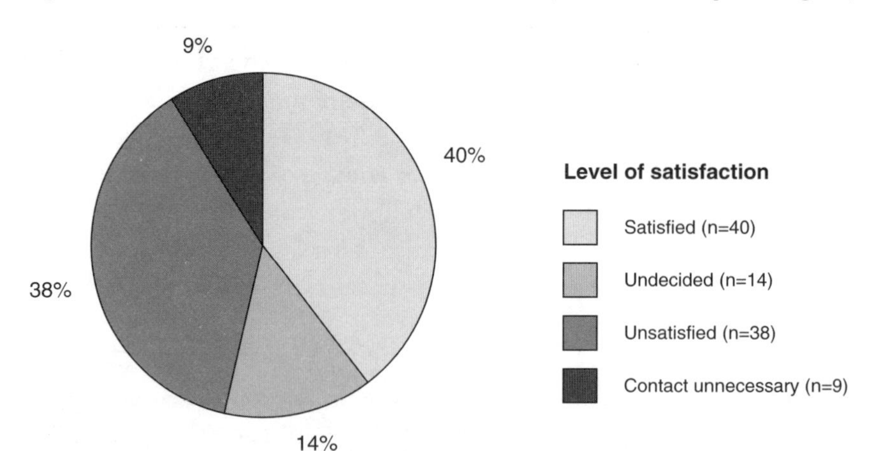

[1] n=101; those having no contact with SSD omitted

collected did not allow differentiation in the analysis between those who were unsatisfied and those who were dissatisfied, a point to be borne in mind when future studies are being designed. General unhappiness at the way in which enquiries had been made about a child protection concern accounted for a large proportion of those in the *dis*satisfied group. Satisfaction, or lack of it, has to be seen, therefore, in the context of the serious and/or conflictual nature of the practical and emotional difficulties faced by some of these families. They were looking for someone to make life better for them, and, certainly in the space of a year, it was unlikely that their hopes and aspirations could be satisfied. Thus, ten of the 33 who received services rated by the researcher as 'good' or 'generally good' were dissatisfied or unsatisfied (30%).

Figure 7.2 shows that there was a trend, which did not reach statistical significance, towards a larger proportion of the 'service request' families being either dissatisfied or unsatisfied by the service (44%) than was the case with the 'neglect' referrals (34%), though more of the 'neglect' group of parents were either undecided or considered that there was no need for a service. There was no difference in the proportions 'unsatisfied' or 'dissatisfied' in the three areas (City 1, City 2 and County).

In the city authorities 40% of the white parents and a similar proportion of those of minority ethnic origin expressed satisfaction with the service and roughly equal proportions (35% and 39%) were unsatisfied.

Figure 7.3 shows a trend, which did not reach statistical significance, for more of these families who had long-term or multiple problems (53%) and

Figure 7.2 ***Satisfaction of parent by type of referral (interview sample, Stage 2)***[1]

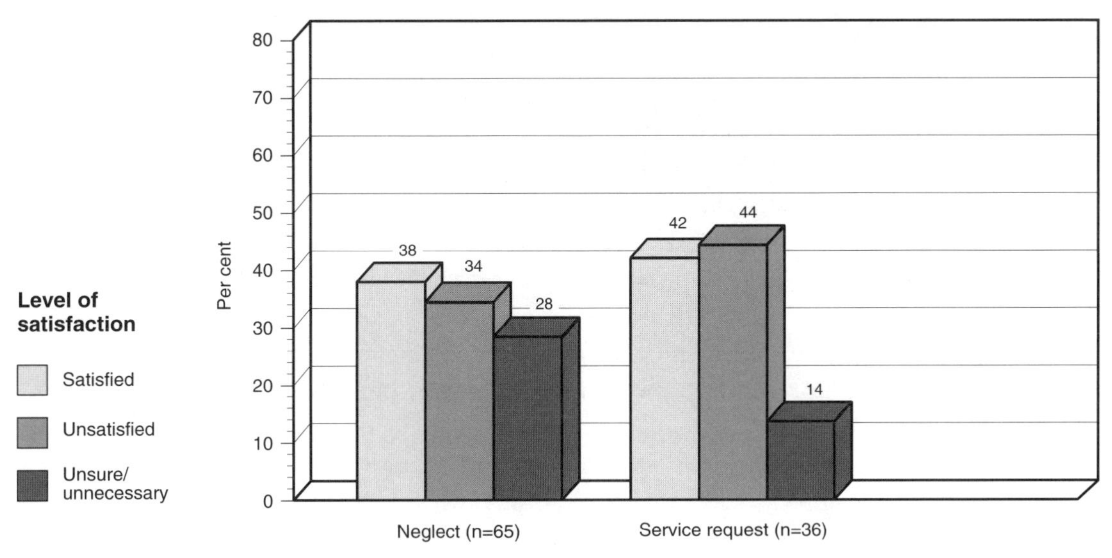

[1] n=101; cases omitted if no contact with SSD; not statistically significant

Figure 7.3 ***Satisfaction by type of family (interview sample, Stage 2)***[1]

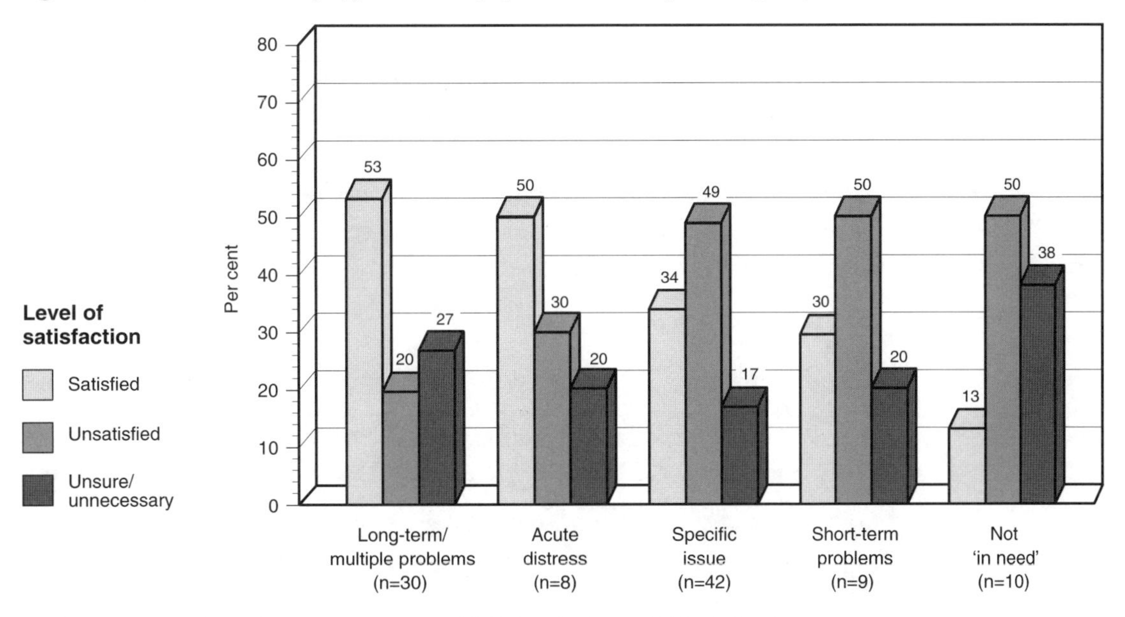

[1] n=99; missing data=2; families having no contact with SSD omitted; not statistically significant

those in 'acute distress' (50%) to express satisfaction with the service. The groups most likely to be *dis*satisfied or *un*satisfied were the 'specific issue' families, those with a short-term problem, and the not 'in need' group, several of whom were upset by a child protection enquiry that proved to be without substance.

Among these families referred because of concerns about maltreatment, those where concerns were expressed about physical neglect were less likely to be satisfied with the service (32%) than those referred because of concerns about emotional neglect (48%) or emotional abuse (50%). This difference is to some extent explained by the fact that those referred because of concerns about physical neglect were more likely to have been upset by a child protection enquiry that did not go beyond the first stage and did not lead to the provision of a service. Those where there were concerns about spouse abuse were most likely to be unsatisfied or dissatisfied (44% were dissatisfied). In the subgroup referred because of concerns about inadequate supervision, only 21% were satisfied (for probably the same reasons as the physical neglect group as a whole, of which they constituted a large proportion).

Parents who went into more detail about what had been helpful usually described packages of services rather than a single one:

> They were helpful with my daughter whilst she was in care. The help I received with my ex-partner and obviously the housing.

> The protection. Financial help. Arranging for the children to live with my mother.

> The help and support – practical provision with the home help and the child minder.

When a specific service was commended, it was likely to be day care, or, in the minority of cases, a social casework service based on a helping relationship:

> Only talking to the social worker.

> Only talking.

> They got my boyfriend to communicate about problems – he didn't think that there were any – he thought they would just go away. They made us both sit down and talk to each other.

Most comments about family or children's centres were positive, especially if they were open-access community resources providing a range of services or activities:

> The family centre was about the best – a group of mums all had problems. We could get away from the kids – do the things we wanted to do – sewing, typing, swimming, learning the computer, having lunch, 'freedom'. Talks on how to deal with children, etc. Hobbies and activities, something different every week.

Help with cash and other practical help was also valued, even if it was of a modest nature:

> Receiving the food parcel and the money.
>
> A parcel of presents.
>
> The wardrobes was the best help I got.

Negotiation and advocacy were also highlighted by several families. Help to put their case appropriately to housing and income support services was particularly valued by those whose first language was not English. Some found that social workers helped them to put their point of view across during the formal child protection process:

> The Social Services are the only people that can intervene to tell the police – 'this cannot happen'.

But, put most simply, what families were most pleased about was the totality of a combined practical help and emotional support service:

> I needed them all equally.

Some parents linked services they received or did not receive with positive or negative outcomes, but others understood that their difficulties were so extensive that a good service would not necessarily lead to a good outcome for them. Those who were unsatisfied because of a lack of services most often spoke of the *lack* of an allocated social worker.

> They helped my wife to have an operation. The contact has made things better than before. It would be better if I had had a social worker.
>
> I feel like if I had a problem I can't go and talk to them about it – but they have helped me with the children.

The researcher's notes on another case show the importance of social work service being provided even when community support was available. The case was closed early and the researcher noted that the father appeared acutely depressed at the second interview:

> The father said he got a great deal of help from the church, where many members were from his own country. He would appreciate having a social worker allocated even though he has sources of practical and emotional support. He thinks members of his community in London are 'mostly

interfering'. He meets people at church, but would always turn to solicitors, social workers, income support if he needed help, and not to the church or people from his country of origin. He did not complain about the rather poor service he received, and was extremely worried about his immigration status and the future of his children. He was somewhat fatalistic, but also greatly helped by his religious faith. When asked who he would turn to first, his simple reply was 'God'.

In terms of practical services the lack of day care or after-school care was most frequently commented on:

> Things are worse because I thought – lovely, seven more weeks with nothing for them to do. I thought it wasn't fair on the children. It gave me an attitude problem for a while. Mind you, I did take them out with a packed lunch one day and they thought it was wonderful.
>
> Being denied the care that we as a family need, and any that they can offer – e.g., the special needs playgroup so that he can mix with other children. Had we got the care, things would have improved. As he gets older his behaviour is getting more bizarre and the quality of family life gets worse.

Some said the biggest service they received was to have their child's name removed from the Child Protection Register:

> Better, with regards I don't have to worry about the children being on the At Risk register. But really no difference. I would still like help with my daughter.

Some never got over the complex emotions they felt at the start of the child protection enquiry:

> We feel 'bound' and we can't get out of this feeling.

Others were more specific about a particular service that they found unhelpful. Whilst advice was sometimes greatly appreciated, it had to be provided in the context of carefully listening to their difficulties:

> The suggestions for discipline did not work, and that was all she had to offer.

'Service request' families linked their lack of satisfaction to the feeling that the social workers did not sufficiently care about the well-being of the children to provide services. Their understanding of 'protection' included protection from the sort of long-term harm that would occur if adequate services for children with disabilities or behaviour difficulties were not made available:

> I feel totally frustrated. It's like hitting your head on a wall. I thought they would be more helpful. Because I managed to look after [step-child with disabilities] as my own child, they have just let me get on with it. They haven't bothered to check on him. I feel they don't give a damn.

In Chapter 8 we consider the outcome for these families in more detail and explore whether any particular aspects of service appeared to be associated with better or worse outcomes.

Summary

Leaving aside the generally (though not invariably) negative comments about the way in which the investigative part of the formal child protection system was handled, the 'sins' complained about by parents were mostly those of omission rather than commission. In light of the high levels of need and the risk to the impairment of the development of the children, a level of dissatisfaction – particularly among parents who were managing 'well enough' in these difficult circumstances – is inevitable. Towards the end of our study all three authorities had enthusiastically accepted the challenge of the policy change that encouraged them to put more of their resources into helping families through the general provisions of Part III of the Children Act 1989. County had re-organised in a way that was beginning to lead to better first stage assessments and to more sensitive services to those who might be in need of protection as well as to those who knew they needed a service and sought it directly or were referred by other professionals. In the two city authorities we were told of a deterioration in the support services available, such as family centres and nurseries. This was due to cuts in resources and made worse by the unanticipated requirement to meet the basic needs of substantial numbers of asylum seekers. Without knowing exactly why, families commented with regret on the deterioration in service as they lost facilities, or on the fact that a caseworker whom they had come to trust had to hand them on to someone else because of the regrouping of social work teams. In one of the authorities, the reduced number of social workers was intended to be compensated by the ability to buy into the voluntary or private sector. However, some of those interviewed said this was not cost-effective since, after the immediate crisis was over, some families refused to be referred elsewhere and tell their story all over again to someone else. It seemed inevitable that some of these parents and children would be re-referred in a worse state of mental health.

In Chapter 9 we pick up on those suggestions made by the social workers and the families that might lead to more rational and more clearly understandable ways of deciding which of the very many children 'in need' can be provided with more comprehensive services; and how early assessments can help judgements to be made about when the formal child protection route is needed and when a more general family support service under the provisions of Part III of the Children Act 1989 will be more appropriate.

8 Outcomes for the families; accounting for the differences

Whilst the majority of the families either saw improvements to their own and their children's well-being during the 12-month period or considered there had been little change, others found that their quality of life and their own or their children's well-being had deteriorated. During the second interviews with the families we sought their views on the original difficulties that had brought them into contact with Social Services and asked them whether, with the benefit of hindsight, they thought things had got better or worse. We sought their views about informal sources of family support and about changes in their support systems and any services provided by professionals. This information was supplemented by data from the files in respect of those cases that received any service at all after the first few weeks. For 18 of the 44 who received a longer-term or episodic service, detailed information about the family and the services was available from interviews with the social workers.

Changes in family circumstances and the parents' well-being

Family composition, economic situation and housing

Whilst the pattern that emerged from the statistical analysis was broadly similar to that at the time of referral, this concealed considerable change for individual families, with problems increasing for some and decreasing for others.

Of the 108 families who were interviewed on the second occasion, a partner had left the home in nine cases and the main parent had a new partner or had remarried in a further nine cases. Nine parents talked about problems with a former partner. Eighteen were pregnant or had had another child in the interim. In six cases a sibling or step-sibling had left the household during the year.

In six cases the parent interviewed had got a job and in a further four cases the parent had started a course of study or training. In seven cases a parent or partner had lost a job in the intervening period. Eight said that they had experienced serious housing problems during the 12-month period and 33 (38% of the sample) had moved house. Whilst at the first interview 36% were dissatisfied with their present housing, this was the case for 30% at the Stage 2 interview. During the first interview 68% said they would like to move house and this was still true for 54% at the time of the second interview. Thus, although there was improvement for some, there was still a high level of dissatisfaction with housing amongst these families.

Support available at Stage 2

The general picture that emerged in respect of family support was very similar to that gained during the first interview. Slightly more parents had no one to whom they could turn for advice or talk about their private feelings (possibly because of the larger numbers of mothers now living alone). However, possibly indicating that the contact with Social Services had had some practical benefits – or perhaps reflecting the fact that more children were in school – there was a smaller proportion (13%, compared with 18% at the time of the first interview) who said they had no one to whom they could turn for help with the children. The advice given by social workers and the referral to advice agencies may be reflected in the finding that a smaller proportion had no one to whom they could turn for material help (19%, compared with 25% 12 months earlier). However, these small differences could have resulted from the different composition of the smaller number of families interviewed at Stage 2.

At the second interview only four people could not name anyone in their personal support system. The proportion who said there was no one with whom they had had a disagreement within the past month had increased from 33% at the first interview to 44% at the second interview, again perhaps reflecting the numbers who were now lone parents (reported disagreements were often with partners).

For some families there had been improvements in the availability of social and emotional support; for others the situation had deteriorated. Thirty-two of the 108 interviewed at the 12-month stage (30%) reported that they were dissatisfied with the amount of emotional support they could call upon (a slight increase on 26% at Stage 1). This conceals the extent of change. Figure 8.1 shows that whilst the extent of social contact problems as rated by the main carer improved for 29%, it deteriorated for 25% and stayed the same for 45%.

Figure 8.1 ***Changes in social contact scores (parents interviewed twice)***[1]

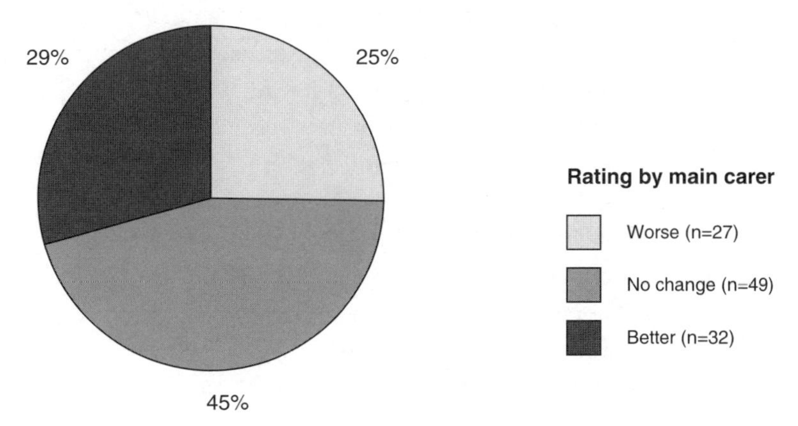

[1] n=108

Eleven (16%) of those for whom lack of emotional support was *not* a problem at Stage 1 reported dissatisfaction with the extent of social and emotional support a year later. On the other hand, 21 of the 41 for whom it was a problem at Stage 1 reported that they felt less socially isolated at Stage 2. As at Stage 1, there was no difference between white families and those of minority ethnic origin in terms of emotional support (Table 8.1).

Table 8.1 ***Availability of emotional support by ethnicity of child, city areas only (interview sample, Stage 2)***[1]

Emotional support	**White**		**Minority ethnic origin**		**All**	
	No.	**%**	**No.**	**%**	**No.**	**%**
Some emotional support	9	60	23	60	32	60
Poor emotional support	6	40	15	40	21	40
Total	**15**	**100**	**38**	**100**	**53**	**100**

[1] Not statistically significant

[2] At Stage 2, although smaller proportions in all groups lacked emotional support, the biggest change was in respect of the 'acute distress' families, with only two of the eight interviewed at that stage reporting poor emotional support. Thirty-eight per cent of the 'long-term problem' families, 27% of the 'specific issue' families and three of the eight 'short-term problem' families still lacked emotional and social support.

Health and emotional problems

Whilst 26% of those interviewed at Stage 1 said that a parent in the household had a physical disability, a learning disability or a long-term or serious physical illness, this applied to 34% at Stage 2. (This may reflect the fact that a smaller number were interviewed and also the different composition of the sample.) There was a smaller difference in respect of children, with around a quarter of the households having a child with a physical disability, learning difficulties or a long-term or serious physical illness. A slightly smaller proportion of the 108 families interviewed twice had marked emotional stress or high emotional stress scores than was the case for the 122 interviewed at Stage 1 (45% at Stage 2 compared with 55% at Stage 1). Taking only those families interviewed twice, the 'malaise' rating (Rutter et al. 1981) remained the same for 70 (65%) and there had been improvements for 27 (24%), although nine of these were still showing signs of marked emotional stress. The emotional well-being of 11 (10%) was worse than at Stage 1.

Family and relationship problems

Turning to more general problems as indicated by answers to the family problems checklist (Gibbons 1990), there was little change in the *proportions* reporting problems in the areas of social contact, finances, health, parenting, and partner relationships in the course of the two interviews. Table 8.2 shows that this apparent stability covers considerable change for individual families. The financial situation for 28% got worse, whereas this was the case for only 17% in terms of marital or partner problems, perhaps reflecting the fact that partner problems were one reason for the original referral and that a partner had since left the home. It is to be particularly noted in respect of this study focusing on the needs of children that the category for which most improvement was reported concerned parenting (34% noted some improvement in this respect and 28% noted deterioration). For many there was improvement in some respects and deterioration in others.

Table 8.2 *Changes in family problem scores (interview sample, Stage 2)*

Family problem	Better		Same		Worse		Total no.
	No.	%	No.	%	No.	%	
Social contact	31	29	49	46	27	25	107
Finance	29	28	46	44	29	28	104
Health	25	23	59	55	24	22	108
Parenting	35	34	39	38	28	28	102
Marital/partner relationships	9	17	35	66	9	17	53

Taking into consideration all the dimensions of family problems and the different sources of data, Figure 8.2 shows that almost half of the parents were

Figure 8.2 ***Changes in well-being of parents (researcher rating, parents interviewed twice)***[1]

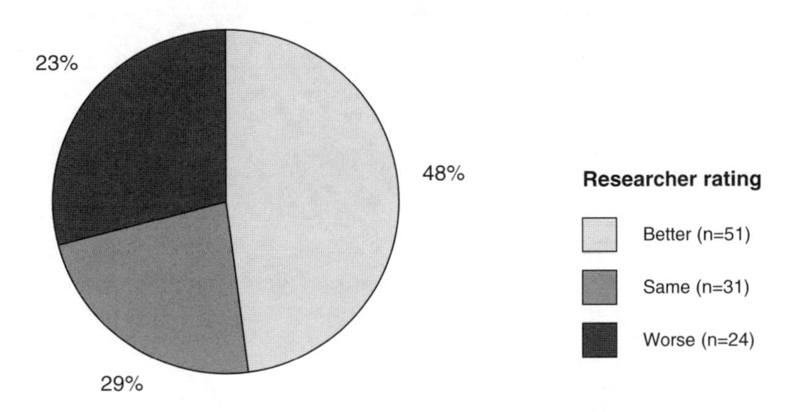

[1] n=106; missing data=2

rated by the researchers as having improved well-being, almost a quarter were seen to be worse and 29% were judged broadly unchanged. As well as using the family problems checklist (Gibbons) and the standardised Rutter 'malaise' schedule (which can be compared with other populations), the families themselves were asked whether they considered that life had got better or worse for them since the first interview. Tables 8.3 and 8.4 show that families were more positive when asked this general question than they were when asked to talk about individual aspects of their lives. Deterioration was reported by 17% (21% if one includes those who noted improvement in some respects and deterioration in others) as compared with 28% who had higher problem scores on the family problems checklist. Only 9% had higher 'malaise' scores. The 54% improvement rate reported by parents is more positive than the 25% improvement rate on the 'malaise' score.

Table 8.3 ***'Malaise' score (interview sample, Stages 1 and 2)***

Social malaise score[1]	**Stage 1**		**Stage 2**	
	No.	**%**	**No.**	**%**
Low emotional stress (score 0–6)	54	44	59	55
Marked emotional stress (score 7–14)	53	43	40	37
High emotional stress (score 15 or more)	15	12	9	8
Total	**122**	**100**	**108**	**100**

[1] Rutter et al. (1981)

Table 8.4 ***Changes on social 'malaise' score and parents' overall view of changes in their lives (interview sample, Stage 2)***

	Better		No change		Worse		Total no.
	No.	%	No.	%	No.	%	
Self-report changes in circumstances	58	54	32	30	18	17	108
Changes in Rutter[1] 'malaise' score	27[2]	25	69	65	10	9	106

[1] Rutter et al., 1981

[2] Includes nine who were still, despite improvement, showing signs of emotional stress

The children 12 months after referral

Changes in general well-being

As with the parents, apparently small changes in the percentages having problems (as indicated by the research instruments used at Stage 1 and Stage 2) may conceal marked improvements for some and deteriorations for others. For those in the 5–7 age group, 18 of the 46 (40%) were described by their parents as having many health or behaviour problems.

Figure 8.3 ***Changes in well-being of children (researcher rating, parents interviewed twice)***[1]

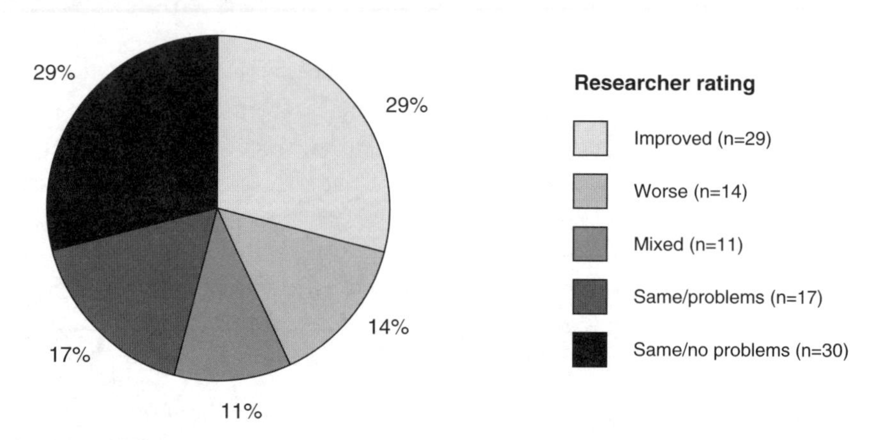

[1] n=101; missing data=7

Using data from the adapted *Looking After Children* schedules (Ward 1995), the 65 health visitor reports available at both stages, the views of the parents interviewed and data from the records, a 'researcher rating' (cross-checked in a proportion of cases and in more complex cases with a second researcher) was made as to whether the index child's overall well-being appeared to have deteriorated, improved or remained largely unchanged. Figure 8.3 shows that 29% of the children were not considered to have problems at Stage 1 and still did not have problems beyond what might be considered to be the normal ups and downs of childhood. Disregarding those with no marked problems and one child with a serious disability who had died, 29% were considered to have improved, 14% to be of lower well-being, 11% to have improved in some respects and gone downhill in others, and 17% still to have problems and to have neither improved nor deteriorated over the past year. If the latter group is combined with those whose well-being appeared to have deteriorated, there is a 'did not improve' rate of around 30% of the 108 cases in the intensive sample interviewed twice.

Table 8.5 shows that there was an improvement in the well-being of a larger proportion of children referred because of concerns about neglect or emotional maltreatment (35% improved) than was the case for 'service requests' (16% improved). Whilst 7% of the children referred because of concerns about neglect or emotional maltreatment showed signs of deterioration in their well-being, this was the case for 28% of the children in the 'service request' families.

Table 8.5 ***Changes in child's well-being by type of case (families interviewed twice)***[1]

Change in well-being	Neglect/ emotional abuse		Service request		All	
	No.	%	No.	%	No.	%
Better	24	35	5	16	29	29
Same	19	28	9	28	28	28
Worse	5	7	9	28	14	14
No problems[2]	21	30	9	28	30	30
Total	**69**	**100**	**32**	**100**	**101**	**100**

[1] Missing cases=7; p:9.509 df:3 p<.05

[2] Whilst some of these were found to be not 'in need' as defined by the Children Act 1989, in most cases it was stresses on the parents that led to the conclusion that a child who was not currently experiencing problems was a child 'in need' under the terms of the Children Act 1989 in that his or her health would be likely to suffer if help were not made available to the parents.

Possible explanations for these differences are complex. To some extent the differences are accounted for by the fact that all the 'service request' families had children who were already experiencing difficulties, whereas some of those referred because of concerns about neglect were, in the light of further enquiry, found not to have sufficient problems to require intervention.

Episodes of maltreatment during the year

There were 308 re-referrals of the 180 children in these 108 families during the 12-month period. In eight cases difficulties with the child's behaviour was given as one of the reasons for re-referral, but this was the *main* reason for re-referral in only four cases. Neglect was mentioned as a reason for re-referral 20 times, inadequate care or supervision 22 times, physical abuse 26 times, sexual abuse 14 times and emotional maltreatment six times.

There were 13 strategy meetings, eight in respect of cases in the 'neglect' group and three in respect of 'service request' cases. We noted that some meetings designated as 'strategy meetings' fitted within the guidelines in *Working Together under the Children Act 1989* (DoH 1991c) and planned how an investigation of abuse should be handled, but others appeared to be inter-agency child protection conferences held without the presence of the parents. Nine child protection review conferences, but only two core group meetings, were recorded in respect of the 'neglect' referrals and two child protection review conferences and one core group meeting in respect of 'service request' families. Table 8.6 shows that, in the period after the Children Act 1989 and while the 're-focusing' debate on the appropriate place of the formal child protection system was going on, several different types of meetings were being held in respect of these families. For some, parents and young people were present; others did not include them. Some were attended by social work staff only and others were interagency meetings. Thoburn and Bailey (1996) document a similar process in a London Borough where the numbers

Table 8.6 ***Number of meetings held in respect of the families (intensive sample, Stage 2)***[1]

Type of meeting	Neglect cases	Service request cases	All
Strategy meeting	8	3	11
Initial child protection conference	9	2	11
Transfer child protection conference	2	–	2
Review child protection conference	6	2	8
Assessment child protection conference	1	–	1
Joint assessment team meeting	2	1	3
Core group meeting	2	1	3
Planning meeting	6	4	7
Placement meeting	4	–	4
Meeting *re* 'looked after child'	3	–	3
Statutory review meeting	1	–	1
Education department meeting	2	–	2
Meeting *re* a parent	3	–	3

[1] More than one meeting was held in some cases

on child protection registers dropped substantially. White (1998) has called attention to the need for clarity about the purpose and appropriate attendance at these different types of meetings. In 14 cases there was one meeting, but in four cases six or more meetings were held.

In only 11 cases did re-referrals lead to an initial child protection conference. Nine of the index children and seven of their siblings had their names placed on the Child Protection Register during this follow-up period, and two of the children and four of their siblings still had their names registered at the end of the 12-month period. Two of those registered were in the 'service request' group, one in the neglect category and one was registered under 'physical abuse'. Of those in the 'neglect' group, two were jointly registered under physical abuse and neglect, one because of concerns about physical and emotional abuse, three for emotional abuse and one for neglect.

Respite care, accommodation or care was provided for 14 of the children or their siblings during the follow-up period and five were still being looked after at the 12-month stage. Although it is likely that a small number of the children remaining at home would have benefited from out-of-home placement on a long- or short-term basis, the small proportion who left home indicates that, of all those referred because of concerns about emotional maltreatment or neglect, only a minority will be in the group needing the most intrusive services.

In total there was information about further maltreatment, or concerns about possible maltreatment, in respect of 28% of the cases (11 of the 57 'service request' cases (22%) and 34 of the 123 'neglect' cases (30%). Thus there was not, as might be expected, a statistically significant difference between the 'neglect' group and the 'service request' group. This bears out the conclusion in Chapter 3 that both groups were living in the sort of stressed circumstances that could only too easily lead to emotional or physical neglect or other forms of maltreatment.

Overall changes in family well-being

Four variables contributed to a 'researcher rating' of overall changes in family well-being. These were:

- the composite rating of any improvement or deterioration in the child's well-being (Figure 8.3);
- changes on the family problems checklist (Table 8.2);

- changes on the Rutter 'malaise' schedule (Table 8.4); and
- the opinion of the interview respondent as to whether their well-being had improved or deteriorated (Figure 8.4)

Figure 8.4 shows that on this composite rating just over half of the 108 families about whom we had sufficient information appeared to have made improvements, around a quarter appeared to have slipped backwards and the well-being of a quarter had either not changed or had improved in some respects and deteriorated in others.

Figure 8.4 ***Overall family outcome (researcher rating, parents interviewed twice)***[1]

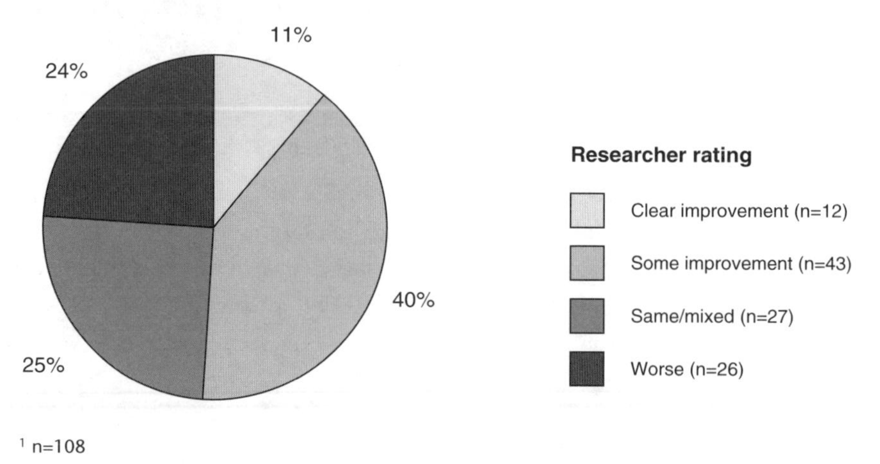

[1] n=108

Since it was only a minority who had anything other than a short-term contact with social services workers, we have to turn to other factors to tease out 'what made a difference'. *Before doing so it is important to emphasise that with a fairly small number of families and a large number of often overlapping variables that might have influenced outcomes, our conclusions, based on a one-way analysis of variance, can only be tentative. There are few statistically significant variables and the tables are provided essentially for descriptive purposes.*

Geography and environment

Figure 8.5 shows that there is no significant difference in the overall outcome for families in the three areas, although there is a trend towards a larger percentage of City 1 families showing improvement (70%) than was the case in either City 2 or County (both less than 50%). A similar pattern is found when the improvements in the well-being of the *main parent* are considered (59% of the parents in City 1 and 51% in County but only 42% in City 2 rated their

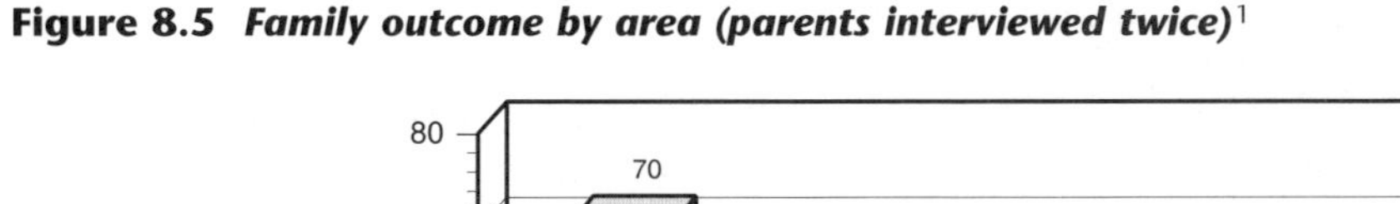

Figure 8.5 ***Family outcome by area (parents interviewed twice)***[1]

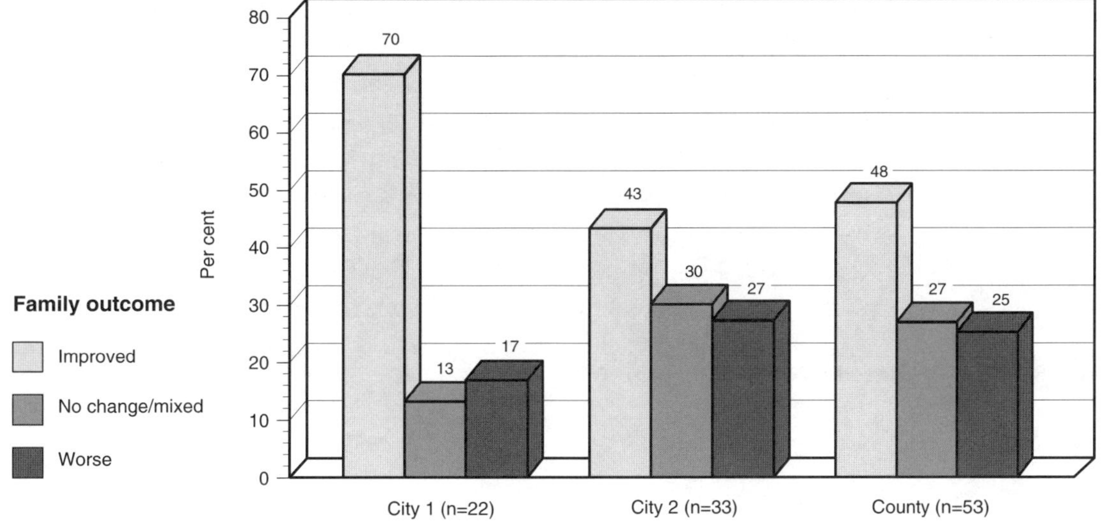

[1] n=108; not statistically significant

own well-being as being better than when they were first in contact with Social Services. Whilst 50% of the main carers rated their well-being better, the well-being of the index child was rated as better in only 29% of cases. However, in 30% of cases, the index child him/herself did not have any specific problem, and it was the more general family problems that might threaten the child's well-being in the future for which assistance had been sought. If only those with problems are included, the well-being of 40% of the children was considered to have improved. Whilst the main carers' well-being had deteriorated in 21% of the cases, there were fewer instances when the child's well-being deteriorated (14%). It was more likely that the children's well-being would have deteriorated in County (20%) than in either City 2 (11%) or City 1 (where no child's well-being appeared to have deteriorated). However, caution is urged in interpreting these data in view of the small numbers of children in each area who had problems.

There may be some relationship between the types of families being referred and the different outcomes for the different areas, although the direction of any association is not clear. A larger proportion of the families referred in County were, in retrospect, rated as not 'in need' as defined by the Children Act 1989 (20% in County compared with 8% in City 2 and 7% in City 1). However more County families (33%) than City 1 or City 2 families (29% and 19%, respectively) were categorised as having long-standing and multiple problems.

Type of referral

It might be anticipated that more progress would be made by those requesting a service than by those referred because of neglect or maltreatment. However, this did not appear to be the case. Figure 8.6 shows a trend, which did not quite reach statistical significance, towards a higher proportion of cases referred because of neglect or emotional maltreatment showing improvement than was the case for those requesting a service. The corollary was also found, with 38% of those requesting a service showing signs of deterioration in the overall well-being of the family compared with 18% of those referred because of concerns about neglect or emotional abuse.

Figure 8.6 ***Family outcome by type of referral (parents interviewed twice)***[1]

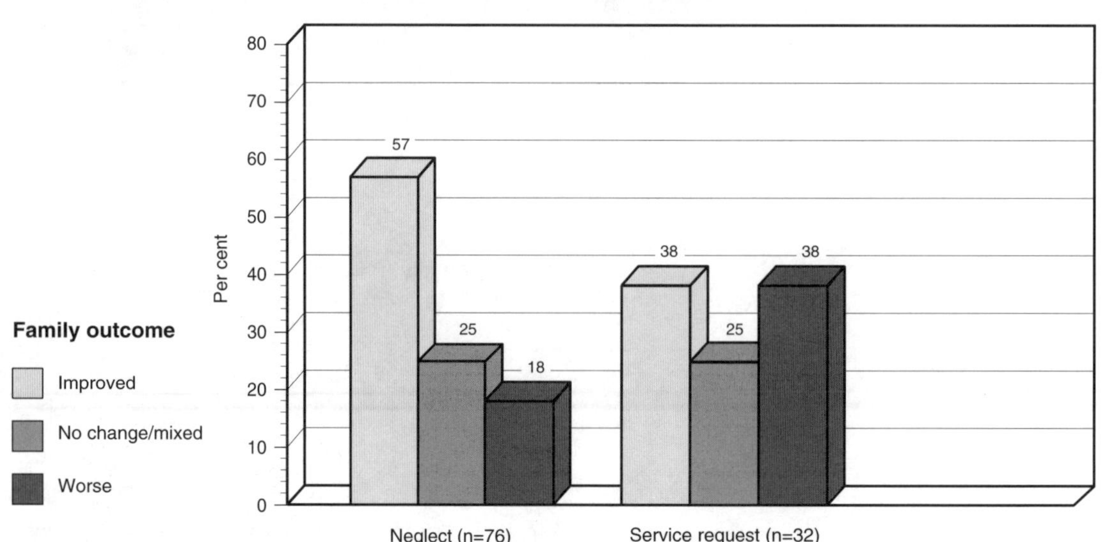

[1] n=108; not statistically significant (p:.081)

When the different categories of maltreatment are considered separately, there was a trend, which did not reach statistical significance, towards a more negative overall outcome for families in the 'emotional abuse' group (half of these ten cases were rated worse) than for those in the 'emotional neglect' (five out of 26 (19%) were worse) or 'physical neglect' cases (13 out of 47 (28%) being rated worse). Half of the 21 parents in 'extreme spouse abuse' cases were rated as being of higher well-being and 38% were rated worse. However, there is a different picture for the children in these cases, with 36% being in the 'improved well-being' group (fewer than the parents) but only 9% appearing to be worse.

There was not a statistically significant difference in overall outcome for the different *types* of families, in part because of the small numbers of families in some groups. Not surprisingly, Figure 8.7 shows that those rated as not 'in need' or as having 'short-term problems' were likely to show overall improvement. Well over half of those in 'acute distress', those with short-term problems and those where the family did not appear to cross the 'in need' threshold had improved well-being at the end of the year. This compared with around 40% of the families with long-term and multiple problems and 41% of the 'specific issue' families. These two groups were more likely than the others to experience a deterioration in their well-being.

Figure 8.7 ***Family outcome by type of family (parents interviewed twice)***[1]

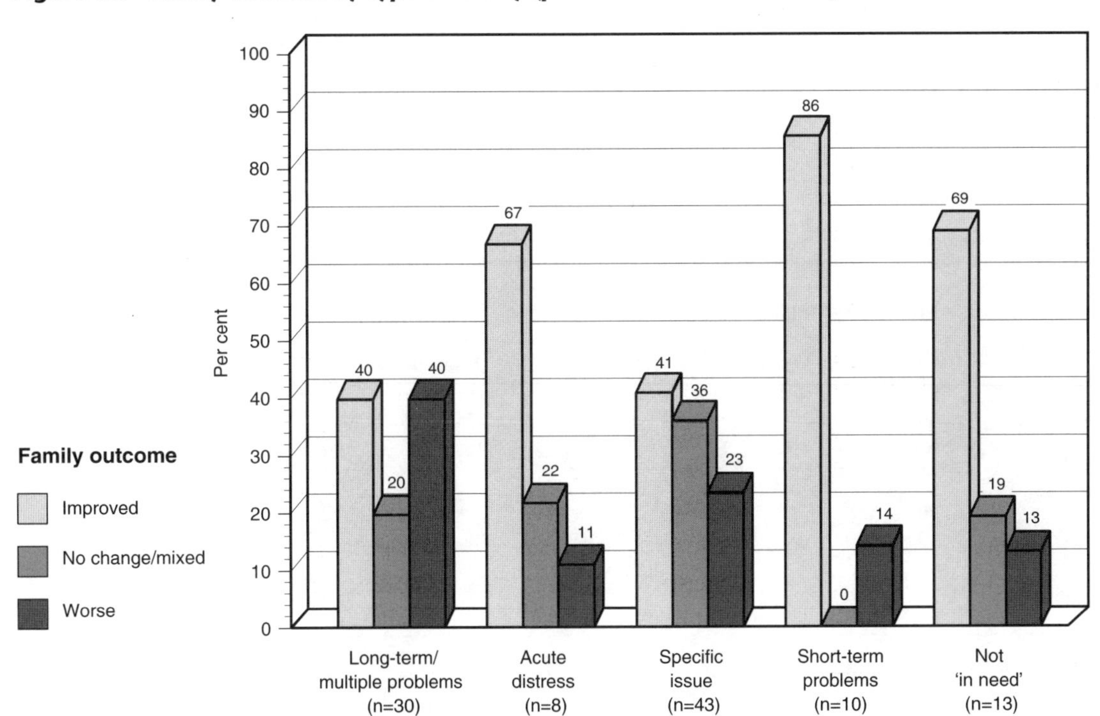

[1] n=104; missing data=4; not statistically significant (p:.078)

Table 8.7 shows a similar pattern in respect of changes in the *parents'* well-being. However, Table 8.8 shows differences between the different types of family in terms of improvement or deterioration in the *child's* well-being. This table is influenced by the number of children who had not (at least yet) developed problems of any marked seriousness. It is however worth noting that the well-being of none of the children of the 'acute distress' families had deteriorated, indicating that, despite their many difficulties, most parents were managing to protect their children from adverse consequences. The well-being of over a quarter of those living in families who had 'long-term and multiple problems' deteriorated, as did that of 14% of the 'specific issue' families.

Table 8.7 ***Changes in parents' well-being by type of family problem (families interviewed twice)***[1]

Well-being	Type of family problems											
	Long-term problems		Acute distress		Specific issue		Short-term problems		Not in need		All	
	No.	%	No.	%	No.	%	No.	%	No.	%	No.	%
Better	13	43	4	50	17	40	7	88	10	67	51	50
No change	7	23	3	38	17	40	–	–	3	20	30	28
Worse	10	33	1	12	9	20	1	12	2[2]	13	23	22
Total	**30**	**100**	**8**	**100**	**43**	**100**	**8**	**100**	**15**	**100**	**104**	**100**

[1] Missing cases=4; not statistically significant

[2] This is the result of deterioration in a parent's health even though the child's needs are being met

Table 8.8 ***Changes in child's well-being by type of family problem (families interviewed twice)***[1]

Well-being	Type of family problems											
	Long-term problems		Acute distress		Specific issue		Short-term problems		Not in need		All	
	No.	%	No.	%	No.	%	No.	%	No.	%	No.	%
Better	10	38	3	43	13	29	1	14	2	12	29	29
No change	9	35	3	43	14	32	1	14	–	–	27	27
Worse	7	27	–	–	6	14	1	14	–	–	14	14
No problems	–	–	1	14	11	25	4	57	14	88	30	30
Total	**26**	**100**	**7**	**100**	**44**	**100**	**7**	**100**	**16**	**100**	**100**	**100**

[1] n=100; missing data=8; not statistically significant

Ethnic origin of family

Turning to ethnicity, Figure 8.8 and Table 8.9 give data for the families in the city areas only. Differences between the white and ethnic minority families were not statistically significant, although there was a trend (Figure 8.8) towards more of the white families showing overall improvement *or* deterioration, and more of the families of minority ethnic origin experiencing little change or mixed outcomes. Nineteen per cent of families of minority ethnic origin were rated as worse in *overall family* well-being at the end of 12 months, as were 29% of the white families.

Figure 8.8 ***Family outcome by ethnicity of child, city areas only (parents interviewed twice)***[1]

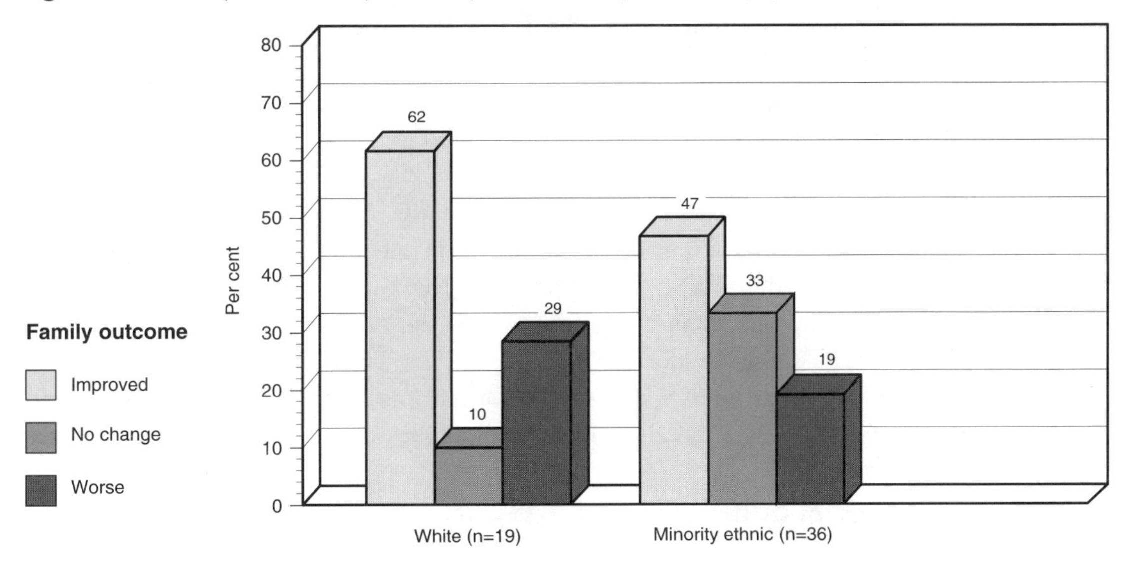

[1] n=55; not statistically significant

When considering the well-being of the *parents*, whilst more of the white parents considered that their own well-being had improved (62%) than was the case for the parents of minority ethnic origin (47%), more of the white parents also talked about a *deterioration* in their overall well-being (29%) than was the case with the parents of minority ethnic origin (19%).

Turning to the relationship between the outcome for the *children* and their ethnic origin, Table 8.9 shows a statistically significant difference between the white children and those of minority ethnic origin: 53% of the white

Table 8.9 ***Changes in child's well-being by ethnicity, city areas only (families interviewed twice)***[1]

Well-being	**White**		**Ethnic minority origin**		**All**	
	No.	**%**	**No.**	**%**	**No.**	**%**
Better	8	53	4	12	12	25
No change	4	27	12	36	16	33
Worse	1	7	3	9	4	8
No problems	2	13	14	42	16	33
Total	**15**	**100**	**33**	**100**	**48**	**100**

[1] Missing cases=7; x^2:9.33 df:3 $p<.05$

children showed some improvement compared with only 12% of the children of minority ethnic origin. However, 42% of the minority ethnic children and only 13% of the white children had no specific problems of their own at this stage of the study. When these are left out, the difference is still there. Just over half of the white children and around one in five of those of minority ethnic origin showed improvement over the 12-month period. It is of concern that only four of the 19 children of minority ethnic origin who displayed problems at the start of the study had actually improved in their overall well-being. Other studies have found that even though the well-being of parents may improve, it takes more time before signs of improvement in the children can be noted. As we saw when considering the families and children in more detail in Chapters 3 and 4, some of those of minority ethnic origin had experienced very serious difficulties and upheavals in their short lives.

Social and emotional support

It has been hypothesised that lack of social support is an important factor in the maltreatment of children and is also related to maternal depression. In this study there was no statistically significant association on any of the three outcome measures (overall family functioning, parents' well-being, child's well-being) between outcome at Stage 2 and lack of support at Stage 1. However, the trend was in the direction of better outcomes for those who *had* support: 54% of those with adequate support had improved overall outcomes compared with 39% of those who reported inadequate support.

The service provided and outcomes after 12 months

Some aspects of the service provided are linked with characteristics of the family, such as whether there has been a previous child protection enquiry or whether the case had been known to the social services department before this re-referral. Indeed a scrutiny of the relationship between service factors, family factors and outcome suggests that it is the *characteristics of the family* that have the greatest influence on both the likelihood that a certain sort of service will be provided and the outcome for parents and children. Put simply: a family referred when there are already concerns about child maltreatment is more likely to be assessed before any service is provided and is more likely to see a social worker and be allocated to a longer-term worker than is the case for a family not previously known to the social services department and where there are no child protection concerns. Because of the shortage of resources and the need to prioritise, those receiving services start off with more intractable problems than those who are refused or provided with minimal services. It is in this

Table 8.10 ***Relationship between social work or service variables and outcome for the family (families interviewed twice)***

Service variable	Variable applies[1]		Variable does not apply		Significance x^2
	% better	% worse	% better	% worse	(One-way analysis of variance)
Ever any interview with a social worker	46	29	74	4	p<.05
Service rated as 'good' or 'adequate'[2]	53	12	37	28	p<.05
Previous referrals to SSD	55	20	59	27	ns
Previous child protection enquiry	54	15	53	28	ns
Short piece of focused work only	49	27	40	28	ns
'Revolving door' type service	53	35	57	25	ns
Long-term service provided at start of case	31	25	53	25	ns
Case remained closed after four weeks	48	22	53	25	ns
Parents willing to accept/requesting help (excludes no next cases)	43	27	64	18	ns
Ever any recorded assessment	44	33	56	16	ns
Any family support plan recorded	50	33	54	26	ns
Resources provided	43	29	58	22	ns
Social worker allocated to family	42	36	57	18	ns
Any choices given *re* service	43	38	54	20	ns
Examples of good practice noted	50	31	53	21	ns

[1] Percentages do not add up to 100% since those cases in which there is 'no change' are omitted from the table
[2] Those not needing a service have been omitted

context that Table 8.10 should be read. In the majority of cases, social workers appear to have been successful in targeting services on those whose problems would be least likely to be resolved without intervention. Although those refused a service might have benefited from greater social services involvement, most did 'well enough' without it.

The reasons underlying the exercise of discretion about the type of service to be provided in each case may not necessarily be recorded, and much reliance is placed on 'practice wisdom' when judgements about prioritisation and types of service are made. The research interviews with the parents and the social workers give a fuller picture of what actually took place than can be grasped by merely scrutinising the files.

In broad terms, the analysis shows that those with the most problems are likely to be provided with services and to be allocated to a social work caseload. That those who are not allocated generally improve or get no worse is an indication that, in the majority of cases, those assessing the referrals 'get it right'.

An inherent obstacle to social workers' attempts to demonstrate effectiveness lies in the fact that hard-pressed social workers' allocate only the most difficult cases; therefore 'allocated' families tend to have less positive outcomes than 'unallocated' families. At its most obvious, this can be seen from the finding that 74% of those who were never interviewed by a social worker had a positive outcome and only 4% a negative one. Looked at another way, these data could be taken as indicating that, with only four 'false negatives' (that is, cases that were judged not to need a service and got worse), the system of sifting the high volume of referrals can be said to be working well enough.

It is at the next two stages that there appeared to be more cause for concern: when decisions were taken as to whether the case should be allocated for a fuller assessment of need and whether a planned social work service of shorter or longer duration should be provided.

The outcome was worse for 22% of the families whose case was closed quickly and remained closed. Would a more careful assessment have led to these parents receiving a more effective service? If there is some social work contact, the deterioration in the parents' condition (with the likely eventual impact on the child's well-being) might have been picked up and possibly halted with the provision of appropriate services.

Leaving aside the cases sifted out early – which improved or got no worse without the provision of further service – there are clues in the quantitative and interview data about how a cost-effective assessment and service might be provided in the context of the high volume of families under stress. Some of the families interviewed had only one office interview or phone conversation with a social worker and spoke positively of the advice given, some saying that it helped them get through a particularly difficult set of circumstances. Moving on to those who had some form of assessment or help beyond a single interview, it is not useful to compare patterns of intervention and outcome, since the assessment process generally ensures that the most complex and difficult situations are the ones receiving longer-term services and resources. So long as thresholds for allocation to social work caseloads remain high, positive short-term outcomes are likely to be few. *High thresholds and complex problems mean that almost no model of intervention will be shown to be effective within as short a timescale as 12 months. If thresholds for intervention were lower and social work services provided at an earlier stage, a range of short-term, more focused methods might be effective, and indeed there is support in our data for this conclusion.*

Fifty-two per cent of those parents who received a short-term service had improved well-being, despite the fact that much short-term work was rated by the researchers and the families as being of poor quality or ill-matched to the needs of the family. More skilled social workers providing a short-term service might have spotted the 15% of families whose well-being deteriorated when services were removed. A switch to a longer-term or episodic service (rather than case closure) might have avoided this deterioration, which was likely to result in more serious problems for the children.

Although 40% of the *parents* who received a longer-term service had poor well-being 12 months later, there was not the same deterioration in the *children's* well-being. As noted in Chapter 7, the researchers recorded examples of particularly good or poor practice and rated the overall quality of the service. There were more instances of the well-being of the child improving among those cases where examples of good practice were noted. *It should also be remembered that, although only 40% of parents rated the service as satisfactory overall, they tended to link this with whether or not their lives had improved rather than whether they found the social worker to be generally helpful. Seventy-one per cent of those who had contact with a social worker, including some with poor outcomes, described them as helpful.*

Figure 8.9 shows that there was a trend, which did not reach statistical significance, for outcomes for those who expressed satisfaction to be better than for those who were *un*satisfied or *dis*satisfied with the service received. This lack of a statistically significant difference emphasises the point that the biggest differences in outcome are accounted for by family strengths and circumstances. However, proportionately more of the families who expressed satisfaction with the service did show improvement in overall well-being

Figure 8.9 ***Family outcome by parental satisfaction (parents interviewed twice)***[1]

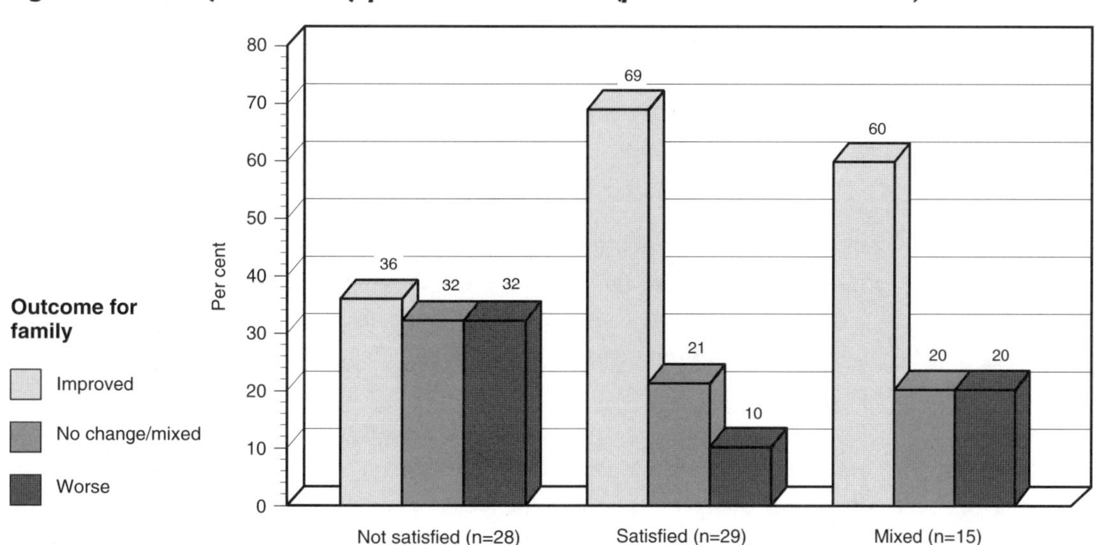

[1] n=72; missing data=7 (those not needing a service omitted); not statistically significant

during this 12-month period. Figure 8.10 shows that, when those who did not need a service are omitted, more of those who received a generally good service had improved well-being at the end of 12 months (p<.05).

These data suggest that the pragmatic and often ill-recorded method of sifting the very large volume of cases works reasonably well: it does not result in the provision of a service to many families (if any) who do not need it, but it does not exclude from service too many families who *do* need it.

Figure 8.10 ***Family outcome by service adequacy (parents interviewed twice)***[1]

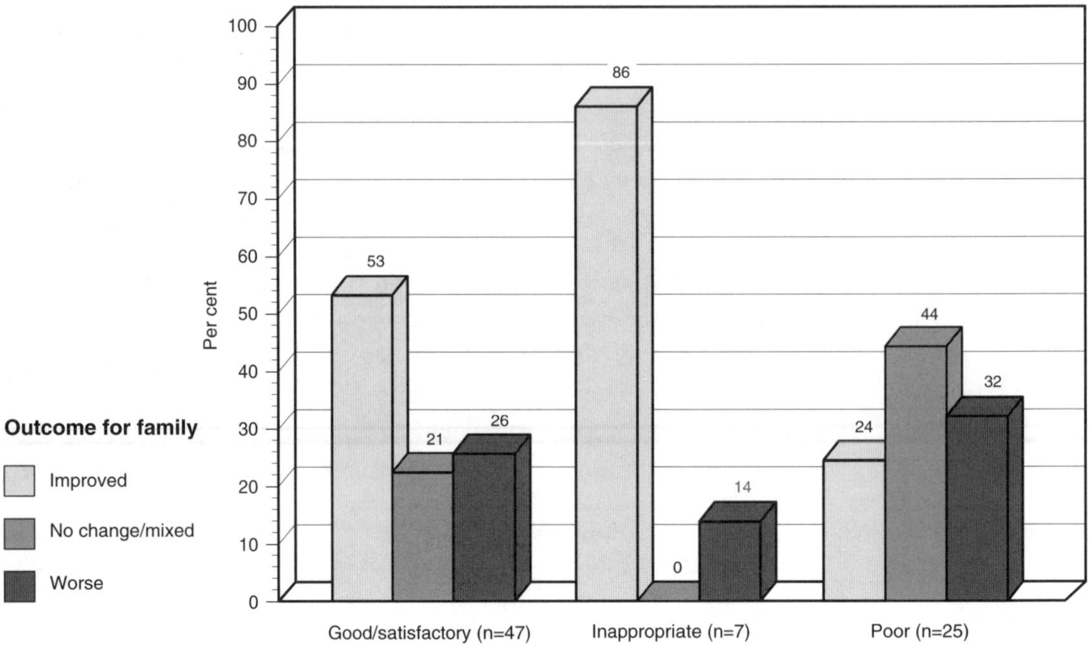

[1] n=79; x^2:11.36 df:4 p<.05

However, improvements *could* be made in the assessment process, which might lead to better outcomes for more families at lower cost. It is particularly important that those cases that are turned away only to be re-referred when problems are considerably worse are provided with services at an earlier stage. Most of these families are seeking help – or at least willing to accept a service if it were offered sensitively – even though the original referral might be occasioned by concerns about neglect or maltreatment. Providing short-term help or advice alongside a 'first stage' assessment for *all* cases of any complexity should make it possible to identify those families whose well-being may deteriorate without the provision of services as well as to undertake a more comprehensive assessment that leads to the type and duration of service appropriate to the circumstances of a particular family. Our data suggest that it is not sufficient to sift simply according to factual information about need, reasons for referral or causes for concern. Time, knowledge and skills must contribute to an understanding of the complex interactions and biographies of the family members – in the context of their willingness or otherwise to accept services – and of the patterns of family and community support available to them.

Summary

Taking the practical and emotional aspects of their lives together, the well-being of 48% of the parents interviewed twice had improved, for 23% it had got worse and for 29% there had been no change.

Twelve months after referral it was noted that some parents (mainly fathers) had moved out and others moved in. Fewer of those interviewed had serious problems with housing, but there was still a high level of dissatisfaction about this area of their lives. The financial circumstances of 28% had got worse.

In terms of support, during the year the situation improved in respect of help with the children and financial help, perhaps indicating that social services' involvement had had a positive impact in these areas.

Twelve months after referral the health and development of 29% of the 108 children whose parents were interviewed twice was considered to have improved; 14% were rated, on all the evidence available, as having lower well-being; 17% still had problems that had neither improved nor got worse. One child with a disability had died, and 29% of children who did not appear to have problems at Stage 1 still had no problems at Stage 2.

There were 308 re-referrals of the 180 children in the intensive sample during the year. There was information about further possible maltreatment or neglect in respect of 28% of cases in this sample (22% of those in the 'service request' group and 30% in the 'neglect' group).

An initial child protection conference was held on only 12 of the 180 children, and only nine 'index' children and seven of their siblings had their names entered on the Child Protection Register at any time during the research period. Two of these were in the 'service request' group. Two of the index children and four of their siblings were still registered at the end of the year.

An *overall* 'researcher rating' of changes in family well-being was made in respect of the 108 families interviewed twice.

There had been an improvement in the general well-being of just over half of the families, and the well-being of almost a quarter had deteriorated. For a quarter there had either been no change or the outcome was positive in some respects and negative in other respects.

More of those referred because of concerns about neglect or emotional maltreatment had improved outcomes than was the case for those referred with a request for a service. The general well-being of more of the families in the 'service request' group *had deteriorated*, but there was no change for a quarter of the families in each group. To some extent this is explained by the fact that, after further assessment, some of those in the 'neglect' group did not have problems that resulted in a conclusion that the child was 'in need'. The 'service request' families, on the other hand, were all families with a child 'in need'.

Those rated as not 'in need' or as having 'short-term problems' were, not surprisingly, likely to show overall improvement. The well-being of over a quarter of the children living in families with 'long-term and multiple problems' deteriorated, as did that of 14% of the 'specific issue' families. However, the well-being of none of the children in the 'acute distress' group of families deteriorated, indicating that, despite the pressures under which they lived, most of the parents were managing to protect their children from the ill-effects of their own stress.

There was a trend towards more of the white families showing overall improvement *or* deterioration, and more of the families of minority ethnic origin experiencing little change *or* mixed outcomes.

Contrary to what we might have anticipated, there was no statistically significant association between outcome and the lack of support to the main parent at Stage 1, although the *trend* was in the direction of better outcomes for those who did have emotional and practical support.

A review of the relationship between service factors, family factors and outcome suggests that the *characteristics of the family*, rather than the nature of the service provided, has the greatest influence on outcome for parents and children.

So long as thresholds for allocation to social work caseloads remain high, positive short-term outcomes that can be attributed to models of intervention are likely to be few. Those allocated to social workers were those with the most serious problems and, therefore, less positive outcomes. Those provided with no service or a short-term service were assessed as having fewer problems, and therefore most likely to improve or show no change whether or not a service was provided.

However, proportionately more of the families *who expressed satisfaction* with the service did improve in overall well-being during the 12-month period, an indication that attempts to work in partnership with families may be justified in terms of better outcomes as well as for reasons of ethics and social justice.

Very few service variables on their own were associated with better outcomes for the family as a whole, the parents or the children.

Not surprisingly, since these were the families who had fewer problems in the first place, more of those who were never interviewed by a social worker improved and fewer got worse.

Services rated by the researchers as good or adequate, whether they involved brief or longer-term interventions, *were* associated with better outcomes for many of the families.

No one *type* of service was associated with better or worse outcomes.

There was no association between better or worse outcomes, and the *recording* of an assessment or a family support plan. Indeed, when the outcome for the parents is considered, those whose files did not include a recorded assessment were more likely to improve and less likely to deteriorate. This may be explained by the fact that those who were most likely to improve received a quick and usually unrecorded assessment before a decision was taken that the case would be closed.

These data suggest that the pragmatic and often ill-recorded method of sifting the very large volume of cases works reasonably well: it does not result in the provision of services to many families who do not need it, but does not exclude from services too many families who *do* need assistance. However, in a small number of cases the inappropriate closure of a case without an adequate assessment led to unnecessary harm to children and to unnecessary expense.

9 Conclusions and implications for policy and practice

The child protection and the child welfare systems

This study was planned, and the first round of interviews completed, just as what has come to be known as the 'refocusing initiative' was being taken on board by the multi-agency groups drawing up Children's Services Plans. The three authorities in which the study took place welcomed the recommendation that they should seek to help a larger proportion of families under the provisions of the family support clauses of the Children Act 1989, and, when it was safe to do so, to divert them away from the formal child protection system.

From the family interviews and discussions with social workers and managers at the end of the study, it is clear that to many people there is confusion about the relationship between the *formal child protection system* (as described in the Guidance *Working Together under the Children Act 1989*) (DoH 1991c) and the *child welfare system* , which, broadly understood, is about protecting children from all forms of harm whatever the cause. The confusion started when the term 'child abuse' was dropped and replaced by 'child protection'. In effect, the *formal* child protection system still concerns itself with children who have been significantly harmed, or are likely to be harmed, by acts of commission or omission by parents and others within the family network or in positions of authority in the residential care sector or community groups. Even with this latter group, once it becomes clear that the child has parents who are able to be protective, the case is moved from the formal system, and the child welfare system takes over the provision of services (if any services are provided). Thus the group of children who are *most likely* to be *most significantly* harmed – those looked after by the local authority and not yet in planned long-term placements – tend not to be on the Child Protection Register and to be viewed as not in need of protective services because there is no identified likely abuser.

On reflecting on the conversations that have taken place during this study about the nature of emotional maltreatment and neglect, it seems unfortunate that, among users of services as well as professionals, the term 'child protection' has become so linked with acts of maltreatment that it is no longer an appropriate description for the whole of child welfare work. This is a particular feature of the child protection system in the UK, since in other countries (encouraged by the UN Convention on the Rights of the Child) child protection and child welfare are synonymous. Thus child welfare or child protection services cover all those children who, in the language of UNICEF and other international bodies, are 'in need of special protective measures'. They may be street children, they may be at risk of attempting suicide because of bullying or racism at school, they may be lacking basic amenities or have parents who are dying of HIV Aids or other chronic diseases, or they may have parents who have mental health problems or addictions. A tiny minority of these parents will not have their welfare at heart and will seek to harm them. Others, because of their own problems, may be inadvertently harming their children or unable to meet their needs for protection. For many children in the UK, as across the world, protection is a major issue, even though they may have parents who, with appropriate assistance, can meet their needs adequately.

This study, then, is about child protection in the broadest sense and focuses on that group of children about whom there is most choice as to whether the formal child protection system should be brought into play or whether the child protection aspects of general child welfare and family support services, as provided for under Part III of the Children Act 1989, should be the appropriate route for service provision. Throughout the research period, and especially at the analysis stage, there has been much discussion about the impact of the refocusing initiative. Most recently this has centred on the publication of the Social Services Inspectorate report on family support services (*Responding to Families in Need*, SSI 1997a). Debate has also focused on ways to counteract the social exclusion of so many young people, which for many has its origins in their experiences in pre-school and early school years. There is broad agreement between the findings detailed in this report and the conclusions of the SSI Inspection Report. However, there are four main ways in which our study differs from the inspection report and earlier child protection studies.

1 It concentrates on children under the age of 8 – although some information was obtained on older siblings – and gives an indication of what might lie ahead for them if appropriate services are not offered.

2 It explores the territory between family support and the formal child protection system and thus addresses some of the issues covered by the SSI report (SSI 1997b) *Messages from Inspections: Child Protection*

Inspections 1992–1996. In particular, it focuses on that group of children in respect of whom there is most scope for discretion among referrers and social workers as to whether the case should be channelled down the formal child protection route or the family support route (that is, children referred because of concerns about emotional maltreatment or neglect).

3 In contrast to most earlier research, the sample includes a large proportion of families of minority ethnic origin, these families being the majority of those who were interviewed in the city areas.

4 Whilst the SSI report on family support focused on the period from the decision to accept a referral to the completion of the case plan, this study also includes families who were offered no service, following them, and those who did receive a longer-term service, for a 12-month period. Our study, therefore, has something to say about those who were *not* provided with a service and can contribute to the debate about whether appropriate decisions are taken about the 'in need' threshold and about prioritisation.

Before returning to the question raised in earlier chapters of how social services departments might best respond to the high volume of children 'in need' who may be eligible for a service, the questions formulated at the start of the research are addressed in summary.

Quantifying neglect and emotional abuse: separate problems or part of a continuum?

The main sources of information about referrals concerning emotional abuse and neglect are the Department of Health statistics prepared by the government's statistical service (DoH 1997c). These show that over 29,000 children (26 per 10,000 children under 18) were registered as in need of protection during the year ending March 1997, and over 32,000 were actually on the Child Protection Register at the end of the year (a rate of 29 children per 10,000 population). Of these, 29% were registered for reasons of neglect alone and 14% for emotional abuse alone. If combined categories are added, neglect or emotional abuse were among the reasons for registration of 51% of those registered in 1997, an increase of 4% over the previous year.

However, registration rates are an inadequate indication of the extent of emotional maltreatment or neglect, as is demonstrated by the variations of rates of registration per 10,000 children in similar authorities. No statistics are kept on a national basis of the numbers of families referred to social services departments for whom neglect and emotional maltreatment are mentioned as causes for concern. Such figures would be more accurate in that they would avoid the distortions resulting from different policies about the use of the formal child protection system and the Child Protection Register. However, the *Child Protection: Messages from Research* studies (Dartington Social Research Unit 1995a) and other research in the child protection field, including the present study, suggest that in some areas professionals use the abuse label in order to access services, whereas in other areas it is easier to access services by requesting help for a family.

The situation is further confused by a lack of clarity about the difference between emotional *harm* and emotional *abuse*. The Children Act 1989 concentrates on the health and development of children and the *likely impairment* to their health and development if appropriate services are not provided. Even in the Sections considering parental maltreatment that might lead to measures of protection sanctioned by the courts (Parts IV and V of the Act), the threshold for the making of an order is harm to the child and not abusive behaviour by a parent or person with parental responsibility (although the position is complicated by the confusion of harm to a child [the noun 'harm'], with acts of ill-treatment [the verb 'to harm'] by the statement (Section 31 (9)(b): '"Harm" means ill-treatment or the impairment of health or development'). This confusion is extended to the formal child protection system as described in *Working Together under the Children Act 1989* (DoH 1991c). Child protection conferences may only decide to register a child if there is evidence of actual or likely significant harm that can be attributed to an act or acts of commission or omission by those with parental responsibility. This focuses child protection conferences on harm to the child. However, at the point of registration, decisions have to be taken on the category of abusive behaviour that appears to have led to the harm or to be likely to lead to it. A parallel study of cases of significant or likely significant harm (Brandon et al. 1999) showed that, although only 9% of the children were registered in the emotional abuse category (and a further 6% if joint categories are included), the major form of significant harm that was occurring or was likely to occur was *actual* emotional harm in 30% of the cases and *likely* emotional harm in a further 6% of the cases. The research described here supports the conclusion that the extent of significant emotional harm is considerably greater than the extent of emotionally abusive behaviour.

The encouragement to think more carefully about whether it is necessary to use the formal child protection system in order to provide services to children who may be being emotionally maltreated or neglected will make the formal child abuse registration figures an even less adequate guide regarding the extent of emotional abuse, let alone emotional harm. The Children Act 1989 uses the term 'significant impairment to health or development' (Section 17(b)) as one of the triggers for 'in need' services, and emphasises that health includes mental health and development includes intellectual, emotional, social and behavioural development. In so doing, it opens up the possibility for a choice to be made between the use of Section 17 (which does not require culpability to be established) and Section 31, where 'harm means ill-treatment' but also means 'impairment to health or development' attributable to parental fault.

By looking at the records it would be impossible, except in a tiny minority of cases, to know whether the cases we were considering were considered by social workers and managers to be Section 17(a) cases 'unlikely to achieve a reasonable standard of health or development', or Section 17(b) cases in which concerns were about the significant or likely significant impairment to health or development. Within either of these two definitions there was rarely any clarity about whether the particular aspects of development that were jeopardised included emotional development. When specifically asked this question by researchers in this study and in the Brandon et al. (1999) study, few social workers said that they analysed cases in terms of the wording of the Children Act 1989. If reliable statistics are to be available on the extent of actual and likely emotional maltreatment and emotional harm, it will be necessary for better records to be kept of the reasons why children are considered to cross the 'in need' or the 'likely significant harm' thresholds.

Turning to the data on the extent of emotional abuse and maltreatment identified by this study, concerns about emotional abuse or neglect were expressed about 23% of all the children referred, if one includes those cases where these were secondary reasons for referral (48% of the 337 referrals mentioned a child protection concern). It was clear from the scrutiny of the records and in discussion with families that this was an over-estimate of the extent of neglectful or emotionally abusive *parental behaviour*, but an under-estimate of the proportion of children referred whose emotional development was being or likely to be significantly impaired if services were not provided. Similarly there was an over-estimate of those families who were *culpably neglecting* their children, but an under-estimate of the numbers of children (in the 'service request' as well as the 'neglect' group) who were vulnerable to accidental harm because their parents were either physically or emotionally unable to provide the supervision they needed at all times. It is also likely that a substantial proportion of the 82 children about whom physical abuse concerns were expressed, of the 47 about whom there were concerns about sexual maltreatment and of the 67 referred for 'other' child protection reasons (see Table 3.4), would include children who were being emotionally harmed or at risk of accidental harm through neglect of their physical and emotional needs. Impairment of intellectual development is also likely to be linked with emotional harm, since those children who cannot make use of the learning opportunities offered in schools may well be the subject of bullying or ridicule from other children. In none of the records did we see specific mention of impairment to intellectual development, yet many of the families spoke about their worries over their children's lack of progress or difficulties in school.

Thus, whether or not the words 'neglect' or 'emotional abuse' appeared in the referral notes, our conclusion is that significant numbers crossing social services thresholds are suffering or are likely to suffer harm to their emotional development. It is, however, important to look at sub-categories within these broad headings, since different types of service will be appropriate in different circumstances. The more recent 'unpicking' of the term 'emotional abuse' and the identification of overlaps between the different types of maltreatment should help managers to plan better the types and quantity of services needed by the different groups. The neglect and emotional abuse referrals will, after an initial assessment, be found to fall into three broad groups:

Some allegations will be found to be *unsubstantiated* and the children will be found to be not 'in need' as defined by the Children Act 1989. Provided that the enquiry itself does not cause harm by weakening the confidence of the parents, these cases can be taken out of the statistics. From the evidence available to the researchers at the end of the study, it appeared that 19% of those children in the interview sample who had been referred because of concerns about emotional maltreatment or neglect were not at risk of maltreatment. Twenty-two per cent of the 'inadequate supervision' referrals required no further action or service, compared with 15% of the interview sample as a whole. Twenty per cent of all the 'physical neglect' referrals but only 1 of the 12 'emotional abuse' referrals (8%) and 1 (5%) of the 21 'emotional neglect' cases were also not in need of services.

The second group consists of those who are vulnerable to accidents or who are generally failing to make appropriate progress in their health and developmental milestones because *their parents are emotionally unavailable or leave them without adequate supervision.* A proportion of families in respect of whom maltreatment or neglect concerns are substantiated will improve if services can be made available to provide (in some cases) practical help, emotional support (in others) so that parents can be more available to provide adequate supervision to their children and meet their emotional and physical needs.

The third group comprises those whose parents have *more serious and longer-term problems.* They will need more sustained help so that change can be achieved in their own emotional functioning and relationships before they can adequately meet the needs of their children. Although only around a half of these under-eights were already suffering impairment to their health or development (as indicated by problems in social, behavioural and educational performance), there were clear signs, particularly in those families where there were older children, that among this group long-term emotional harm was likely to ensue if more sustained and creative services were not provided. Fewer than a third of the 'neglect or emotional maltreatment' group and a small minority of the 'service request' referrals came into this category, which roughly equates to the 'high criticism, low warmth' families identified by the researchers contributing to *Child Protection: Messages from Research* overview (Dartington Social Research Unit 1995a), and by other writers on neglect and emotional maltreatment, as being particularly harmful to children (Stevenson 1998; Iwaniec 1995).

A sub-group of those with longer-term problems comprises those parents who will be most difficult to help, and whose children are most likely to need *long-term, out-of-home care.* Because of lack of attachment or concern for their children, but more often because of mental health problems (almost invariably originating in their own childhood relationships), these parents behave in a way that is intended (at least at the time that it happens) to cause harm to the child. They made up a very small proportion of our interview sample.

It is this third group who are most likely to need the most intensive and creative services if the long-term separation of parents and children is to be avoided. A major challenge to those sifting referrals is to detect and provide services to the second group at an earlier stage of problem formation to prevent them succumbing to stress and slipping into the third group.

Thus, the question posed at the start of the study – whether neglected and emotionally maltreated children are two distinct groups and whether either can be distinguished from other children referred to social services departments – has to be answered in terms of the different groups of children and families being referred under these broad headings. In order to do this it becomes necessary to consider the *patterns of problems and problem formation* of families requesting or referred for service, since there may be children at risk of suffering the ill-effects of neglect or emotionally harmful parenting among any of the families crossing the child care team threshold. In order to provide an appropriate service to avoid future impairment to health or development, it is not sufficient to look at whether any particular type of abuse was mentioned in the referral, although it is necessary to do so. Nor can likely harm be predicted from the *needs* identified at the time of referral. Two families referred because they need support in seeking rehousing, or immediate financial assistance because a crisis loan application is pending and there is no food for the children, may have totally different relationships with their children. This will mean that, beyond the crisis, one family will need no further assistance, whilst the children in the other family will be emotionally harmed if no provision is made for intensive and/or extensive services.

In the light of the fact that assistance is sought by a very large numbers of families with apparently similar environmental and practical difficulties, ways have to be found to sift referrals so that the most effective service is provided to those who can make use of it at an early stage (thus avoiding further impairment of the children's health and development) and so that cost-effective longer-term help is provided for those whose children are already suffering significant harm and are likely to continue to do so without sustained support. The notion of *triage*, more often used when considering health services, provides a way forward. Central to this sifting process is the continuum of types of assessment (SSI 1999) which are being developed by several local authorities, including those in our study. The sifting process starts when families themselves or other professionals or neighbourhood support workers decide whether or not to make a referral. In the final section of this chapter we make specific suggestions about assessments based on our interview data and our study of the outcomes in these cases.

Who refers cases of emotional abuse and neglect?

There are different referral routes for the different types of behaviour that come under the broad headings of emotional abuse and neglect. This study has followed the sub-divisions used by the US Department of Health and Human Services (1988), with the broad categories of emotional abuse, physical neglect and emotional neglect being further sub-divided. The police were the major referrers of the 'inadequate supervision' cases, but otherwise referrals were fairly evenly divided between health professionals, schools and the families themselves. We noted that referrals by neighbours and family members, and particularly non-resident parents, were least likely to be taken seriously and result in a service being provided. A small number of referrals came from social services personnel, usually working in day centres, who expressed concerns about children attending their centres who were not allocated to a social work caseload and may be likely to suffer harm because of neglect or emotional maltreatment. Within the 'service request' group, there were more self-referrals, and families were more likely to be referred by health professionals.

Although other professionals were not interviewed, and we only had comments written by a proportion of health visitors and school nurses on the health monitoring forms, additional information about the referrers was gained from letters on file and also from the families themselves. It was clear that all groups of referrers (parents, social services staff and other professionals) made choices as to whether a case should be referred as a family in need of support, or as a family where there were concerns about neglect or emotional maltreatment. There were only one or two examples of families referred for services being reframed by the assessment team as child protection referrals. From the small number of cases leading to a child protection conference, it can be seen that, after preliminary enquiries, social workers and team managers decided to treat the majority of emotional abuse and neglect cases as cases for which a support and social work service should be provided under the provisions of Part III of the Children Act 1989. From the review of the circumstances of families referred because of concerns about the possibility of maltreatment and those referred for a service, this seems entirely appropriate. In terms of background and environmental stresses, the two groups were similar. However, more of the 'service request' families scored highly on the emotional stress scale, but more of the families referred because of concerns about maltreatment had problems of addiction, mental health problems and personal and relationship problems that sometimes resulted in partner violence.

Assessment and the patterns of service provision

How then are decisions taken about which cases will be the subject of a child protection enquiry and which will be reviewed by a child protection conference; which will be further assessed before a decision is taken about whether services should be made available; and which will receive a service or be told that they are not of sufficiently high priority (without any more assessment than a few phone calls) and, less often, an interview with a social worker)?

The conclusions from this research are similar in many respects to those of the recent SSI inspection report (SSI 1997a): on many of the files we did not see reasoned accounts of the processes that led to the decision to channel a family down one route rather than another. In discussing this question with groups of social workers and with the 18 workers who provided a longer-term service to some of the families, it became clear that a proportion of them *were* basing their judgements on theories and knowledge gained during their initial and post-qualifying training. Some were able to articulate the principles that underlay their decisions, whilst others had to work hard during the interview to get back in touch with the theories that informed their everyday 'practice wisdom', based not only on research and theory but also on experience accumulated over the years.

All three authorities (City 1, City 2 and County) had guidelines about the priority to be given to cases, but there was confusion in the minds of some of the workers interviewed about the difference between criteria for crossing the 'in need' threshold and thus being *eligible* for services and the criteria for *prioritisation*. It was this latter set of guidelines on which workers appeared to be basing their decisions. During the research interviews with the families and the social workers, questions were asked about the extent to which decisions were based on the wording of Sections 17 and 31 of the Children Act 1989. It became clear that few social workers turned regularly to the legal definition, particularly that of the 'in need' threshold. It was, therefore, not surprising that families seemed unclear about whether they had any rights to services, and thus any rights to make representations about the non-availability of services. This applied particularly to those who requested a service, or an assessment as to the type of help that might be made available and had their request refused, and especially to those who themselves had disabilities or whose children had disabilities.

The second threshold, or more often the first, since few social workers appeared to differentiate between the 'in need' threshold and this one, was the decision about whether a child and family were of high enough priority to be provided with services. This applied especially to services that were more expensive and in short supply, such as allocation to a social worker caseload, day care, family aide, and accommodation or respite care for a child. In all three authorities the records of the under-eights and home care workers were not routinely placed on the main family file, even when the case was closed, so it was not possible to know how the decisions about allocation of practical help in the home and day care were taken. Towards the end of the research the language of 'first stage' and 'second stage' assessments was being used, and the process was formalised, but without this it was clear that there were indeed three sorts of assessments taking place – the quick, rough-and-ready decision about whether the extent of risk or need justified proceeding further; a somewhat pragmatic assessment about whether a specific service or resource should be provided; and a more comprehensive assessment once it was decided that further services would be provided. This last group included assessments that were part of the formal child protection process and broadly followed DoH (1988) Guidance.

These assessments led to judgements being made (either on the basis of this or subsequent referrals, and almost always in consultation with a team leader) on which of the five broad patterns of service would be provided. These were:

- no service other than a referral to another agency;
- a 'first stage' assessment of need and priority, accompanied by a practical service or advice before case closure;
- a short-term social casework service, sometimes including one or more practical services;
- an episodic social casework service, usually accompanied by practical help; and
- a longer-term casework service combining emotional support and practical services.

The 'no further action' or 'referral elsewhere' response (pattern 1) accounted for just over a quarter of the cases in both the 'neglect' and the 'service request' groups. The short-term service response (pattern 2) was by far the most frequent, being used in 35% of the referrals (for slightly more of the 'neglect' than the 'service request' families). From our interviews with social workers and managers, it is clear that – though those doing the sifting often failed to record their reasoning – they were making professional judgements based on the information available. However, without even a short meeting or conversation with most of the families (and they were even less likely to meet the children in this young age group), 'false negatives' and 'false positives' are inevitable. Although from our interviews with families in the 'intensive' sample and scrutiny of the records there were few if any families who received a service when no service was needed, some received an *inappropriate service* when a more careful assessment at the early stage might have led to more effective provision. Given the shortage of resources to meet the very high need for day care, after-school care, and family aide work in particular, it is important that these services are not provided inappropriately when other services would better secure the longer-term well-being of children and parents. It may also be that, with a more appropriate assessment of families' needs and preferences, these resources would be more appropriately designed around their varying needs, thus avoiding the non-take-up and drop-out rates, which, though not high, indicate some lack of satisfaction. Generally these practical services – together with the provision of cash and material help – and negotiation and advocacy with other agencies were well received by families.

There was little evidence recorded on file that those making the assessments that led to no service or a short-term service took into consideration the *likelihood of any particular service being more or less effective.* Services tended to be matched with the needs or reasons for crossing the threshold, as advocated by the Dartington Social Research Unit (1995b), but less often with the cluster of practical, emotional and relationship difficulties and the competences and support available to the family. Nor did we find that, in the process of assessing need, the need for protection from significant impairment of the different aspects of health or development was systematically recorded. Whether or not the referral mentioned the possibility of maltreatment was certainly considered, but there was a lack of recording of the *significance and type* of any harm that might occur, or the likelihood of it happening if particular services were or were not made available. Whilst all these considerations may have been part of the thought processes of the social workers, in only a minority of the cases was it clear that all these different factors were weighed before decisions were taken about which route the case would follow. As has been mentioned in Chapter 6, recorded assessments and family support plans were found on only a minority of the records. When they were available, they sometimes included all the considerations referred to in this section, and there were some particularly good examples of case closure or transfer summaries that contained descriptions and evaluations of the services provided, the reactions of family members to them, and the reasons why some services offered had not been accepted. Without such summaries the assessment of re-referrals by a new intake worker would certainly have been more time-consuming and probably less effective.

The service most often provided, though rarely systematically recorded in these 'no further action' or 'short-term service' cases, was a first or second stage assessment of risk, and, in a smaller proportion of cases, need. Generally, decisions taken to proceed no further in making enquiries about maltreatment or in providing family support services were appropriate, in that most of those cases where no further assistance was provided did well enough during the ensuing year. In other words, as discussed in Chapter 8, there were few 'false negatives' (families whose position deteriorated when a service was not provided). There were also very few 'false positives' (families provided with a service who did not need it). Even in the small number of cases that were inappropriately referred, it was necessary for an enquiry to be made as to whether, for example, a child not being collected from school indicated a one-off incident or a 'pattern'. There were examples of sensitive one-off interviews that families found helpful. However, in some cases, requests for services were refused without any full discussion with the family about the extent of need; in others, allegations of maltreatment were insensitively handled, leaving parents anxious about possible future consequences and determined not to seek help even if they might need it.

The third, fourth and fifth types of response, which sometimes started off as an assessment of risk in the shape of a Section 47 enquiry and sometimes as a fuller assessment of need that included the need for protection services, comprised the provision of a package of services co-ordinated by a case-accountable social worker. Sometimes (patterns 3 and 4) this was provided on a *short-term* or *episodic basis*, usually by the worker from the assessment team. In other circumstances (pattern 5) the case was transferred to a social worker in a long-term team.

Our more detailed data are available only for those in the intensive sample who were referred because of concerns about emotional maltreatment and neglect or because a service was requested. Twenty-three per cent received a longer-term service, the intensity and nature of which might fluctuate, and 15% a more episodic service, which we termed a 'revolving door' type service because on each occasion, after the case had been closed, the family had to find their way back into the system, going yet again through the referral, assessment and allocation process, often with a different set of workers, though sometimes with the same referrer.

The service provided to the 'revolving door' and 'longer-term' families as well as to some of the 35% who received a short-term service, can best be described as a social casework service. Families were offered a supportive relationship with a social worker, who also discussed with them and sought to provide a range of practical services including day care, family aide, negotiation with other agencies and practical and financial help. In a minority of cases the social worker adopted a 'case-management' approach, putting together and monitoring packages of services but being minimally involved with the family. Sometimes this was at the request of the family members, but more often parents regretted that they did not see more of the social worker, whom they saw as potentially helpful but too distant for them to feel able to talk through personal feelings and relationship difficulties. There was a greater risk in these 'case-management' type cases that the services provided would be inappropriate, since the worker did not get sufficiently close to the parents and children to understand what was really needed or likely to be effective. In a minority of cases, this co-ordinated package of services involved the social worker linking in a planned way with those (often mental health professionals) providing therapy to parents or children, or with neighbourhood workers who provided high levels of support. In the city areas some

Asian and African–Caribbean workers had developed excellent working relationships with neighbourhood resources provided for particular ethnic groups and used these to very good effect. In such cases the supportive and therapeutic service was provided by the neighbourhood resource, and the good relationship between the neighbourhood worker and the case-accountable social worker ensured that, if changes to the services were needed, a quick response could be made.

Do families find the services helpful, and do they appear to be effective in preventing further impairment of children's health and development?

The answer to this question has to be set in the context of the very high levels of need presented daily to child and family social work assessment teams. Without the provision of a very much higher level of resources, there will inevitably be families who are unsatisfied by the response – in other words, the parents are not provided with a service that would improve the quality of life for themselves and their children and make it more possible for them to fulfil their responsibility and ensure that their children achieve, in the words Section 17(a) of the Children Act 1989 'a reasonable standard of health or development'. It is also inevitable that some parents will be *dis*satisfied, particularly those who are the subject of enquiries about whether they are responsible for emotionally harming their children, or not adequately protecting them from a range of accidents and adversities, or failing to meet their emotional needs.

It is in the light of the very high level of unmet need and the consequent pressure on front-line social workers that our findings on satisfaction, adequacy of the service and outcome, as discussed in Chapters 7 and 8, have to be set. In drawing attention to this, we reinforce the points made in the Social Service Inspectors' report, which listed the challenges for social services departments. These include:

- reduced expenditure on the personal social services;
- changes in the responses of NHS Trusts, which diminished the services available to children and families with disabilities;
- problems resulting from a higher rate of school exclusions (which impacted on some of these families who had older children); and
- the necessity to provide financial and practical support to asylum seekers with less than full financial compensation. (SSI 1997b, p. 223)

We would add to this list the extreme complexity of practical and emotional problems of the majority of families who cross the thresholds of social services departments. This complexity presents a major challenge to those responsible for devising assessment processes. Neither the *reason for referral,* including whether the case is referred because of concerns of maltreatment or for a specific service, nor the *type of services requested in response to the type of need identified by the referrer* are adequate bases for a quick decision about the sort of service to be provided. Although somewhat rudimentary, our categorisation of families may be helpful to service planners. Adapting the typology of Cleaver and Freeman (1995) and Brandon et al. (1999), we found that most families came into one of five broad groupings, each requiring a different pattern of service provision. These were:

1. those who, although experiencing difficulties, would be able to manage without the provision of the extra services available under the terms of the Children Act 1989;
2. those with short-term problems, often of a practical nature;
3. those with a specific issue, which distorted the way in which they were able to conduct their lives;
4. those in acute distress, but with strengths that might see them through if the overwhelming pressures of the moment could be alleviated; and
5. those with multiple and longer-term problems.

This categorisation proved fairly robust as a means of predicting the sort of services that would be most likely to be needed by different groups of families. However, it is not possible to differentiate between families without obtaining information about personal, family and community strengths and difficulties, and about interpersonal relationships between adults and between parents and children. Our interview data suggest that most of those assessing referrals do, indeed, take note of these less tangible characteristics of family members and also of departmental guidance about prioritisation according to type of need and extent of risk. They are certainly included in guidance on first- and second-stage assessments, which is beginning to be adopted by local authorities in order to help their front-line workers (SSI 1999). Consequently, the apparently pragmatic and often ill-recorded methods of sifting the very large volume of cases work reasonably well. They do not result in the provision of inappropriate services to too many families who do not need them, but do not exclude from services too many families who *do* need them. However, some very worrying cases were referred as often as eight times before they were recognised as families in which the children's health or development was being significantly impaired without the provision of services. Had help been provided at an earlier stage, harm to the children's long-term well-being could have been avoided. In other words, 'false negatives', though a minority of the cases studied, proved to be more costly and also resulted in more serious harm to children, harm that it would be more difficult if not impossible to alleviate.

Turning specifically to outcomes, given the complex nature of the difficulties experienced by many of these families, it would be unrealistic to anticipate that their problems would be resolved within a 12-month timescale. It was concluded that the characteristics of the families had a greater impact on whether or not there was improvement or deterioration during this period than the nature of the services provided. It is a particular problem for social services departments seeking to demonstrate effectiveness that, if they successfully target their services on those in greatest need, good outcomes will be hard to achieve, and the departments will be less able to demonstrate that services have been effective in terms of alleviating the difficulties. If they can intervene when problems are less serious, it is more likely that a range of interventions will be seen by the families as helpful and these cases will be associated with more successful outcomes.

Given the generally negative public image of social work, it is worth noting that 71% of parents who received a social work service described their social worker as helpful, even though a larger proportion remained unsatisfied by the resources (or lack of resources) that could be provided (see Chapter 7).

Implications for policy and practice

The implications for policy and practice differ for the different sorts of families who may need a service. It is a central theme of the research conclusions that, in the face of high levels of need, referrals to social services departments should be more carefully and methodically sifted than has often been the case. Parents, relatives, neighbours and professionals do not make these referrals without good cause. Even with the small number of referrals of families who were found not to have a child 'in need' or 'in need of protection', there was a *prima facie* case for a check to be made, or else the family was 'needy' but was managing in adverse circumstances to provide good enough care and was able to make use of advice and information about eligibility under the Children Act 1989 should their circumstances change.

Central government level

1 In its fight to combat social exclusion and to target resources where they are most needed, central policy-makers will find that data on families who cross Social Services thresholds provide a rich source of information on the families and children who are most likely to be excluded from playing a full part in society. These data will be more accessible as a basis for planning the types and quantity of services that should be available (at primary, secondary, tertiary and quaternary levels) if more systematic assessments can be better recorded at local level and collected at a central level.

2 In the revised guidance on *Working Together under the Children Act 1989* (DoH 1998) there should be greater clarity about the term 'child protection'. It is frequently used as synonymous with the formal child protection system, and therefore with protection from parental or carer maltreatment. However, protection from impairment of development, whatever the cause, is part of all family support services. It may be necessary to return to using the words 'child abuse' or 'child maltreatment' to highlight the essential role still to be played by Area Child Protection Committees in protecting children from being significantly harmed by acts of omission or commission on the part of parents or carers.

3 Within the formal child protection system confusion is caused by the switch from 'significant harm', as the *threshold* to registration, to parental behaviour (types of maltreatment) for the detailed *categories* for registration. If registration were to be based on categories of harm to the child (with a distinction between present harm and likely future harm), protection and family support plans would better fit the protection and other needs of the children. Registration under more than one category of harm or likely harm should be encouraged when appropriate, thus allowing a fuller picture of the extent and nature of harm to be collected at central and local level. It may be appropriate to have categories that combine the type of harm with its likely cause, particularly in the areas covered presently by 'neglect' and 'emotional abuse'. These registration categories are inadequate for the purposes of providing information about the type and volume of services needed nationally and locally. Based on the present study, possible registration categories might include: physical harm through inadequate supervision; emotional harm resulting from emotional neglect; emotional harm resulting from emotionally abusive behaviour. These categories might have sub-divisions for the major known causes of

harm: emotional harm through persistent and inappropriate methods of discipline; emotional harm through failure to protect the child from the adverse consequences of marital conflict; physical harm through neglect occasioned by addiction.

4 The consultation document on revisions to child protection guidance (DoH 1998) proposes a continuing role for Area Child Protection Committees. It is clear from our study that coercion is sometimes needed to ensure the provision of co-ordinated intervention in cases of emotional maltreatment or neglect to those families who cannot be helped without it. These ACPCs (or Area Child Maltreatment Committees) should retain their present membership but also routinely include adult mental health staff and workers from the drugs and alcohol services. They should operate as sub-committees of the Area Children's Services Planning Groups, which should broaden their membership to include housing managers, Benefits Agency managers, the major statutory and voluntary family support agencies, and health education staff. Their remit should include 'impairment of health or development' cases that result from adverse environmental circumstances, and the avoidance of public policies that are significantly harmful to children.

5 More clarity is needed about the 'in need' status of children with disabilities. The clause 'without the provision of a service under this Act' which is part of Sections 17a and 17b of the Children Act 1989 is not included in the clause about disability (17c). It appears difficult for social workers and other advisers to explain to families of children with the types of disabilities listed in the legislation why services are refused. Yet prioritisation is inevitable given the volume of need arising from childhood disability. Departmental guidance prepared in consultation with parents and older children with disabilities would be helpful.

6 There is a long way to go before the communication and consultation systems of agencies – and social work practice – make a reality of partnership-based service planning and practice. The Department of Health Guidance *The Challenge of Partnership in Child Protection* (DoH 1995b) is not widely used and could usefully be relaunched alongside new guidance on joint working and assessment.

7 Agencies should be reminded of the Guidance on Part III of the Act, which makes clear that they may not redefine the 'in need' threshold, although they may develop protocols for deciding about the priority

and allocation of services for those who *do* cross the threshold. From this study and from the parallel study of cases of 'significant harm' (Brandon et al. 1999) it appears that social workers do not routinely refer to the legislation and are unfamiliar with the 'in need' definition. For the wording of Section 17 they substitute the departmental guidance, which lists priorities for the receipt of services. This may deprive families of the possibility of making representations if they are never informed whether their child crosses the 'in need' threshold.

8 The complexities of providing an appropriate, skilled and cost-effective assessment and support service to families under stress require a more highly qualified workforce than is presently available. Managers of assessment teams, senior practitioners, and social workers providing longer-term services to vulnerable children and their families should undertake additional training within the post-qualifying framework. Although some examples of very high quality practice were commended by the parents, their accounts of practice and what we read in the records indicate that a minority of social workers lack adequate knowledge (including legal knowledge) and assessment and casework skills to undertake competent social work practice with children and families. Without appropriate knowledge and skills the work will be ineffective and a waste of scarce resources, and in some cases increase the harm experienced by children.

Implications for local authority planners and senior managers

1 If available resources are to be used to best effect, and if cases are to be made for further resources, information is needed about the sorts of families seeking assistance and the volume and nature of the different types of services needed. This will involve some way of categorising the sorts of families as well as the reasons for referral. This study has suggested ways of broadly categorising families so that management information can be obtained about the numbers of those who will need a longer-term service; of those who will need a short-term focused service; and of those for whom an efficient and knowledgeable advice and referral service will be appropriate.

2 Guidelines on prioritisation for the more expensive services – such as respite care, accommodation, day care and the allocation to a social worker's caseload – are essential. Rather than basing these guidelines on the reason for referral or on the services specifically requested, it is

suggested that those in the highest priority group should be *children who are assessed as most likely to be most significantly harmed or whose health or development will be significantly impaired if a service is not provided*. It is also important to identify families who can be provided with a short-term service at an earlier stage of problem formation, i.e. those families who would otherwise be highly likely to succumb to stresses at a later stage, by which time the children would have been more significantly harmed and would be much harder to help. The rates of improvement amongst the 'specific issue' group of families in this study were disappointing. They tended to get a less adequate service than those in the 'long-standing and multiple problem' group, but our data suggest that a more carefully thought out brief and focused service might have avoided deterioration in the well-being of some of these children and parents.

3 Multi-agency groups planning children's services should identify those high need areas within their localities from which most family referrals come and locate neighbourhood family centres within them. They should also profile their referrals to ascertain the clusters of family problems that result in requests for different levels of services. From this study, parents experiencing severe marital or partner difficulties, and particularly those who are having difficulty separating without emotionally harming their children, should be an important sub-group. Parents involved in the abuse of drugs or alcohol should be another. Working groups drawn from the statutory and voluntary agencies and self-help groups should then devise strategies for a co-ordinated approach to particular problems, including responses at primary, secondary, tertiary and quaternary level. A public health style approach involving education about the harm that may result would be particularly helpful – for example, in reducing the numbers of parents who are emotionally neglectful of their children because of marital or partner problems.

Implications for team leaders and social workers

1 When assessing families referred because of concerns about emotional maltreatment and neglect, the categories of emotional neglect, physical neglect, and emotional maltreatment should be used and further sub-divided along the lines suggested by Glaser and Prior (1997) or the categories used in this study. All assessments should conclude with a clear statement of the sort of behaviour that is causing concern, and the type of harm or impairment to health or development that either

has been caused or is likely to be caused. An estimate of the significance of this harm or impairment, and the likelihood of it continuing, is also necessary. The assessment should also profile the family: identify any strengths, sources of family and community support and personal difficulties as well as relationship problems. These areas should always be covered, in brief or in greater depth, depending on the existence of harm or impairment, its significance and its likelihood of recurring.

2 If there is no mandate to intervene compulsorily and the family is reluctant to receive a service, the assessment is likely to be a brief one. If the family is seeking help, and effective methods of helping in those particular circumstances are available, a fuller assessment will be appropriate. In cases where the child is likely to be significantly harmed, or his/her health or development impaired, a more comprehensive assessment will be necessary whether or not the family is initially willing to take part.

3 Assessments should contain a section that reviews previous intervention and reasons why such intervention was considered effective or ineffective. This should include the views of family members about what they have found helpful or unhelpful in earlier interventions.

4 Family support social workers usually provide a casework relationship and act as case manager for the provision of a package of services. Packages of services that are co-ordinated by a caseworker who does not have a good relationship with the family are least likely to be effective, and most likely either to be inappropriate or to be provided for either too long or too short a period to be effective.

5 A particularly difficult problem is posed by those referrals that result from concerns about physical neglect or child safety and, after phone calls and a review of the available information, are considered to need no further action. Given the numbers of such referrals, it is appropriate that a quick response and case closure is the most frequent response. If a decision is taken that the family should be notified that a referral has been made, and no further action is to be taken, it is not helpful – and *may* be harmful if a letter tells the family that they may seek assistance if they wish. If it is considered necessary to send a letter telling parents that a child protection referral has been received, a specific appointment should be offered or a date should be given

when the social worker will visit. Without this it is not possible to tell whether the referral has had a negative impact on the family and will lead to adverse consequences for the child. Opportunities to provide advice or short-term help are also missed.

In conclusion, the most important recommendation for practice stemming from an analysis of these cases is that a careful assessment should lead to an acceptance that an important minority of cases will need a longer-term, relationship-based casework service, and that this should be provided earlier rather than later. A major challenge to managers, practitioners and theorists is to find cost-effective ways of providing long-term services to those parents and children who need them. Family centres, which can provide continuity of buildings and support staff even when key workers move on, provide a particularly appropriate service setting. The intensity of services provided to each family will rise and fall in response to the stresses on family members. The service will be effective only if a wide range of resources is available from different professionals and if family members are consulted about what they find helpful. Above all, if multiple referrals and the consequent waste of time on repeated assessments are to be avoided, ways have to be found to enhance parental self-esteem and reduce stigma when it is recognised that long-term support is likely to be needed.

References

Aldgate, J. and Statham, J. (forthcoming) *Research on the Implementation of the Children Act 1989*, London: The Stationery Office

Aldgate, J. and Tunstill, J. (1995) *Implementing Section 17 of the Children Act – The First 18 Months*, Leicester: Leicester University Press/Department of Health

Andrews, B., Brown, G. and Creasey, L. (1990) 'Intergenerational links between psychotic disorder in mothers and daughters', *Journal of Child Psychology and Psychiatry*, Vol. 31, No. 7, pp. 1115–29

Audit Commission (1994) *Seen but not Heard: Co-ordinating Community Child Health and Social Services for Children in Need*, London: HMSO

Baldwin, N. and Spencer, N. (1993) 'Deprivation and child abuse: implications for strategic planning in children's services', *Children and Society*, Vol. 7, No. 4, pp. 357–75

Barn, R., Sinclair, R. and Ferdinand, D. (1997) *Acting on Principle*, London: British Agencies for Adoption and Fostering

Bebbington, A. and Miles, J. (1989) 'The background of children who enter local authority care', *British Journal of Social Work*, Vol. 19, pp. 349–68

Beck, A.T., Steer, R. and Garbin, M. (1988) 'Psychometric properties of the Beck Depression Inventory', *Clinical Psychology Review*, Vol. 8, No. 1, pp. 77–100

Bilson, A. and Thorpe, D. (1997) 'A new focus for child protection?', *Professional Social Work*, July, pp. 8–9

Bowlby, J. (1971) *Attachment and Loss*, London: Penguin

Brandon, M., Lewis, A. and Thoburn, J. (1996) 'The Children Act definition of "significant harm" : interpretation in practice', *Health and Social Care in the Community*, Vol. 4, No. 1, pp. 11–20

Brandon, M., Lewis, A., Thoburn, J. and Way, A. (1999) *Safeguarding Children with the Children Act 1989*, London: The Stationery Office

Brière, J., Berliner, L., Bulkley, J.A., Jenny, C. and Reid, T. (eds) (1996) *The APSAC Handbook on Child Maltreatment*, Thousand Oaks, California: Sage

Brown, G. and Harris, J. (1978) *Social Origins of Depression: A Study of Psychiatric Disorder in Women*, London: Tavistock

Brown, G., Andrews, B., Harris, T., Adler, Z. and Bridge, L. (1986) 'Social support, self-esteem and depression', *Psychological Medicine*, Vol. 16, No. 4, pp. 813–31

Burrell, B., Thompson, B. and Sexton, D. (1994) 'Predicting child abuse potential across family types', *Child Abuse and Neglect*, Vol. 18, No. 12, pp. 1039–49

Butt, J. and Mirza, K. (1996) *Social Care and Black Communities: A Review of Recent Research Studies*, London: HMSO

Central Council for Education and Training in Social Work (1978) *Good Enough Parenting*, London: CCETSW

Claussen, A.H. and Crittenden, P.M. (1991) 'Physical and psychological maltreatment: relations among types of maltreatment', *Child Abuse and Neglect*, Vol. 15, Nos 1 and 2, pp. 5–18

Cleaver, H. and Freeman, P. (1995) *Parental Perspectives in Cases of Suspected Child Abuse*, London: HMSO

Coffin, G. (1993) *Changing Child Care*, London: National Children's Bureau

Coulton, C.J., Korbin, J.E., Su, M. and Chow, J. (1995) 'Community level factors and child maltreatment', *Child Development*, Vol. 66, No. 5, pp. 1262–76

Crittenden, P. (1996) 'Research on maltreating families: implications for intervention', in Brière, J. et al. *The APSAC Handbook on Child Maltreatment*, Thousand Oaks, California: Sage, pp. 158–74

Crittenden, P. (1999) 'Child neglect: causes and contributors', in Dubowitz, H. (ed.) *Neglected Children: Research Practice and Policy*, Thousand Oaks, California: Sage, pp. 47–68

Dartington Social Research Unit (1995a) *Child Protection: Messages from Research*, London: HMSO

Dartington Social Research Unit (1995b) *Matching Needs and Services*, Totnes: Dartington Social Research Unit

Department of Health (1988) *Protecting Children: A Guide for Social Workers Undertaking a Comprehensive Assessment*, London: HMSO

Department of Health (1991a) *The Children Act 1989 Regulations and Guidance*, Vol. 2, London: HMSO

Department of Health (1991b) *The Children Act and Local Authorities: A Guide for Parents*, London: HMSO

Department of Health (1991c) *Working Together under the Children Act 1989*, London: HMSO

Department of Health (1995a) *Children and Young Persons on Child Protection Registers – Year ending 31 March 1994, England*, London: HMSO

Department of Health (1995b) *The Challenge of Partnership in Child Protection*, London: HMSO

Department of Health (1997a) *Social Services: Achievement and Challenge*, Cmnd 3588, London: The Stationery Office

Department of Health (1997b) *Children in Need – Report of an SSI National Inspection of Social Services Departments Family Support Services 1993–1995*, London: The Stationery Office

Department of Health (1997c) *Children and Young People on Child Protection Registers – Year Ending 31 March 1997, England*, London: Department of Health

Department of Health (1998) *Working Together to Safeguard Children: New Government Proposals for Inter-Agency Co-operation – Consultation Paper*, London: Department of Health

Department of Health and Social Security (1982) *Child Abuse: A Study of Inquiry Reports 1973–1981*, London: HMSO

Department of Health and Social Security (1985) *Review of Child Care Law*, London: HMSO
Department of Health and Welsh Office (1994) *Children Act Report 1993*, London: HMSO
Dubowitz, H. (ed.) (1999) *Neglected Children: Research, Practice and Policy*, Thousand Oaks, California: Sage
Eckenrode, J., Laird, M. and Doris, J. (1993) 'School performance and discipline problems among abused and neglected children', *Developmental Psychology*, Vol. 29, No. 1, pp. 53–62
Egeland, B., Sroufe, A. and Erickson, M. (1983), 'The developmental consequence of different patterns of maltreatment', *Child Abuse and Neglect*, Vol. 7, No. 4, pp. 459–69
Feeney, J. and Noller, P. (1996) *Adult Attachment*, London: Sage
Frost, N. (1997) 'Delivering family support: Issues and themes in service development', in Parton, N. (ed.) *Child Protection and Family Support*, London: Routledge, pp. 193–211
Garbarino, J. and Sherman, P. (1980) 'High risk neighbourhoods and high risk families: the ecology of child maltreatment', *Child Development*, Vol. 51, No. 1, pp. 188–98
Gardner, R. (1992) *Preventive Social Work with Families*, London: National Children's Bureau
General Household Survey (1993) London: HMSO
Gibbons, J. (1990) *Family Support and Prevention: Studies in Local Areas*, London: HMSO
Gibbons, J. (1991) 'Children in need and their families: outcomes of referrals to Social Services', *British Journal of Social Work*, Vol. 21, pp. 217–27
Gibbons, J. (ed.) (1992) *The Children Act 1989 and Family Support: Principles into Practice*, London: HMSO
Gibbons, J., Conroy, S. and Bell, C. (1995) *Operating the Child Protection System*, London: HMSO
Gibbons, J. and Wilding, J. (1995) *Needs, Risks and Family Support Plans: Social Services Departments' Responses to Neglected Children* Interim report to the Department of Health, Norwich: University of East Anglia
Glaser, D. and Prior, V. (1997) 'Is the term child protection applicable to emotional abuse?', *Child Abuse Review*, Vol. 6, pp. 315–29
Goodyer, I.M. (1990) 'Family relationships, life events and childhood psychopathology', *Journal of Child Psychology and Psychiatry*, Vol. 31, No. 1, pp. 161–92
Hall, A.S. (1974) *The Point of Entry: A Study of Client Reception in the Social Services*, National Institute Social Services Library No. 27, London: George Allen & Unwin
Hardiker, P., Exton, K. and Barker, M. (1991) 'The social policy contexts of prevention in child care', *British Journal of Social Work*, Vol. 21, pp. 341–59
Harris, T. (1993) 'Surviving childhood adversity', in Ferguson, H., Gillgan, R. and Torode, B. (eds) *Surviving Childhood Adversity: Issues for Policy and Practice*, Dublin: University of Dublin Press
Hashima, P.Y. and Amato, P.R. (1994) 'Poverty, social support, and parental behaviour', *Child Development*, Vol. 63, No. 3, pp. 394–403

Hegar, R.L. and Yungman, J.J. (1989) 'Towards a causal typology of child neglect', *Children and Youth Services Review*, Vol. 11, pp. 203–20

Home Office (1946) *Report of the Care of Children Committee* (Curtis Committee Report), Cmd 6922, London: HMSO

Home Office, Department of Health, Department of Education and Science, and Welsh Office (1991) *Working Together under the Children Act 1989*, London: HMSO

House of Commons Social Services Committee (1984) *Report of the Social Services Committee Children in Care* (The Short Committee Report), London: HMSO

Howe, D., Brandon, M., Hinings, D. and Schofield, G. (1999) *Attachment Theory, Child Maltreatment and Family Support: A Practice and Assessment Model*, London: Macmillan

Iwaniec, D. (1995) *The Emotionally Abused and Neglected Child: Identification, Assessment and Intervention*, Chichester: Wiley

Iwaniec, D. (1997) 'Emotional maltreatment and failure-to-thrive', *Child Abuse Review*, Vol. 6, pp. 370–88

Jones, A. and Bilton, K. (1994) *The Future Shape of Children's Services*, London: National Children's Bureau

Jones, M.A. (1985) *A Second Chance for Families – 5 Years Later*, New York: Child Welfare League of America

Kurtz, P.D., Gaudin, J.M., Wodarski, J.S. and Howing, P.T. (1993) 'Maltreatment and the school-age child: school performance consequences', *Child Abuse and Neglect*, Vol. 17, No. 5, pp. 581–9

Lidbetter, E.J. (1993) *Heredity and the Social Problem Group Vol. 1*, London: Edward Arnold and Company

Long, G. (1995) 'Family poverty and the role of family support work', in Hill, M., Hawthorne-Kirk, R. and Part, D. (eds) *Supporting Families*, Edinburgh: HMSO

Macdonald, G. and Roberts, H. (1995) *What Works in the Early Years?*, London: Barnardos

McGlone, F., Park, A. and Smith, K. (1998) *Families and Kinship*, London: Family Policy Studies Centre

Mann, C. (1997) *Children in Need: The Role of the Voluntary Sector*, Dissertation for the degree of MA in Social Work (unpublished), Norwich: University of East Anglia

Margolin, L. (1990) 'Fatal child neglect', *Child Welfare*, Vol. 69, No. 2, pp. 309–19

Martin, M.J. and Waters, J. (1982) 'Familial correlates of selected types of child abuse and neglect', *Journal of Marriage and the Family*, Vol. 44, No. 2, pp. 267–76

Moncher, F. (1995) 'Social isolation and child abuse risk', *Families in Society*, September, pp. 421–31

Mortley, E. (1999) *'Good Enough Parenting': The Role of Parenting Education*, Norwich: University of East Anglia Monographs

Noble, M. and Smith, T. (1994) 'Children in need: using geographical information systems to inform strategic planning for social services provision', *Children and Society*, Vol. 8, No. 4, pp. 360–76

O'Hagan, K. (1993) *Emotional and Psychological Abuse of Children*, Buckingham: Open University Press

Olds, D.L., Henderson Jr, C.R., Chamberlin, R. and Tatelbaum, R. (1986) 'Preventing child abuse and neglect: a randomized trial of nurse home visitation', *Paediatrics*, Vol. 78, pp. 65–78

Parker, R.A. (ed.) (1980) *Caring for Separated Children: Plans, Procedures and Priorities*, London: Macmillan

Parton, N. (1991) *Governing the Family: Childcare, Child Protection and The State*, London: Macmillan

Parton, N. (1995) 'Neglect as child protection: the political context and the practical outcomes', *Children and Society*, Vol. 9, No. 1, pp. 67–89

Philp, A.F. and Timms, N. (1957) *The Problem of the Problem Family*, London: Family Service Units

Polansky, N. (1981) *Damaged Parents: An Anatomy of Child Neglect*, Chicago: University of Chicago Press

Reder, P., Duncan, S. and Gray, M. (1993) *Beyond Blame: Child Abuse Tragedies Revisited*, London: Routledge

Roberts, I. (1996) 'Family support and the health of children', *Children and Society*, Vol. 10, pp. 217–24

Robins, L.N. and Rutter, M. (1990) *Straight and Devious Pathways from Childhood to Adulthood*, Cambridge: Cambridge University Press

Rose, W. (1994) *An Overview of the Developments of Services – The Relationship Between Protection and Family Support and the Intentions of the Children Act 1989*, Department of Health paper for the Sieff Conference, 5 September 1994

Rutter, M., Tizard, J. and Whitmore, K. (eds) (1981) *Education, Health and Behaviour*, London: Longmans

Seagull, E.A.W. (1987) 'Social support and child maltreatment: a review of the evidence' *Child Abuse and Neglect*, Vol. 11, pp. 41–52

Shaw, D.S. and Vondra, J.I. (1993) 'Chronic family adversity and infant attachment security', *Journal of Child Psychology and Psychiatry*, Vol. 34, No. 7, pp. 1205–15

Shemmings, D. (1991) *Client Access to Records*, Aldershot: Avebury

Sheppard, M. (1997) 'Social work practice in child and family care: a study of maternal depression', *British Journal of Social Work*, Vol. 27, pp. 815–45

Sieff Foundation (1994) *Family Support in Protecting the Child*, Surbiton: Michael Sieff Foundation

Sinclair, R. and Carr-Hill, R. (1997) *The Categorisation of Children in Need*, London: National Children's Bureau

Sinclair, R., Garnett, L. and Berridge, D. (1995) *Social Work and Assessment with Adolescents*, London: National Children's Bureau

Smith, M. (1998) 'What does research tell us?', paper given at cross-departmental review on provision for young children, London: Thomas Coram Research Unit

Social Services Inspectorate (1997a) *Responding to Families in Need*, London: The Stationery Office

Social Services Inspectorate (1997b) *Messages from Inspections: Child Protection Inspections 1992–1996*, London: The Stationery Office

Social Services Inspectorate (1998) *Responding to Families in Need: Planning and Decision-making in Family Support Services*, London: The Stationery Office

Social Services Inspectorate (1999) *Assessment in Child Protection and Family Support: A Report to the SSI*, London: Department of Health

Stevenson, O. (1996) 'Emotional abuse and neglect', *Child and Family Social Work*, Vol. 1, No. 1, pp. 13–18

Stevenson, O. (1998) *Neglected Children: Issues and Dilemmas*, Oxford: Blackwell Science

Sutton, P. (1995) *Crossing the Boundaries: A Discussion of Children's Service Plans*, London: National Children's Bureau

Thoburn, J. (1993) 'The role of the local authority', in Triseliotis, J. and Marsh, P. (eds) *Prevention and Reunification in Child Care*, London: Batsford, pp. 24–38

Thoburn, J. and Bailey, S. (1996) *Inter-Agency Working in Child and Family Cases in Kensington and Chelsea: An Independent Evaluation of Current Practice*, Norwich: University of East Anglia Centre for Research on the Child and Family

Thoburn, J. and Lewis, A. (1992) 'Partnership with parents of children in need of protection', in Gibbons, J. (ed.) *The Children Act 1989 and Family Support: Principles into Practice*, London: HMSO, pp. 49–62

Thoburn, J., Brandon, M. and Lewis, A. (1997) 'Need, risk and significant harm', in Parton, N. (ed.) *Child Protection and Family Support*, London: Routledge, pp. 165–92

Thoburn, J., Lewis, A. and Shemmings, D. (1995) *Paternalism or Partnership? Family Involvement in the Child Protection Process*, London: HMSO

Tunstill, J. (1992) 'Local authority policies on children in need', in Gibbons, J. (ed.) *The Children Act 1989 and Family Support: Principles into Practice*, London: HMSO

Tunstill, J. (1995) 'The Children Act and the voluntary child care sector', *Children and Society*, Vol. 5, No. 1, pp. 76–86

Tunstill, J. (1996) 'Family support: past, present and future challenges', *Child and Family Social Work*, Vol. 1, pp. 151–8

US Department of Health and Human Services (1988) *Study Findings: National Incidence and Prevalence of Child Abuse and Neglect (NIPCAN)*, Washington, DC: Department of Health and Human Services

Utting, D. (1998) *Suggestions for the UK: An Overview of Possible Action*, report prepared for the cross-departmental review on provision for young children, York: Joseph Rowntree Foundation

Ward, H. (ed.) (1995) *Looking after Children: Research into Practice*, London: HMSO

Weismann-Wind, T. and Silvern, L. (1994) 'Parenting and family stress as mediators of the long-term effects of child abuse', *Child Abuse and Neglect*, Vol. 18, No. 5, pp. 439–53

White, R. (1998) 'The Founders' Fund Lecture', *Child Abuse Review*, Vol. 7, pp. 6–12

Wilding, J. and Thoburn, J. (1997) 'Family support plans for neglected and emotionally maltreated children', *Child Abuse Review*, Vol. 6, pp. 343–56

Wilson, H. and Herbert, G.W. (1978) *Parents and Children in the Inner City*, London: Routledge and Kegan Paul
Wodarski, J. (1990) 'Maltreatment and the school-age child: major academic, socio-emotional and adaptive outcomes', *Social Work*, Vol. 35, No. 6, pp. 506–13

Index